D1233741

The Sokolov Investigation

Nicholas Alexeyevich Sokolov

THE
SOKOLOV INVESTIGATION

OF

The Alleged Murder

OF

The Russian Imperial Family

A Translation of Sections

of

NICHOLAS A. SOKOLOV'S

The Murder of the Imperial Family

Translation and Commentary

by

JOHN F. O'CONOR

Robert Speller & Sons, Publishers, Inc.
10 East 23rd Street
New York, N.Y. 10010

Publisher's Preface

The Romanov Dynasty, during its three-hundred-year history as rulers of Russia, was often marked by the assassination of its members, including the assassinations, both by terrorists, of the Emperor Alexander II Nicholayevich in St. Petersburg in 1881 and of his fifth son, the Grand Duke Serge Alexandrovich, in Moscow in 1905. It is an ironic touch of history that the name Ipatiev figures in the fate of both the first and the last rulers of the Romanov Dynasty, as the first Romanov Tsar, Michael I Feodorovich, was in hiding in the Ipatiev Monastery at Kostroma, near Moscow, at the time of his election as Tsar of All the Russias in 1613, and the last Romanov Tsar, the Emperor Nicholas II Alexandrovich, was imprisoned in the Ipatiev House at Ekaterinburg, at the time of his disappearance and that of his immediate family in 1918.

Paradoxically, on the eve of the removal of the Romanov Dynasty from the throne of Russia, one of its members, the Grand Duke Dimitri Pavlovich (a first cousin of the last Emperor), together with Prince Felix Felixovich Yusupov, the husband of Princess Irina Alexandrovna Yusupova (born a Princess of Russia and the only niece of the last Emperor) and Vladimir Mitrofanovich Purishkevich (a Right-Wing member of the Duma, the Parliament of the Russian Empire) involved themselves with several other persons, some not yet known to history, in the assassination in St. Petersburg in 1916, of Gregory Yefimovich Rasputin, the notorious charlatan who held sway during the last decade of the Russian Empire. Rasputin had prophesied that if he should die as a result of a conspiracy of members of the Romanov Dynasty and of the nobility then the Russian Empire would fall and its sovereigns and their immediate family as well as other members of the Dynasty and members of the nobility would die a similar death.

Just two-and-a-half months after the death of Rasputin came the collapse of the Romanov Dynasty and within less than two years afterwards came the alleged deaths (alleged, as none has ever been substantiated) of eighteen members of the Dynasty, in addition to innumerable members of the nobility. The eighteen members of the Dynasty whom history has generally recorded as having been assassinated by Bolsheviks were the Grand Duke Michael Alexandrovich (the third and youngest brother of the last Emperor), near Perm in 1918; the Emperor Nicholas II Alexandrovich (the last Emperor), his wife, the Empress Alexandra Feodorovna, their only son, the Grand Duke and Tsarevich Alexei Nicholayevich, and their four daughters, the Grand Duchesses Olga, Tatiana, Maria, and Anastasia Nicholayevny, all seven in Ekaterinburg in 1918; the Grand Duchess Elizabeth Feodorovna (the widow of the Grand Duke Serge Alexandrovich and the second sister of the last Empress), Prince Vladimir Pavlovich Paley (a first cousin of the last Emperor), the Princes Ivan, Constantine, and Igor Constantinovichi of Russia (all second cousins of the last Emperor), and the Grand Duke Serge Mikhailovich (a first cousin, once removed, of the last Emperor), all six near Alapayevsk in

1918; and the Grand Duke Paul Alexandrovich (the fifth and youngest uncle of the last Emperor), and the Grand Dukes Dimitri Constantinovich and Nicholas and George Mikhailovichi (all first cousins, once removed, of the last Emperor), all four in Petrograd in 1919. None of these alleged deaths has ever been substantiated.

The published version of the investigation of Nicholas Alexeyevich Sokolov dealt primarily with the alleged deaths of those presumed murdered in Ekaterinburg, and only briefly with those presumed murdered near Alapayevsk and near Perm, and not at all with those presumed murdered in Petrograd. Another published account of the alleged deaths of the afore-mentioned eighteen members of the Romanov Dynasty is the book by Serge Nicholayevich Smirnov entitled *Autour de l'assassinat des Grands-Ducs, Ekaterinbourg, Alapaïevsk, Perm, Pétrograd* (Paris, Payot, 1928).

The Sokolov and Smirnov books are two of the main accounts published outside Russia of these alleged murders. As the Smirnov book deals primarily with those alleged deaths at the three places other than Ekaterinburg, it is therefore the Sokolov book which has been the main source from which historians have based their account of the Ekaterinburg mystery, and it has thus been analyzed by John F. O'Conor, who has also translated from the Russian-language edition of the Sokolov book the pertinent parts of the investigation, and has compared the essential statements of the Sokolov report with those of the contemporaries of Sokolov with the result being that in the final analysis, there is much evidence that the Emperor Nicholas II and his wife, their only son, and their four daughters were not murdered at Ekaterinburg, and nothing that would be accepted by legal standards as evidence of their murder.

The Commentary by the translator does not delve into the innumerable reports of the escape and subsequent activities of the last Emperor and his immediate family, nor into the various claimants to their identities. Two of the most intriguing reports were printed in *The New York Times* in early 1924 · and mentions a mysterious trip to the United States by Sokolov and the man who assisted him in the preparation of his book, Prince Nicholas Vladimirovich Orlov. With them was also Orlov's first wife, Princess Nadejda Petrovna Orlova (born a Princess of Russia and a second cousin of the last Emperor). The first report (on January 29) stated that these Russian exiles had made the long journey from France to visit a woman who claimed to be one of the four daughters of the last Emperor. The second report (on February 6) was a denial of the previously stated reason for their visit, and instead gave other rather intangible reasons for the visit. This visit to a Romanov claimant coming on the eve of the publication of the French-language edition of the Sokolov book certainly demonstrates that Sokolov and the Orlovs did not really believe the conclusion of the book which they were nurturing towards publication.

Later on that year, the French-language edition of the book was published, and in the latter part of the same year, 1924, Sokolov died. His colleague, Prince Orlov, who had been thanked by Sokolov for his assistance in the preparation of the French-language edition of the book, then wrote a brief appreciation of Sokolov for the Russian-language and German-language editions of the book, both of these editions appearing in 1925. Prince Orlov ended his commentary on Sokolov by repeating the inscription which adorns the cross of the grave of Sokolov in a French country graveyard: "Your Truth is Truth eternal." Yet, today, his "Truth" is being investigated with the result that the final analysis will be quite different for eternity.

This is just one of the many reports and interviews that could easily fill another book.

TABLE OF CONTENTS

TABLE OF CONTENTS

List of Illustrations and Diagrams

No. 59. Objects found in Ekaterinburg after the murder of the Imperial Family. At the left in the top row is an ikon of the Savior. This was found on the breast of the Grand Duchess Elizabeth Feodorovna, whose corpse was found at the bottom of a mine shaft near the city of Alapayevsk. (Publisher's Note: The Grand Duchess Elizabeth Feodorovna was allegedly murdered; her "corpse" has never been indisputably identified. The Grand Duchess was an older sister of the Tsarina and the widow of the Grand Duke Serge Alexandrovich, who was an uncle of the Tsar and who was murdered in 1905. One day after the alleged murder of the Tsar and his family occurred the alleged murder of the Grand Duchess at Alapayevsk. Allegedly murdered along with her, were the Grand Duke Serge Mikhailovich—a first cousin, once removed, of the Tsar—,the Princes Ivan, Constantine, and Igor Constantinovichi—all second cousins of the Tsar—,and Prince Vladimir Pavlovich Paley—a first cousin of the Tsar. None of the "corpses" of these five gentlemen has ever been indisputably identified. In January, 1919, in Petrograd, four other gentlemen of the Imperial Family were allegedly murdered. They were the Grand Duke Paul Alexandrovich—an uncle of the Tsar—,and the Grand Duke Dimitri Constantinovich and the Grand Dukes Nicholas and George Mikhailovichi—all first cousins, once removed, of the Tsar. None of the "corpses" of these four gentlemen has ever been indisputably identified, in fact, has ever been seen. Mysterious was the disappearance of the Grand Duke Michael Alexandrovich, the youngest brother of the Tsar. The Grand Duke disappeared from Perm in June, 1918, allegedly murdered, and his "corpse" has never been found. In all, 18 missing Romanovs.).

No. 60. Ikons belonging to the Imperial Family, which were given to it by Rasputin.

No. 61. The reverse sides of these ikons with the inscriptions of Rasputin. (See p. 280). [Page 280 of the Russian-Langauge Edition.]

No. 62. Effects of the Imperial Family and of persons murdered with it, found in Ekaterinburg after the murder.

No. 63. Effects of the Imperial Family found in Ekaterinburg after the murder. The photograph shows toys of the Tsarevich and a parasol of the Tsarina.

No. 64. Grade crossing No. 184. The corpses of the Imperial Family were brought by here.

No. 65. The Koptyaki Road, along which the corpses of the Imperial Family were brought. Two pine stumps: remains of four pines, "The Four Brothers."

No. 66. General view of abandoned shafts in the vicinity of the mine.

No. 67. General view of abandoned shafts in the vicinity of the mine.

No. 68. General view of abandoned shafts in the vicinity of the mine.

No. 69. Open shaft, in which the Imperial Family were destroyed.

No. 70. The same shaft during the excavations in the spring of 1919.

No. 71. The opening of the shaft of the mine in which the Imperial Family were destroyed.

No. 72. Location, near grade crossing No. 184, of the barrier set up by the Bolsheviks.

No. 73. Excavations made in the vicinity of the mine in the spring and in the summer of 1919.

No. 74. Excavations made in the vicinity of the mine in the spring and in the summer of 1919.

No. 75. Rope and pieces of pine board found at the mine.

No. 76. Ramp laid down by the Bolsheviks on the Koptyaki Road, where the auto-truck which brought the corpses of the Imperial Family to the mine got stuck.

No. 77. Small fire used for smudge against mosquitoes, near which the small pine boards were found.

No. 78. Documents signed by Voikov, concerning the delivery of the sulphuric acid.

No. 79. Bonfire near the open shaft, where the corpses of the Imperial Family were destroyed.

No. 80. Bonfire at the old birch tree.

No. 81. Found in the mine shaft: relics of the Imperial Family. Icons.

No. 82. Found in the mine shaft: relics of the Imperial Family.

No. 83. Found in the mine shaft: relics of the Imperial Family.

No. 84. Found in the mine shaft: relics of the Imperial Family.

No. 85. Found in the mine shaft: relics of the Imperial Family.

No. 86. Buckle from an officer's style belt.

No. 87. The Emperor. Compare his buckle to the buckle in No. 86.

No. 88. Belt buckle, of small style, found at the mine.

No. 89. Diamond-studded shoe buckles found at the mine.

No. 90. Shoe buckle found at the mine.

No. 91. Vial of salts found at the mine.

No. 92. Lens from spectacles, found at the mine.

No. 93. Frame-mounting of a pince-nez, found at the mine.

No. 94. Lenses from a pince-nez, found at the mine.

No. 95. False teeth found at the mine.

No. 96. Remains of a small (mustache) brush, found at the mine.

No. 97. Collar button and tie clasp found at the mine.

Nos. 98, 99, 100 and 101. Parts of corsets, found at the mine.

Nos. 102 and 103. Parts of corsets, found at the mine.

No. 104. Buckles from men's clothing, found at the mine.

No. 105. Springs from suspenders, found at the mine.

Nos. 106, 107, 108, 109, 110 and 111. A buckle from suspenders, a ladies' belt buckle, military style buttons, buttons and parts of buttons, hooks, eyes and buttons, brilliant and cross, found at the mine.

No. 112. Pearl ear-ring found at the mine.

No. 113. The Empress in pearl ear-rings.

No. 114. Parts of another pearl ear-ring.

No. 115. Pearls found at the mine.

No. 116. Parts of a broken brilliant, found at the mine.

No. 117. Two gold fragments of bracelets, found at the mine.

No. 118. Gold parts of an ornament, found at the mine.

No. 119. Topazes found at the mine.

No. 120. Human finger found at the mine.

No. 121. The corpse of the dog, "Jemmi," belonging to the Grand Duchess Anastasia Nicholayevna, found at the mine.

No. 122. "Jemmi" in the arms of the Grand Duchess Anastasia Nicholayevna. (Publisher's Note: Seated from left to right are: the Grand Duchess Olga Nicholayevna, the Heir Tsarevich, the Grand Duchess Anastasia Nicholayevna with her dog, "Jemmi," and the Grand Duchess Tatiana Nicholayevna.)

No. 123. The receipt of Medvedyev for money given him by Yurovsky to pay off the Sysertsky guards after the murder of the Imperial Family.

No. 124. P. Yermakov.

No. 125. S. Vaganov.

No. 126. Clearing with pine stump near the open shaft where the bodies of the Imperial Family were destroyed.

No. 127. Found near Koptyaki.

No. 128. Pieces of a German language newspaper.

No. 129. The telegram of Beloborodov to Goloshchekin with respect to the replacement of the internal guard with Chekists.

No. 130. "Tell Sverdlov that entire family suffered same fate as head officially family will perish in evacuation."

No. 131. (Telegram whose text appears on page 250.) [Page 250 of the Russian-Language Edition.]

No. 132. (Telegram whose text appears on page 251.) [Page 251 of the Russian-Language Edition.]

No. 133. The telegram from Yurovsky.

No. 134. The telegram from Beloborodov to the Alapayevsk Soviet.

No. 135. The telegram of Beloborodov with respect to the pretended abduction of the prisoners of Alapayevsk.

No. 136. The corpse of the Grand Duke Serge Mikhailovich. (Publisher's Note: The Grand Duke, allegedly murdered, was a first cousin, once removed, of the Tsar. His "corpse" has never been indisputably identified.)

No. 137. The corpse of the Grand Duchess Elizabeth Feodorovna. (Publisher's Note: The Grand Duchess, allegedly murdered, was an older sister of the Tsarina and the widow of the Grand Duke Serge Alexandrovich, who was an uncle of the Tsar and who was murdered in 1905. Her "corpse" has never been indisputably identified.)

No. 138. The corpse of the Prince Ivan Constantinovich. (Publisher's Note: The Prince, allegedly murdered, was a second cousin of the Tsar. His "corpse" has never been indisputably identified.)

No. 139. The corpse of the Prince Constantine Constantinovich. (Publisher's Note: The Prince, allegedly murdered, was a second cousin of the Tsar. His "corpse" has never been indisputably identified.)

No. 140. The corpse of the Prince Igor Constantinovich. (Publisher's Note: The Prince, allegedly murdered, was a second cousin of the Tsar. His "corpse" has never been indisputably identified.)

No. 141. The murderers of Alapayevsk.

No. 142. Countess A. V. Hendrikova.

No. 143. The corpse of Countess A. Hendrikova, found in Perm.

No. 144. The corpse of E. A. Schneider, found in Perm.

No. 145. The plan of the lower floor of the house of N. N. Ipatiev. The plan of the upper floor of the house of N. N. Ipatiev.

No. 146. The map of the property of N. N. Ipatiev in Ekaterinburg, with identification of buildings:
Key:
I. Two-story stone house.
L. Terrace.
II. Two-story stone building of the servants.
III. One-story bath-house and laundry.
IV. Wooden building of the servants, with stone foundation.
M. Wooden summer-house (pergola).
V. Shed on wooden posts.

No. 147. Sketch of the locality in the tract of the Four Brothers.

No. 148. The Dowager Empress Maria Feodorovna, in exile in Denmark, 1924. (Publisher's Note: The Dowager Empress, the mother of the Emperor, maintained, until her death on October 13, 1928, that the Emperor and all his family had not been murdered and that they would all reappear in due time.)

No. 149. The Russian Imperial Family, 1913. Seated are the Grand Duchess Olga Nicholayevna, the Emperor Nicholas II Alexandrovich, the Heir, Tsarevich, and Grand Duke Alexei Nicholayevich, and the Grand Duchess Tatiana Nicholayevna. Standing are the Grand Duchess Maria Nicholayevna, the Empress Alexandra Feodorovna, and the Grand Duchess Anastasia Nicholayevna.

Publisher's Note: Photographs Nos. 1-144 are from the Russian-language edition of *The Murder of the Imperial Family,* and are numbered identically in this book. Nos. 145, 146, and 147 are also from the same edition but were not numbered, but have been done so here for order. The frontispiece was the frontispiece of the same edition. Nos. 148 and 149 have been added to this book for the benefit of the reader. It is obvious from the point of view of this book, that although the descriptions of the photographs from the Russian-language edition constantly mention the Imperial Family and members of their suite as having been murdered, we have let stand the original descriptions of the photographs, and have made comment on many of the descriptions; "murder" really means "alleged murder", and is applicable throughout the List of Illustrations and Diagrams as none of the "corpses" has been indisputably identified.

TRANSLATOR'S COMMENTARY

I. Introduction

THE TRANSLATOR AND THE publisher of an historical work, and indeed of any work based upon research and investigation, are normally presumed to support its conclusions. In this case there must be no such presumption. The purpose of this translation is simply to present in clear English, adhering as closely as possible to the meaning and spirit of the original, Nicholas A. Sokolov's description of the evidence of *The Murder of the Imperial Family*.[1] The reader will be able to judge for himself the nature and value of the evidence described.

The purpose of the Commentary, on the other hand, is to call attention to the weakness of that evidence, and to call the reader's attention to conflicting evidence described in Sokolov's account and in the accounts of other persons closely connected with the investigation of the Imperial Family's disappearance. Although the authors of these accounts reach similar conclusions, their explanations, and even the evidence described, are frequently contradictory—in some cases self-contradictory.

Those sections of Sokolov's work which do not deal directly with the evidence of murder have not been translated. In the untranslated sections, which comprise almost two-thirds of the published account,[2] Sokolov relates the experiences of the Imperial Family from the time of the Tsar's overthrow in March, 1917,[3] to the time of the Imperial Family's disappearance in the summer of 1918, shortly before the city of Ekaterinburg,[4] the Imperial Family's last known place of imprisonment, was captured by White, anti-Bolshevik forces.

As Sokolov relates, the Imperial Family was first imprisoned in the palace at Tsarskoye Selo. In August, 1917 they were transferred to Tobolsk, in northwestern Siberia. There was a second transfer, in the spring of 1918, to Ekaterinburg, in the Ural Mountains.

Sokolov also discusses a number of controversial issues affecting the Imperial Family, such as the influence of Gregory Rasputin, the Tsarina and others upon government policy; accusations that the Tsar and the Tsarina were disloyally attempting to negotiate a separate peace with Germany;[5] and the allegation that the Provisional revolutionary government, which was overthrown by the Bolsheviks in November, 1917, shares indirect responsibility for the Imperial Family's asserted execution.

Finally there is an account of the apparent murder, near Perm, of certain relatives of the Imperial Family, said to have occurred on July 17-18, 1918; and of the disappearance in June, 1918, in the same locality, of the Grand Duke Michael Alexandrovich. The Grand Duke Michael was the brother in whose favor the Tsar had abdicated.

II. Other Accounts of the Investigation

Because Sokolov was the last-appointed investigator in the case, his published account had been regarded by many as a kind of "official" report of the investigation. It should be noted, however, that it does not contain or describe all of the testimony and material evidence gathered, and represents, in actuality, only a statement of Sokolov's personal views and conclusions, supported by partial quotations from affidavits and selective descriptions of the physical evidence and tests. It was not published, moreover, until the year of his death, 1924, several years after the defeat and dissolution of the governmental authority which had appointed him. The first edition of his work was in French. The Russian edition, which differs somewhat from the French, was published in 1925, posthumously.

Other accounts describing evidence collected in the course of the investigation would appear to have an equally "official" character. They were written by persons who had an official part in the conduct of the investigation, or who acted as witnesses, or who obviously had more or less complete copies of the record in their possession.

The Siberian phase of the investigation was ended with the defeat of the anti-Bolshevik forces in that region, at the end of 1919. Sokolov, however, continued the inquiry in western Europe, questioning many additional people who had fled the Soviet regime.

His records were brought out of Manchuria by General Maurice Janin, Chief of the French Military Mission to Siberia and Commander of the Allied Forces there. In his memoirs [6] General Janin states that there were three heavy suitcases and a strong-box. The inventory included 311 items, all of which, he says, were turned over to the senior Russian Ambassador, M.N. de Giers.

Janin also mentions a proposal to send this material to General

3

Wrangel in the Crimea, and a further proposal, opposed by relatives of the Imperial Family, to store the material in the archives of the French Foreign Ministry.

Further light on the disposition of this material is provided by Sokolov's assistant in the investigation, Captain Paul Bulygin. Bulygin states that it was the original plan to bring the records to the Dowager Empress, Maria Feodorovna, and continue the work under her patronage.[7] Although she eventually directed Sokolov "not to come" to Denmark, where she lived until her death in 1928, Bulygin relates that she contributed 1,000 pounds to the furtherance of the work. As a result of this, he says, "the Investigation was saved."

The Tsar's cousin, the Grand Duke Nicholas Nicholayevich, also refused to accept the records. According to Bulygin, they were ultimately kept in Sokolov's and Bulygin's joint apartment. At some unspecified date "seven volumes of the official Journal of the Investigation" were carried off by an armed band of Russian and German communists in Berlin, and "according to the information obtained by the German police, these were sent on to Moscow, via Prague."[8] The "official inventory", however, still existed and remained "to this day" [in 1935] in "the box that received the bones found amongst the ashes at the spot where the bodies of the Imperial Family were burnt." There were also "thirteen drops of blood," carefully preserved "in arsenic capsules," and "the Tsaritsa's finger", which had been "placed in alcohol".[9]

Bulygin's story, however, appears to be in contradiction with still another account,[9a] which indicates that the entire dossier, together with the "relics," remained in the custody or control of de Giers (and others whom de Giers declined to identify) at least until 1930, for use at such time as "the investigation interrupted in 1919 might be reopened in a resurrected Russian state."

The first to get into publication with the "complete" story of the investigation was, as might be expected, a newspaper correspondent, Robert Wilton, of the London *Times*. Wilton spent a great deal of time with the investigators, both in Ekaterinburg and elsewhere in Siberia, and according to Bulygin, returned to Europe in Sokolov's company. His book was published in 1920,[10] the year of the evacuation. In it he relates that he had in his possession "the complete history and documents of the case," including the "signed depositions of eye-witnesses," with Sokolov's authorization to use them.[11] There must have been more than one copy of the record at this time[12] because, as Wilton explains, he "took charge of one dossier" in Harbin, where Sokolov had hidden it in his car.[13]

Wilton's book also contains the complete text of four depositions which had been brought from Omsk by the last Minister of Justice in Admiral Kolchak's government, George Telberg. Prior to the revolution Telberg had practiced law in the Urals and lectured at the Universities of Moscow, Tomsk and Saratov.

Second to get into publication was Pierre Gilliard, a French tutor of Swiss nationality who shared the fate of the Imperial Family until its arrival in Ekaterinburg, where he was released. After the city was taken by the Whites he assisted in the investigation. The full text of his deposition appears in Wilton's book. His own book, consisting of personal memoirs, was published in 1921.[14]

In 1922 a two-volume work was published in Vladivostok by General Michael Constantinovich Dieterichs.[15] General Dieterichs was a Russian general staff officer who had been offered, and rejected, the post of Minister of War in the Provisional Government of Alexander Feodorovich Kerensky. When the Bolsheviks seized power in Petrograd, General Dieterichs opposed the submission of the Staff to their authority and took refuge with the French military mission. Subsequently he became chief of staff of the pro-Allied, Czechoslovak national force which was evacuated through Siberia after the Peace of Brest-Litovsk. Travelling with the first echelons of the Czechs when they turned on the Bolsheviks, General Dieterichs participated in the liberation of Vladivostok in June, 1918 and later became associated with the newly-organized, anti-Bolshevik, Russian army in Siberia. In January, 1919 he was vested with general supervision of the Romanov investigation. In July, 1919 he was appointed commander-in-chief of the White armies in Siberia and on August 10, 1919 chief of staff and minister of war in the government of Admiral Alexander Vasil'yevich Kolchak. Following the collapse of this government he remained for a time in the Far East where, for a brief period in 1922, he acted as governor of the Japanese-occupied Maritime Region.

Sokolov has high praise for General Dieterichs' account [15a] criticizing only the assertion that Dieterichs' role in the investigation was superior to his own. General Dieterichs in turn has high praise for the accounts of Wilton and Gilliard. It thus appears that even though the participation of the two foreigners was not "official," their accounts were approved and accepted, As General Dieterichs says:

5

In presenting the terrible and bloody drama played out within the walls of the Ipatiev House, the works of Wilton and Gilliard alone accomplished what had not been done before— first, in sounding the notes of a sympathetic attitude and regard for the victims of the historic drama and second, in removing this murder, perhaps only instinctively, from the category of the usual Bolshevik atrocities of the time to that of an event of national significance for the Russian people.

Wilton and Gilliard were foreigners, but nevertheless, having for a long time lived in Russia, among the Russian people, and being men of pure and sensitive heart, men who deeply and sincerely loved the Russian people, men observant and by nature sincere, and having lived with the Russian people through the tragedy of their disintegration—the revolution, the abyss—they felt instinctively, with their hearts, the truth: *these murders were completely out of the ordinary*, not only for the Russian people, but for the entire world.[16]

Bulygin's account was published in 1935. He had been an officer in the Imperial Life Guards and after the Bolshevik seizure of power took part in the first Kuban ("Icy") campaign of General Lavr Georgiyevich Kornilov. In the summer of 1918, he reports, he led an unsuccessful effort to rescue the Imperial Family, travelling incognito to Vyatka, and finally to Ekaterinburg, where he was imprisoned by the Reds.

Escaping after a brief period, he returned south to be appointed commander of the personal guard of the Dowager Empress Maria Feodorovna then in the Crimea. In January, 1919, at the request of the Dowager Empress, mother of the Emperor, and the Grand Duchesses Xenia and Olga Alexandrovny, sisters of the Emperor, he set out for Siberia in another effort to ascertain the fate of the Imperial Family. Reporting to Admiral Kolchak's headquarters at Omsk, he was officially informed of the Imperial Family's execution. Some time prior to August, 1919 he was appointed Sokolov's assistant.

Bulygin states that the "first object" of his account, entitled "The Sorrowful Quest", was to "popularise Sokolov's work" and "present it to the public in a simpler form." [17] The same volume contains an account by Alexander Feodorovich Kerensky entitled "The Road to the Tragedy".

Every one of the writers mentioned above reached the same conclusion—that all members of the Imperial Family, the Tsar Nicholas II, the Tsarina Alexandra Feodorovna, and their five children, the Tsarevich Alexei Nicholayevich and the Grand Duchesses Olga,

6

Tatiana, Maria, and Anastasia Nicholayevny were shot to death in Ekaterinburg, July 16-17, 1918 and their bodies destroyed in the neighboring forest by fire and sulphuric acid. The remains, it is asserted, were scattered in the grass or thrown into an abandoned mine shaft.

In reaching this conclusion the White investigators contradicted the initial announcement of the Soviet authorities who at first asserted that only the Tsar was executed. The Soviet position was apparently changed in September, 1919, when, according to Wilton, the Bolsheviks announced the trial at Perm of twenty-eight persons for the murder of "the Tsar and all the members of his entourage." [18]

The White investigators regarded this "trial" as staged, or even fictitious. Its announcement, nevertheless, confirmed their conclusions, stating that "in all, eleven persons were assassinated." This seemed to eliminate the possibility that even one member of the family had escaped. The "eleven" would cover all of the last known members of the Tsar's group—seven members of the Imperial Family and four others: Dr. Eugene Sergeyevich Botkin, who was the family physician; the maid, Anna Stepanovna Demidova; the cook, Ivan Mikhailovich Kharitonov; and the servant, Alexei Yegorovich Trupp.

Finally, in 1921, three years after the event, the murder of the entire family was confirmed by another Soviet source, Paul Mikhailovich Bykov. Bykov was described as chairman of the Ekaterinburg Soviet,[19] and his article, "The Last Days of the Last Tsar," appeared in a compendium entitled "The Workers' Revolution in the Urals." [20] It was published in Ekaterinburg.

In 1926 Bykov published a book, "The Last Days of the Romanovs," [21] again confirming that "all the eleven—Nicholas Romanov, his wife, son, four daughters and four of their household— were shot." "On the night of July 16-17," he writes, "the Romanov family ceased to exist." [22]

Since Bykov acknowledged official responsibility for the executions, and because his writings could only have been published with the approval of the Soviet authorities, he seemed to provide the one thing required to make the conclusions of the anti-Bolshevik investigators really "official". His account, however, left much to be desired. It added little to what had already been published by the anti-Bolsheviks, and in fact followed them so closely, sometimes citing them, that one cannot escape the feeling that they are the major sources of his information. It said nothing, moreover, about the unexplained 'trial' at Perm, and apart from the obvious opportunity afforded for anti-counter-revolutionary propaganda, Bykov's main purpose seemed to be, not to throw additional light upon the case, or to answer the riddles arising from the anti-Bolshevik accounts, but only to echo their principal assertions and lend the support of·his own apparent authority to their conclusions.

In this connection there may be some significance in the fact that Bykov's first article appeared shortly after the publication of Wilton's account, and his book shortly after the publication of Sokolov's. It almost seems as though the Bolsheviks were unwilling to commit themselves until after having been assured of what the White investigators had found and of what the final conclusions of these investigators were to be.

These conclusions, however, are far from convincing. A really analytical reading of the published accounts of the White investigation inevitably impresses one with three doubt-raising and predominating considerations. In the first place, the investigation was plagued by admitted disagreements, lack of cooperation, inefficiency, and even bungling on the part of several independently operating investigating authorities. Second, the principal accounts —those of Sokolov, Dieterichs and Wilton—clearly indicate that the Bolsheviks were making a sustained effort to deceive the White investigators, and throw them off the track. Many kinds of false evidence were planted, and many of the witnesses, known to be members of the Bolshevik party, were obviously lying. It was at least difficult to determine which of this evidence, if any, was real or truthful, and which was false. The Bolsheviks, in other words, may have been attempting to conceal murder, or they may have been attempting to conceal an escape or release. The facts concerning either contingency could have been embarrassing to them, in the case of the latter perhaps more so than in the case of the former. Third, there was considerable evidence of German efforts to obtain the release of the Imperial Family, as well as of the removal of the Imperial Family from Ekaterinburg some time in June, 1918, at least three weeks prior to the date on which the murders are supposed to have taken place. If the Imperial Family were removed from Ekaterinburg at that time, then, of course, while they may have been murdered somewhere else, they could not have been murdered in Ekaterinburg, or in the manner indicated by Sokolov and those who accepted his conclusions.

The first factor referred to above is described below in the section entitled "The Conduct of the Investigation"; the second in the section entitled "Evidence of Murder"; and the third in the section entitled "Evidence of Escape".

III. The Conduct of the Investigation

The seeming unanimity of "official" opinion described above did not always exist. Investigation of the fate of the Imperial Family began almost immediately after Ekaterinburg was captured by White forces (July 25, 1918). Sokolov was not appointed until February 7, 1919 seven months later. Prior to his appointment, and for a short time afterwards, there were other investigators who frequently differed with and even competed with each other, both as to their conclusions and as to the appropriate methods of investigation. Some of them reached the conclusion that all or part of the Imperial Family had been spared.

Since these circumstances are not described in Sokolov's account, it is necessary to look for the information in the accounts of the others.

The Officers' Commission

General Dieterichs relates that immediately after the liberation of Ekaterinburg an officers' investigating commission was appointed by the garrison commander to investigate the circumstances of the Imperial Family's disappearance. In order to insure that the work of the commission "would follow the more customary technical procedures," its staff included the court investigator of the Ekaterinburg Regional Court, Nametkin.[23]

The officers, however, soon became dissatisfied with Nametkin. Dieterichs reports that a "feeling of anger and exasperation arose against him and, as was generally characteristic of the period—of distrust, suspicion. Fearing that Nametkin was deliberately making the case obscure instead of bringing it to a disclosure of the facts, the officers began to engage in independent inquiry, independent activity." [24]

In describing the visit to the abandoned mine shaft made on

10

July 30 by the Officers' Commission and Nametkin, Sokolov gives the impression that this was the end of the search in that area until his own arrival a year later. Thus he states, page 169:

> There were no corpses at the bottom of the shaft. Energies quickly flagged. The court investigator went off to the city after remaining at the mine for an hour and a half.

Actually, for the Officers' Commission, this was only the beginning. There was deep water in the shaft and it was impossible to tell if there were corpses at the bottom until the water was pumped out. It was not until August 19, after many difficulties, that all of the water was finally removed. Then, when no bodies were found, the assistant public prosecutor, N. Magnitsky, organized an intensive search of the entire area by mine specialists, people familiar with the terrain and even boy scouts.

Then, as Sokolov says, energies did flag. The officers were demoralized, and as General Dieterichs relates, the members of the Commission went off in various directions:

> The officers divided and began to adopt various positions, if only to escape from the dead-end of insoluble mystery to which they had been brought by the disappearance of the bodies of the Imperial Family. Those who continued to believe firmly in the accomplishment of the foul deed became silent, holding themselves aloof from discussion and questioning. Others, unwilling to accept it, attached themselves to the legend prompted by Yankel Sverdlov:[25] the Tsar had perished, but the whole Family had been spared and removed by the bolsheviks to a safe place. A third group, turning in despair to germanophile sympathies, was carried away with the idea that the Imperial Family had been saved by the Germans and even named people who had allegedly seen this or that Member of the Imperial Family in this or that place of this or that foreign country.[26]

Mistrust, Dieterichs says, "rose to terrible proportions" and continued for long afterwards so that "there were occasions, even after the case had passed into Sokolov's hands, when if he summoned any of the officers who had participated in the investigation in Ekaterinburg, or who were closely connected with it, they were heard to whisper among themselves before testifying: 'can he be told everything we have seen?' "[27]

11

At the same time that the garrison commander created the officers' commission, he also directed the Ekaterinburg Criminal Investigating Division to commence an investigation of the Imperial Family's disappearance.

The criminal investigating divisions were, as Dieterichs states,[29] that part of the military, counter-espionage apparatus attached to the military-administrative authorities in the rear areas and large cities. Much of the work, especially in the lower echelons, was done by personnel drawn from the existing network of civilian agents—police and investigatory workers formerly in the employ of the Ministry of the Interior.

General Dieterichs was extremely critical of their work, especially in connection with the Romanov case:

> The most characteristic trait of the military-criminal investigating divisions was their intolerance of the investigatory work of any other organ or institution, and an over-weening self-assurance both in the matter of personal investigatory talent and in the belief that only that was correct which their own directors had sought out and investigated. This led, first of all, to a lack of coordination between the criminal investigating division and the investigatory work of the prosecutor which it served: while the [judicial] investigation sought to channel the inquiry in one, indicated direction, according to a unified, prepared plan, the criminal investigating division would move independently in an altogether different direction along different channels, not aiding the investigation but threatening it with theories of various agents that were frequently fantastic to the point of absurdity.
>
> The criminal investigating division would detain a great many people, interrogate them, carry out searches and seizures, but all this mass of material would not reach the [judicial] investigating authorities for 1, 2, and even 3 months, during which time several of the witnesses would manage either to die or disappear, thus slipping through the hands of the prosecutor and the investigator.[30]

General Dieterichs also complains that because the criminal investigating division was subordinate to the military authorities, it was "able to insulate itself and its activities from the prosecutor's supervision" and "find support in the military command." "And since," he says, "due to war conditions in the military theater of operations, all civilian institutions were subordinated to the military command, and since, during the revolutionary period, the military authorities were prejudiced against all civilian institutions for political reasons, the units of the military-criminal investigating division were instructed by their superiors, one after another, to conceal their actions from the eyes of the public prosecutor." [31]

In the beginning, according to General Dieterichs, the criminal investigating division of Ekaterinburg proceeded, in the Romanov case, "along quite normal and natural lines, completely as indicated by all the circumstances." [32] But its subsequent activities, he relates, were, like those of the officers, completely thrown off course by the failure to find bodies at the bottom of the infamous mineshaft:

> But from the second half of August, i.e., when the officers did not find the bodies of the Imperial Family in the mine-shaft, the criminal investigating division made a complete about face, setting out upon an individual course of work. In various periods of its subsequent activity it adopted as the basis for its work some one of the currently circulating, invented theories and then, through the approach of various agents, sought facts which might serve to support them. It rejected the facts already pointed out by actual, living events and began to seek material to support previously conceived and adopted notions.
>
> It is possible, of course, by this method to stumble upon the truth, but only by accident. This course is too uncertain, inaccurate, untechnical, unscientific. Most frequently one working in this fashion falls into the nets spread by the opposing side to conceal its crime. This is the fate which befell the military-criminal investigating division. It followed the course prompted by the Soviet regime itself—only the Tsar had been killed, and all His Family were alive. [33]

One feels, on reading General Dieterichs' account, that the escape theory had to be rejected because it was supported in part by the Bolshevik announcement:

> Seizing upon the idea suggested by the leaders of the Soviet regime and the principals in the crime, the criminal investigating division became so attracted by it that it quite soon and readily turned away from the live clues provided to it by the materials gathered in the first days of the investigation. Its work was exclusively directed to the fruitless follow-up of the different variations which appeared on the basic Bolshevik theme and only confused and seriously complicated the investigatory work of the Ekaterinburg public prosecutor. On the other hand the independence in general of the criminal investigating division, already referred to, gave it the opportunity, through rep-

13

resentatives of the military command, to insinuate into the community, and even into the highest government circles, a mass of different rumors, theories and suppositions supported by a kind of officially obtained information, which definitely supported doubts of the facts relating to the murder of the Imperial Family in Ekaterinburg and of the Grand Duke Michael Alexandrovich in Perm, and which at times provided food for a deliberate continuation of the discrediting of the former Tsar, Tsarina and Their Children as having Germanophile tendencies.[34]

The latter statement gives the impression that any theory which might discredit the Imperial Family must also be rejected out of hand. General Dieterichs apparently felt that such discredit would result if people were allowed to think the Imperial Family might have gone or been taken to Germany for any purpose, or by any means, voluntarily or involuntarily.

This may explain the antipathy of General Dieterichs towards the later work of the criminal investigating division because, as he relates, the division did turn to the theory that the Imperial Family had been saved by the Germans:

> Setting out upon its new course of work, the military-criminal investigating division first of all seized upon the rumors which were then circulating vigorously throughout all Siberia and which many people have not yet abandoned—that the Imperial Family was saved by Wilhelm and taken somewhere abroad.[35]

Later, General Dieterichs relates, the division came to the conclusion that the Imperial Family had been moved out of Ekaterinburg by the Bolsheviks. The change in theory occurred after the defeat of Germany by the Allies:

> This theory [of German intervention] was finally dropped when, with the collapse of German power, it became known that the Imperial Family was not in Germany and had not been there.
> This theory disappeared and in its place, still following the same basic idea, the criminal investigating division took to another: the Imperial Family was saved and taken away by the Bolsheviks themselves. This theory had, in its entirety, been indicated by the statements made by the soviet regime with respect to the shooting of the former Tsar.[36]

General Dieterichs does not indicate how it "became known" that the Imperial Family was not, and had not been, in Germany. He simply blames the criminal investigating division for making inquiry in this direction. He also repeatedly complains that because it insisted on doing so—because it would not base its work solely upon the assumption that the Imperial Family had been murdered, it made things much more difficult for the judicial investigators:

> . . . the undue attraction of the criminal investigating division to various theories and rumors immensely increased the work of the investigator, Sokolov, since, for the sake of the completeness and exactitude of the basic data of the investigation, he had to consider and analyse all of the investigatory material relating to these theories and rumors in order to dispose of them, either driving them to the wall or to the source of the theory or rumor, or establishing the complete absurdity of the position taken by the criminal investigating division as the basis for its work. In the majority of cases this resulted in an absolutely useless waste of time.[37]

Finally, after the liberation of Perm, 235 miles to the west of Ekaterinburg, many positions in the criminal investigating division of the liberated city were filled with Ekaterinburg personnel. General Dieterichs relates that these people continued their "secret investigation" until after Sokolov's appointment:

> They continued the secret investigation of the case of the Tsar in Perm, where the assistant public prosecutor of the Perm Regional Court, Tikhomirov, also took part, on his own, even though warned several times by the prosecutor of the need to take a cautious attitude toward the direction of inquiry pursued by the criminal investigating division.
> In Perm the work of the former personnel of the criminal investigating division developed quickly, without departing from the same basic theory that the Imperial Family had been taken from Ekaterinburg by the Bolsheviks themselves. Witnesses appeared, and also material evidence.[38]

As General Dieterichs relates, the views of the criminal investigating division did find favor with the Minister of Justice at Omsk.[39] Nevertheless, sometime after Sokolov's appointment, it was forbidden to do any further work on the case and its materials were all turned over to Sokolov.

The Judicial Investigation

The judicial investigators, prior to Sokolov's appointment, did not

15

escape their share of criticism. Sokolov relates, pages 1-2, that the court investigator, Nametkin, was taken off the case on August 7, 1918, because of his "conduct" and the "situation prevailing at that time." There were accusations, he says, of "cowardice" and other unspecified suspicions.

Nametkin's replacement, Sergeyev, is also criticized by Sokolov, pages 130 and 200, for his failure to photograph the room of execution "in the condition in which he found it," and because he "did not once go to the mine."

Dieterichs more fully explains the reasons for dissatisfaction. They appear to have been largely political:

. . . . the apparati of government, as set up at that time,[40] were, willy nilly, formed of those who had either survived the depravity and corruption of the nation during the Kerensky period, or were special products of its creation. In addition, the very conditions under which governments were created at that time did not insure against the infiltration, even into their most central organs, of persons of the lowest moral caliber but possessed, nevertheless, of the ability to make a noise everywhere and to proclaim their so-called high-humanitarian political slogans and popular democratic principles in a loud voice. In particular, the situation was seriously complicated for the Ural government by the strong, behind-the-scenes influence exerted on the administrative work of government organs by elements of the extreme left which gathered in Ekaterinburg—from former members of the Constituent Assembly led by Chernov,[41] Minor and Vol'ski—and who had the patronage and support of the then influential Czecho-Slovak National Council in Ekaterinburg.

In these conditions the general character of government organization inherited from 1917 was reflected in the activities and views of all government institutions, including the Ekaterinburg Regional Court which was then resuming its activity. First of all, in every matter of even the slightest importance attention was turned to the political side of the question. Did it augur support for reaction? Was it not a threat to the "gains of the revolution"? Was there not food for monarchist conspiracies? And, as in the unhappy year 1917, almost everyone was afraid of appearing conservative, reactionary, and especially monarchist. This led to mutual distrust between employees of the same institution, suspicion of one another, of the mass, of former organizations, whether of officers or of private individuals and politically active people. . . . . .

. . . . . it was necessary, in order to avoid bringing matters to a complete standstill, to act very cautiously and alertly in the conduct of any question which for any reason, in the eyes of government or community intelligentsia, bore the marks of reaction or political danger.

Among such matters in the Urals was the case of the bolsheviks' murder of the former Tsar. The special interest shown by the military command in this event, and the officers' direct, impassioned participation in the investigation, inspired the Chernov-Minor circles with grave fears that the case might form a basis for strengthening monarchistic ideas and tendencies among the popular masses and in the ranks of the young army which was then being born. Through direct, concealed or disguised agents—political activists who brought only ill to Russia and its people—this view of the significance of the Tsar's case was conveyed to the very heart of the Ekaterinburg Regional Court. Its first agents, the investigator, Nametkin, and the member of the court, Sergeyev, irrespective of their personal qualities, characters and political coloration, were, in their investigatory activities, unquestionably under the influence of the sick current of political thought described above, which infected the civil authorities at that time, and of the political parties of former members of the Constituent Assembly which were exercising their influence upon it.[42]

The judicial investigation was initiated on July 30, 1918, by the acting public prosecutor, Kutuzov. According to General Dieterichs the general reaction was unfavorable. Kutuzov's proposal was met with "great lack of sympathy and suspicion," to such an extent that "no member of the 'Oblast Ural' Government, during the entire period of its existence, ever once showed an interest in this case." [43]

Nametkin's dismissal, and his replacement by Sergeyev, are described by General Dieterichs as follows:

From the first days of investigator Nametkin's work the public prosecutor, Kutuzov, saw his complete unfitness for the conduct of such an involved and important matter. Nametkin distinguished himself not only by laziness and carelessness in his work, he simply ignored his plain duties as an investigator. Since no other qualified investigators were available, Kutuzov raised the question of entrusting conduct of the investigation, as the law provided, to one of the members of the court. His choice fell upon two, Mikhnovich and Plyuskov. In preliminary conversations with the president of the court, Glasson, it was finally decided to propose Mikhnovich, an experienced former investigator and a man of integrity, unaffected by the prevailing political currents. Since regulations required that a member of the court proposed for conduct of an investigation should be elected "by a general meeting of the divisions of the Regional Court," interested political groups sought to secure a candidate more pleasing to them—a third candidate for the investigation —Ivan Sergeyev, who was also a member of the court. On

August 7, to the surprise of the public prosecutor, Kutuzov, and in spite of the previous agreement with the president of the court, Glasson, the greatest number of votes was cast for I. A. Sergeyev. The conduct of the preliminary investigation of the case of the murder of the former Tsar was accordingly vested in him.

The regular court prosecutor, V. Iordansky, the man whom Kutuzov merely replaced, soon arrived in Ekaterinburg. The conduct of the civil investigation was completely separated from the investigation being made by the military authorities. The latter maintained an almost hostile attitude towards the appointment of I. A. Sergeyev to conduct the investigation, as he was elected under the influence of definite political currents in Chernov's direction. The military authorities were in general very much prejudiced against I. A. Sergeyev personally.[44]

With respect to Sergeyev himself, General Dieterichs had the following to say:

Although Sergeyev had, in the past, gone through the rank of court investigator, judging by the manner in which he conducted the case of the Tsar, with which he was entrusted, one might have thought that he had never in his life had any connection with this specialized profession. One can only assume that, as the candidate of certain political tendencies, Sergeyev was in general opposed to the case of the Tsar and that he looked upon it as upon the ordinary fulfillment of office work. . . . .

If Nametkin was distinguished for laziness and apathy toward his duties, Sergeyev, in the work accomplished, demonstrated a complete absence of the most modest investigative talents and an absolute lack of understanding of the investigator's profession. His interrogation of witnesses consisted in the mere notation of what the witness, or the criminal himself, wanted to tell. Any effort to direct the questioning in accordance with a definite thought, a definite plan, or a system of complimentary questions, was completely lacking with Sergeyev, or can be observed in the protocol only when the witness himself, accidentally, or the criminal, provided the material for this in his testimony. He [Sergeyev] completely ignored the possibility of establishing facts through investigation and thorough examination of items of material evidence. He only collected them. With Sergeyev the material evidence speaks nothing of itself, it does not help to establish the facts of the crime, it does not open up new paths of investigation, it simply represents "additions" in the narrow sense of the article of the law.[45]

He [Sergeyev] moved to Ekaterinburg during the Kerenshchina, when capacity for, and love of work and knowledge had already lost their significance in the judicial world, and importance was attached only to words, speeches, politics, meetings, democratic principles and other poison emanating from the disorganization of the year passed, 1917. And Sergeyev now adhered, apparently, to that camp once again and was accordingly elected to conduct a historic, national case.[46]

Sergeyev dragged on the investigation for six months, taking almost no step beyond what had been furnished to him by the military-criminal investigating division during its first two weeks of useful work. All that he did on his own was to make a more thorough examination of the Ipatiev House, photograph the rooms, cut pieces of wood with bullet marks from the walls and floor, superficially question six additional people who were run across by chance, accept a few documents from the telegraph office, and that was it.[47] He did not immerse himself in the investigation, he did not develop it or study it. The material evidence and the effects of the Imperial Family which were collected at the Ipatiev House, in the vicinity of the mine shaft, and taken from various persons, remained unsorted, unexamined and even undescribed. He did not show any interest in going to the Koptyaki woods himself, investigating the tracks, or seeing what was being done at the Ganina mine. He did not summon the witnesses indicated by the data of the criminal investigating division, although they were right in the city.[48]

General Dieterichs makes short shrift of the excuses advanced by Sergeyev—lack of funds and the indifference of superiors. Wilton, however, indicates that these problems were quite serious.[49]

According to Wilton, the Governor-General of the Urals even refused to provide Nametkin with "the monthly stipend of a typist." And he further points out that even after the seizure of power by Admiral Kolchak, "perhaps the worst enemies of the investigation were in the Ministry of Justice." At that time, presumably, the "democratic principles and similar poison" of the "Kerenshchina" had been eliminated.

In fairness to Sergeyev it should be noted that Sokolov's tests and extensive second search of the mine area turned up very little, if anything, that was more conclusive than the things already found. Sergeyev, moreover, could hardly be blamed for not going personally to the mine when the officers, who were so "prejudiced" against him, had the search there well in hand. The work there, moreover, was being supervised by his own assistant prosecutor, Magnitsky. Sergeyev would certainly seem entitled to rely upon Magnitsky's report on materials found. And even General Dieterichs concedes that Sergeyev, in the last month of his work, after he had been asked to give an accounting, showed "extraordinary energy and activity." [50]

Sergeyev's conclusions, in any event, were the same as those subsequently expressed by Dieterichs and Sokolov—that the entire family had been shot. He differed only in his refusal to place blame on the central Soviet authorities in Moscow.

General Dieterichs even went so far as to insinuate that Sergeyev's unhurried approach, and his refusal to implicate the central Soviet authorities, were influenced by his Jewish origin. There were persons of Jewish origin in the Bolshevik leadership, both in Moscow and Ekaterinburg, and Dieterichs, whose book contains many anti-Semitic assertions and expressions of opinion, states with bold innuendo: "The investigation was in the hands of a member of the murderers' race—a Jew." [51]

The appointment of Sergeyev's successor, on February 7, 1919, is described, pages 113-115, by the latter himself, i.e., Sokolov. At that time Sokolov was employed as Court Investigator for Especially Important Cases of the Regional Court at Omsk. Previously he had served as Court Investigator for Major Cases at Penza.

Sokolov was a confirmed monarchist. According to General Dieterichs, he "hated Kerensky and everything borne and left as a heritage from the Kerenshchina to the depths of his soul." [52] He escaped to White-occupied Siberia some time after the Bolshevik seizure of power, in disguise—according to some as a peasant, according to Bulygin as a tramp.

Following his appointment to the Romanov case he had only five months to work at the site—in and near Ekaterinburg—because, due to the return of the Bolsheviks, work there had to be abandoned on July 10, 1919. There is no indication that Sokolov ever went to Perm, where the criminal investigating division was working. Perm was retaken by the Bolsheviks on July 1, 1919.

IV. Evidence of Murder

Without in any way impugning the honesty or sincerity of any of the people concerned, it must be stated that the evidence of murder is not conclusive. There was evidence, of course—charred "remains" and oral testimony (largely hearsay)—but the quality and sources of that evidence are open to serious question. The arguments built around it by Sokolov and his supporters are not convincing, and other conclusions, having equal probability with their own, may as reasonably be drawn from the evidence described.

The Room of Execution–Bullet Marks and Blood Stains

Sokolov provides an elaborate description of the room in which the murder is supposed to have occurred. The location of every bullet hole and blood stain is carefully ascertained. There is a lengthy, detailed account of examinations and tests made by unidentified [53] experts. But the results, even if accepted in their entirety, go no further than to demonstrate that there was, indeed, shooting in this room, and that human blood was spilled. They do not establish the identity of the victims, or even the time at which the shooting occurred. The blood could have been anyone's; the bullets could have been fired at anyone, even at random into the walls and floor.

There is a picture presented, Photograph No. 51, of two bullet marks in the floor which are described as having been made by bullets which killed the Tsarevich. But nowhere in the text of Sokolov's account, or in the accounts of the other writers, is there the slightest hint of how these two bullet marks, out of the great number described, were connected with the Tsarevich. The assertion is completely unsupported and one is forced to conclude either

21

that important evidence was suppressed or that great liberties were taken in its interpretation.

Moreover, the time at which the bullet marks and blood stains first appeared is not entirely free from doubt. Sokolov describes thirty-two bullet marks. Dieterichs, however, quotes one of the guards, Michael Letemin, as testifying that on July 18, 1918, he could find only three small holes, and no traces of blood. This was two days after the murder was supposed to have occurred:

> All that I learned about the murder of the Tsar and His Family deeply interested me and I determined to confirm, in so far as possible, the information I had received. For this purpose, on the 18th of July, I went into the room in which the shooting occurred. I saw that the floor was clean, and I did not find any stains on the walls. On the rear wall, to the left as one enters the room, I saw three small holes of a depth of about one centimeter each; I saw no other evidence whatsoever of firing. In general I did not find traces of blood anywhere.[54]

The stains, of course, were supposed to have been "washed away" on the night of the murder. Many of them were in the crevices between the floorboards. As Letemin said, he had to look hurriedly, in the evening, to avoid being caught. And even the investigating court member, Sergeyev, failed to see some of the "spatters". It is possible, therefore, that Letemin might also have failed to see some of the bloody traces of the crime.

But what of the bullet holes? A man who had time to notice three "small" bullet holes could hardly have failed to notice so many of the others. And as for the bloodstains, even under the circumstances described, it is difficult to see how anyone could fail to notice them entirely. According to Sergeyev "stains of a reddish hue" were still "visible on the surface of the floor" more than a week after Letemin's look (see page 126), and Wilton, reporting his own personal observation, relates that "so much blood had flowed that the marks of the red-stained swab were distinctly visible a year later."[55]

There are other unexplained discrepancies in the descriptions of this room. Dieterichs states, for example, that there were bullet holes "in the upper cornices",[56] whereas Sokolov, who carefully located and listed each mark in accordance with the measurements of Sergeyev, puts the highest bullet hole in the door of the east wall. Its height is given, page 127, as only 173.3 centimeters (5 ft., 8.2811 in.) from the floor.

Finally, there are the seemingly self-contradictory assertions of the witness Gilliard, who visited the Ipatiev House sometime after the latter part of August, 1918. In his sworn deposition, March 5, 1919, he states:

> . . . at the time I left the house I could not believe that the Imperial Family had really perished. There was such a small number of bullet holes in the room which I had inspected, that I thought it impossible for everybody to have been executed.[57]

In his book, on the other hand, which was published in 1921, Gilliard describes his visit to the room of execution as follows:

> I went down to the bottom floor, the greater part of which was below the level of the ground. It was with intense emotion that I entered the room in which perhaps—I was still in doubt—they had met their death. Its appearance was sinister beyond expression. The only light filtered through a barred window at the height of a man's head. The walls and floor showed numerous traces of bullets and bayonet scars. The first glance showed that an odious crime had been perpetrated there and that several people had been done to death. But who? How?
>
> I became convinced that the Tsar had perished and, granting that, I could not believe that the Tsarina had survived him.[58]

There is certainly a difference in the impressions described in these two accounts of the same visit. The first conforms precisely with Letemin's. The second is vastly different.

How, we must ask, could Gilliard, after many weeks, see "at first glance" stains which Letemin had been unable to observe after an interval of only two days? Was the room later used for some other atrocity? Or had the evidence of execution—the numerous bullet holes and bayonet scars, the sinister and odious blood-stains —been planted in the room for the purpose of deceiving the White investigators?

Sokolov states that "evidence" of a similar nature was planted at Alapayevsk in connection with the disappearance of certain relatives of the Imperial Family.[59] The purpose in that case, as Sokolov describes it, was not to simulate a murder but to conceal one. Nevertheless, the type of "evidence" and the possible implications of callous inhumanity are the same.

The victims at Alapayevsk are believed to have been thrown alive into a deep mine shaft during the night of July 17-18, i.e., one day after the murder of the Imperial Family. In order to cover up their deed, the Bolsheviks are supposed to have staged a fake battle against "white guard conspirators", complete with the planting of the body of a "casualty".

Two of the local Bolsheviks were later caught and arrested. One was a member of the Cheka, the other was from the local Soviet. They "had seen all". They saw "who took the prisoners to the shaft" and who "simulated the attack by pretended 'white guards' ". The "casualty" turned out to be a peasant who had been seized earlier by the Chekists.[60]

Sokolov quotes the testimony of one of the captured Red soldiers who took part in the "defense":

> At three o'clock in the morning of July 18 the alarm was sounded in our barracks: the white guards were attacking. We quickly assembled, dressed and armed. We were taken to the Napolny school and deployed in a ring around it. We maintained this position for about half an hour and then approached the school itself. We saw no enemy, and there were no shots. Commissar Smolnikov was standing at the entrance to the school. He brushed himself off and said to us: "Comrades, we are going to get it now from the Ural Oblast Soviet, because the Princes have succeeded in getting away. The white guards took them off in an aeroplane." People's Court Judge Postnikov was there too, "with a big book in his hands", investigating the Princes' escape. Three or four days later people began to say that the commissars were deceiving the people, that they had made up the story of the Princes' rescue, and that the Princes had actually been killed by them.[61]

General Dieterichs, in describing this incident, even more clearly indicates the method by which the white guard "casualty" was obtained:

> In order to convince the local population of this invention the bolsheviks, after the murder had already been accomplished, staged a provocatory attack with a false enemy, and to make it more convincing shot a peasant who was being held under arrest for drunkenness, dragged his body to the school and presented the corpse as one of the white guards they had killed.[62]

If it was possible for the Bolsheviks to kill a man in order to provide the "evidence" of a "rescue", they would surely have had no difficulty in producing a little human blood, if they had wished to do so, to provide the necessary "evidence" of an execution.

"Remains" and Effects of the Imperial Family Found in Ekaterinburg and in the Vicinity of the Mine Shaft

Sokolov considered the "mute objects" found by the investigators to be the "very best" and "most valuable witnesses" of the murder. (See page 191.) Yet the descriptions of this evidence, and the arguments spun around it, are replete with inconsistencies.

In Chapter 19, for example, Sokolov argues that the Imperial Family could not have been planning to leave Ekaterinburg because "many medicines and various articles for treatment of the Tsarevich were found in the Ipatiev House." "Why," he asks, "did they not take, why abandon, the things he needed the most?"

A similar inference is drawn from the apparent abandonment of certain treasured items. Thus the things found in the Ipatiev House included such indispensable material as religious books belonging to various members of the Imperial Family which, as Sokolov says, "contained their whole moral outlook, their whole soul;" a ribbon of St. George from an overcoat with which the "Emperor never parted," and icons of great religious and sentimental value, including one which was "very nearly the most treasured object of the Empress," without which she "never went anywhere," and to deprive her of which "would be the same as taking her life."

The clear implication is that there was no truth in the rumors "that the Imperial Family had been taken away."

Yet there is other, similar, evidence which completely nullifies this implication, contradicts it, and perhaps even more strongly implies that the rumors were correct.

Many items found at the mine shaft, for example, are consistent only with the assumption that the victims were dressed and prepared for travel. Thus Sokolov describes miniature icons or images which, he says, "ordinarily" hung at the children's beds but which they wore "when travelling;" cloth believed to come from an "overcoat belonging to Alexei Nicholayevich"; a piece of fabric "cut from the Tsarevich's knapsack;" and remnants of a vial of salts such as the Tsarina and the Grand Duchesses "usually" took with them "when travelling."

According to General Dieterichs there was a piece of Dr. Botkin's overcoat.[63] There was also the corpse of Anastasia's dog, found at the bottom of the shaft. As General Dieterichs states, "the presence of the dog, Jemmi, with the Grand Duchess indicates that Anastasia Nicholayevna and accordingly, no doubt, the others, were dressed for the road." General Dieterichs concludes that Anastasia "did not part with the dog when she travelled and had taken it with her when she went down to the chamber of execution."[64]

Because "all of the Members of the Imperial Family were dressed for the road," General Dieterichs asserts, "they must have had with them at the Ganina mine all [of the jewels] that were sewn into their clothing at Tobolsk."[65]

Finally Sokolov himself states, page 237, with no apparent basis and in seeming contradiction of his witnesses,[66] that the Imperial Family was lured from its rooms "with deception, on the pretense of departure from the house."

It would thus appear that there was as much evidence to support the conclusion that the Imperial Family was prepared for a departure from Ekaterinburg as there was for the conclusion that they were not so prepared.

Other inferences drawn by the investigators from the "mute" evidence are equally inconclusive, especially those which relate to the destruction of bodies at the mine. According to the investigators, the bodies of the victims were partly cremated in fires of wood, gasoline and kerosene, and partly dissolved in sulphuric acid. The purpose of this destruction, it is asserted, was to conceal the crime.

Thus Sokolov states, page 191: "Here we have the same picture as in the Ipatiev House: the concealment from the world of the evil that had been committed." The Bolsheviks, he further explains (page 231), were anxious to conceal the murder of all except the Tsar:

". . . the essence of the Bolshevik lie became entirely clear to me. "We shot the Tsar, but not the *family*."

If this explanation is correct,[67] then, one supposes, the Bolsheviks would have made every effort to conceal the "remains". All those noticeable, incriminating items by which the investigators were actually able to identify the victims as members of the Imperial Family would have been thrown into the mine shaft, or even more carefully disposed of, and certainly would not have been left lying about on the surface.

Unfortunately Sokolov does not, in general, disclose which of the discovered items were found on the surface and which in the shaft. Of the 66 numbered items and categories of items listed in Chapter 22, only the "greasy masses, mixed with earth" and some shattered, burned bones are identified as having been found on the surface. For the rest Sokolov simply states, page 190; that "articles noticeable to the eye, as for instance the finger, Jemmi's corpse, many bones, were found in the bottom of the open shaft. . . ."

Sokolov could have given more detailed information about this matter. General Dieterichs, in his account, classifies the items very carefully. Those found during the first examination, made by the officers' commission, are divided by General Dieterichs in two classifications: those found on the surface and those found in the shaft.[68] Those found during the second examination, the examination made by Sokolov, are divided by General Dieterichs into four classifications.[69] In the case of the shaft there is a separate listing of items found in the large and small wells. (The small well was not explored in the first examination.) Items found on the surface are divided between those found under the ashes of the fire near the old birch tree and those found nearer the shaft, including items found in the clay-surfaced area and those found under the ashes of the fire made in that vicinity.

General Dieterichs' classification discloses that some very significant articles identified as belonging to the Tsarina or the children were found *lying on the surface.* They included the following:

A brilliant belonging to the Tsarina, weighing 12 karats. It was mounted in green gold and platinum and belonged to a large jeweled ornament. The experts determined that the value of such a brilliant, before the revolution, was 20,000 roubles.[70]

An emerald cross of Kulm, with pearl pendants. It belonged to one of the Grand Duchesses. It was badly burned, especially the pearls, of which only one still retained its natural color.[71]

Two small diamond-studded shoe buckles belonging to the Grand Duchesses.[72]

A brass buckle with a small coat of arms, with clasp, from a leather belt belonging to the Tsarevich.[73]

Five large brass buttons and one small one, with coats of arms, from military overcoats belonging to the Tsar or the Tsarevich.[74]

There were also a great many articles of feminine attire—shoe buckles, corset stays, buttons, belt buckles and so on—and such a mass of additional incriminating and possibly identifiable items, including smaller jewels, charred items of clothing, as well as burned, chopped and sawed human bones, that it is very difficult to believe that anyone really attempting to conceal a crime would have left them. General Dieterichs lists 54 items and *categories*

27

of items found on the surface. According to Nametkin, the officers, on their first trip to the mine, even found on top of one of the ashy piles what appeared to be a "completely burned rib." When they attempted to pick it up it "crumbled into fine ash."[75]

A far more thorough clean-up job would normally be expected of anyone who wished to destroy all evidence in the manner described in the accounts of the investigators. General Dieterichs lists 33 items and categories of items that were dropped in the shaft. In order to do this it was necessary to cut through a permanent layer of ice. And as Wilton relates, the "criminals" even took the trouble to adjust and anchor under water a "false floor" at the bottom of the smaller well.[76] It was beneath this floor that the corpse of the dog was found. Having gone thus far, why did the criminals not drop in everything?

If the criminals went to the lengths of burning eleven human bodies in open fires, even dissolving parts in sulphuric acid, and if they took the trouble to drop so much material into the mine shaft, why did they not drop it all in? Why did they leave some in piles of ashes? Why did they scatter others in the grass?

The Bolsheviks certainly knew how to dispose of the bodies without a trace. Of the Grand Duke Michael Alexandrovich, also presumed to have been murdered, there were no remains—no traces —at all.

One must also ask why, with the extensive forests of Siberia and the Ural Mountains at their disposal, the Bolsheviks made such a fanfare in a sensitive area, cordonning it off conspicuously, blocking a public road, driving off peasants, setting off explosions and producing a heavy stream of traffic—horses, wagons, trucks with gasoline and sulphuric acid. No such display accompanied the disappearance of the Grand Duke Michael Alexandrovich.

And why, one finally asks, did they even brag of their deed in writing on the wall, with the pretentiously moralizing quotation from Heine (see page 132):

> Belshazzar was that very night
> Seized by his slaves and killed outright.

This is the kind of clue one expects to find in a game or a contest— an amateur "treasure hunt"—but not in an execution supposed to have been planned by professional cutthroats bent on preserving secrecy at all costs, and carried out by agents of the Cheka. The Bolsheviks, pardon the expression, have never been so corny.

There were also other actions quite inconsistent with a real desire for concealment. Dieterichs, for example, relates that on the morning of July 19, after the bodies, supposedly, had been disposed of, Yermakov's group of cremators were sitting in the garden of the communist club at Verkh-Isetsk and talking "in a most frank manner." "They were talking," he says, "about all they had seen and done." "They listed those who had been murdered; they remarked that jewels had been sewn in the belts of the clothing." They related that "the bodies were still warm." And of course they spoke loud enough to be overheard, so that General Dieterichs was ultimately able to report the conversation.[77]

In another, similar, violation of security, some Red soldiers who were "under the strong influence of alcohol," boasted to the peasants of Koptyaki: "We burned your Nicholas and all of them there."[78]

Incriminating table linen, towels and napkins with "large, thick bloodstains," on which someone had "wiped his hands without washing them," were left lying on and under the table in the buffet of the Ipatiev House.[79] They were still there when the first investigators arrived, more than a week after the "crime" was committed.

And finally, as General Dieterichs relates, the director of the destruction, Isaac Goloshchekin, himself helped spill the beans. Thus General Dieterichs states:

> Nicholas Kotechev, while in prison, heard a conversation between two persons who had served in Isaac Goloshchekin's guard, one of whom accompanied Isaac on his trip to Moscow after the murder of the Imperial Family and overheard Isaac Goloshchekin tell his fellow travelers that they had burned the former Tsar.[80]

In view of all this, it seems more likely that the Bolsheviks were trying to call attention to the "evidence" of their "crime" than that they were trying to conceal it. From their point of view it might well have seemed more culpable, more politically inexpedient, and therefore more a matter for concealment, to allow such "enemies of the people" as the Imperial Family were said to be, to escape than it would have been to murder them.

It is admitted, in any event, that the Bolsheviks were planting false evidence of some kind. Both Wilton and Dieterichs refer to it. Wilton states that these efforts were ineffective:

> In vain they drew innumerable red herrings of their own color over the trail, suborning false witnesses to give misleading

information about the whereabouts of the bodies, announcing officially that the family had been removed to "a safe place," etc.[81]

General Dieterichs, on the other hand, bitterly complained that the agents of the criminal investigating division were being duped by such spurious evidence:

Snatching up information from the reports of various, often even unknown agents, the criminal investigating division threw itself time after time into the work-up of those data, those ideas, in that direction and with that tinge desired by the perpetrators of the crime. It was the latter who actually launched and inspired inquiry, through their counter-agents. And the criminal investigating division, without verifying original sources, without establishing whether a particular agent's report was worthy of belief, without ascertaining who had provided the information, whence he had come or who he had been in the past, would seize upon such new information as the basis for its work simply because the information was obtained by it and, above all, would direct its work in such a manner as to prove to others the truth of the evidence it had obtained. Along this path, of course, it ran into planted witnesses and material evidence manufactured by the same agents, and its whole investigation went down the false trails desired by the criminal side, bringing great confusion, obscurity and drivel into the investigatory material of the court investigator.[82]

The question is: which evidence was false and which wasn't? The investigators insist that the evidence of escape was false. But such statements are a two-edged sword. One wants to know why only the criminal investigating division was led down "false trails", and why only that evidence was "planted" which indicated the possibility of escape and which ran counter to General Dieterichs' and Sokolov's conclusions. If false evidence was being planted at all, then all was suspect.

And the manner in which the attention of the investigators was turned to the mine shaft is certainly not above such suspicion. Let us start with General Dieterichs' account of this incident.[83] According to General Dieterichs, on the morning of July 27, 1918, two days after the capture of Ekaterinburg, a certain Lieutenant Andrei Andreyevich Sheremetevsky brought some "burned effects and objects of various parts of clothing, linen and footwear" to the commandant of the 8th city district. Among these items were two of the most significant and identifiable of all the objects found on the surface of the mine area—the emerald cross and the diamond-studded shoe buckles. All, according to Sheremetevsky, had been found by peasants of Koptyaki, the village in which he, Sheremetevsky, had been hiding from the Bolsheviks. "Upon their return to the village they [the peasants] gave everything they had found to him, Sheremetevsky."[84]

Sokolov's account, pages 165-166, is slightly different. According to Sokolov (a) two peasants, not Sheremetevsky, made the first report of events at the mine area, (b) the first such report was made at Verkh-Isetsk, and (c) nothing was removed from the mine until at least July 28.

Whichever account is correct, the information provided was accepted in the same rash, incautious manner in which General Dieterichs complains that the "reports" of "unknown" agents were "snatched up" by the criminal investigating division. General Dieterichs himself describes the reaction to Sheremetevsky's (or the peasants') report as follows:

> This new information caused a great commotion in the commission of officers appointed to the investigation. Examination of the things brought in by Sheremetevsky, and their comparison with the things found in the Ipatiev House left no doubt of the identity of the things and that they had belonged to the Imperial Family. There were exactly the same shoe buckles with brilliants, the same buttons, hooks and eyes, the same suspender and garter clasps, etc. It became clear to everyone that the bolsheviks had burned the clothing of Members of the Imperial Family in the Koptyaki forest. Thence, as a logical result of the impression derived from examination of the Ipatiev House, arose the terrible, definite conviction: the Most August Family had been murdered; the bodies were taken by the criminals to the forest where They were searched, disrobed and thrown into the shaft, while the clothing, linen and other items were burned in order to conceal the traces. All those who from moral convictions had until this time doubted the possibility of such a beastly crime, now cast off their doubts. For all, the fact of the murder of all Members of the Imperial Family became a truth, which for its final reality required only the discovery of the bodies of the victims.[85]

If the Bolsheviks were trying to conceal this murder, they were certainly doing a very poor job. But who was Sheremetevsky? Did anyone question whether he was "worthy of belief," "whence he had come," or "who had he been in the past?" Was any effort made to determine whether he, or perhaps some of his peasants, were not "counter-agents" such as General Dieterichs describes? The ap-

31

parent discrepancy in Sokolov's and Dieterichs' accounts of this incident only increases the mystery which surrounds it.

General Dieterichs recognized the possibility of deception at the mine area and mentions, in this connection, the possible "simulation of the method and the place of concealment of the victims."[86] But he dismisses this possibility. The perpetrators of the crime, he maintains, "would hardly be willing, for the sake of simulation, to sacrifice a brilliant worth 20,000 roubles, pearl earrings, an emerald cross and similar jewelry."

But the question is—why not? If they were willing to go to the lengths to which they had already gone, why should they hesitate over a small part of the Romanov jewels? The stakes were very high. They involved the Emperor of a very large and important domain, for whom the ransom might well have been extraordinary, perhaps the continued existence of the Soviet regime itself.[87]

The evidence of murder found at the mine was no less suspect than the evidence of escape, which the investigators rejected. The Bolsheviks, if they wished to conceal the removal of the Imperial Family, and simulate their execution, could have planted a few jewels, a few scorched items of clothing, and a few charred bones at the mine near Ekaterinburg just as easily as they could have planted the entire human body in the school house at Alapayevsk.

Moreover, there are conflicts and very implausible explanations, even in the accounts of the investigators, with respect to the items of this nature found at the mine near Ekaterinburg. One such conflict relates to Dr. Botkin's false teeth. General Dieterichs says that they were found *in* the shaft,[88] whereas Wilton states that they were found outside, or "*near* the shaft."[89] (Italics added.) The front teeth, Wilton reports, "were deeply encrusted with mire, as if the body had been dragged face downwards and thereby the teeth, catching in the hard clay soil, had dragged the plate out of the dead man's mouth."

Bulygin seems to be in accord with Wilton, stating that the false teeth were found "close by" the human finger.[90] But this, perhaps, is only because Bulygin, in turn, is in trouble with respect to the finger. He reports it as "found on the slope leading down to the No. 7 pit," i.e., the shaft,[91] whereas all of the other writers place it in the shaft itself. There is little chance of misunderstanding as to where the "slope" ends and the "shaft" begins, because General Dieterichs accommodatingly tells us that the finger, like Dr. Botkin's teeth, was found in "muck from the bottom."[92]

There is disagreement also on the sex of the finger. General Dieterichs relates that Dr. Derevenko, the Tsarevich's physician, "categorically" identified the finger as Dr. Botkin's.[93] But the committee of experts in Omsk was "more inclined to believe" that it belonged to a woman. (See page 189.) Bulygin repeatedly and confidently describes it as the Tsarina's.[94]

In addition there are two bullets which General Dieterichs describes as being "very deformed at the tips, in the manner typical of a bullet striking against bone."[95] If all the bodies were burned such bullets would presumably have melted into formless masses. And General Dieterichs' statement is not the result of mere inadvertence because he describes still another bullet, which had a "flattened end, in the manner usual in the event of striking human bone," and which was "also determined to have been in a fire where it was subjected to the intense heat of the flames."[96]

Sokolov does not tax his readers' credulity in this manner. With him such bullets "melted in the fire and then, cooling, retained the irregular shape of a congealed mass." (See page 189.) Nevertheless, he can, on occasion, show equal defiance of the laws of thermal forces. His list of finds includes "pieces of lead foil," collected by the Tsarevich and presumed to have been in the latter's pockets. (See page 183.) These, it would seem, ought to have been more susceptible to fire than the bullets, and thus burned beyond recognition.

Another item which taxes the readers' credulity is Anastasia's dog. General Dieterichs explains its presence at the mine by asserting that "it was so small that the Grand Duchess used to carry it either in the sleeve of her suit, or in her muff." The "murderers," he says, "undoubtedly discovered the dog only when they got the bodies to the clay-surfaced area,"[97] i.e., to the mine.

This hardly explains how the dog was kept quiet during the nightmare scene of mass murder which the investigators describe, including the long, difficult truck ride with eleven corpses and the death agony of its mistress, who, as two of the writers indicate, "at first escaped the bullets," then "rolled about, screamed" and "fought desperately" with one of the murderers.[98]

The best explanation for all these discrepancies would be the planting of evidence by the "criminals", the simulated rather than actual cremation of eleven bodies, and the vivid imagination of some of the investigators. It also must be accepted as a fact that some of the witnesses were lying. One of the depositions reproduced by Wilton contains the following assertion, made by the guard, Medvedyev:

In answer to your question as to where the bodies of the Imperial Family were taken, I can only state the following: On the way from Ekaterinburg railway station to Alapayevsk I met Peter Ermakov and asked him where the bodies had been carried to. Ermakov explained that the bodies had been thrown down the shaft of a mine near the Verkh-Isetsk Works, and that the shaft had afterwards been destroyed by bombs or explosives in order to fill it up. I do not know, and I never heard anything concerning the woodpiles that were burned near the shaft.[99]

This assertion is obviously inconsistent with the theories advanced by the investigators. According to them the bodies were not thrown into the shaft, or exploded, but burned and dissolved in sulphuric acid. The shaft, moreover, was found in good condition.

Furthermore, General Dieterichs indicated that the procedure described by Yermakov was impossible:

. . . to destroy a mine shaft with the aid of hand grenades is absolutely impossible; it is sheer fantasy, and an excellent example of this is the fact that the Nizhny-Semichensk shaft [where the victims of Alapayevsk were killed], in which not only hand grenades were exploded, but also large artillery shells of considerable explosive force were thrown, was not successfully destroyed, but sustained only the ripping out of several planks from a part of the framework. In this respect Yermakov was undoubtedly lying to Pavel Medvedyev and, we must suppose, also lied when he said the bodies were thrown into the shafts.[100]

Presumably it was for this reason that Sokolov omitted the passage from Medvedyev's testimony—without even indicating the omission. But the conflict found its way into Sokolov's account nevertheless. Thus on page 165 he states: "During all of this time [the two days during which the mine area was cordonned off] the explosion of grenades could be heard at the mine." General Dieterichs, on the other hand, states that there were only "2-3 explosions of hand grenades" and thereafter "there was no further firing of any kind."[101]

In this fashion the lies of the witnesses brought inconsistency, conflict and implausibility into the accounts of the investigators themselves. .

34

Sokolov did not put very great faith in the credibility of any of the witnesses. At the end of Chapter 22 he describes the "mute", physical evidence of the murder as "the very best, the most valuable witnesses" and then invites the reader to "listen to what the cunning human tongue has to say." (Page 191.)

He openly questions the veracity of two witnesses: Paul Medvedyev, whom he calls "not very literate", and Anatole Yakimov, whom he describes as "erratic". Medvedyev testified that he did not fire at any of the victims, yet Sokolov asks, page 215: "Did Medvedyev commit murder himself, or was he only a witness of the murder?" Yakimov said that he was in bed the whole time, yet again Sokolov asks, page 216: "Did Yakimov witness the murder with his own eyes, or did he know about it only through the words of others?"

General Dieterichs expresses a low opinion of the veracity of all "the creators of the revolution." They had a "habit" of lying, he says. He discusses this in telling the story of Medvedyev's first appearance.[102]

Medvedyev acted as a sort of chief non-commissioned officer among the guards at the Ipatiev House. He fled with the Bolsheviks upon the liberation of Ekaterinburg and, as General Dieterichs relates, later defected and turned up at the Whites' 139th Evacuation Hospital near Perm. He first disclosed his true identity in a conversation with one of the nurses, Lydia Semenovna Guseva. Apparently she was not one to carry tales, and Medvedyev finally had to tell his story to the authorities himself.

The authorities—the public prosecutor of the Perm Regional Court and an agent of the criminal investigating division—also had their troubles with Guseva. When they went to the house of the Red Cross Association, where she was then living, they were told she was ill. She could not be seen. Thus spoke the Directress, Alexandra Mikhailovna Urusova. But the authorities were undaunted. The state of Guseva's health would have to be verified— by medical examination. At this point she turned out to be quite well and quickly appeared.

Even then Guseva denied that she had ever talked with Medvedyev about his work at the Ipatiev House or the fate of the Imperial Family. She changed this story only when confronted with Medvedyev himself.

Dieterichs was quite naturally annoyed with this uncooperative attitude:

She [Guseva] was no longer a child, no longer an adolescent; she was a mature, experienced, responsible woman who could not fail to be aware of what she was doing. But nevertheless she lied. She lied to the point of making herself a criminal, concealing an assassin, concealing a crime of which she was well aware. And her Directress, Urusova, lied with her, like a young school girl. And she lied so unsuccessfully that she was at once exposed. Neither of them were bolsheviks; they were adherents of the new regime, of the new political trend. There was nothing to fear.

What, then, was the difficulty?

What was the reason for this useless, harmful and dangerous lying?

Habit. The conditions of normal life, environment, society, had dulled the sense of a need to live "with a clear conscience" and affixed in human nature the perverted idea that life can be made to conform to a "false conscience". The entire composite of life bred the basis of criminality in the soul, breaking down the moral basis of the state and uniting society with crime.[103]

In a similar vein Dieterichs speaks of two other potential witnesses, who are not mentioned by Sokolov, but from whom some very helpful information was apparently expected.[104] One of these was Dr. Nicholas Arsen'yevich Sakovich, former Oblast Commissar of Public Health in Ekaterinburg. At a meeting held in March or April, 1918, Sakovich heard several commissars discuss the possibility of murdering the Tsar during the transfer from Tobolsk.[105] Dieterichs describes Dr. Sakovich as a person who could change color at will and as often as circumstances directed:

In January, 1917 he was a monarchist, in March of the same year he declared himself a social-democrat, at the end of the year a social-revolutionary, in January 1918 he became a bolshevik commissar, and in August of that year he declared himself non-party.[106]

He died, according to Dieterichs, in the Omsk prison, in June, 1919, of galloping consumption.[107]

The other man, Semen Georgiyevich Loginov, was reportedly a Social-Democrat [Menshevik] who had acted as a secret political agent for the Bolsheviks. His ultimate fate, and the nature of his testimony, are not revealed.

Dieterichs angrily denounced both for their false and incomplete testimony:

Both of them had been caught, as it is said, "at the scene of the crime." Both were well aware that the evidence against them was so serious that their testimony could not in any way affect their fate, that the death sentence was assured for both. Their stories were their last word—the confession before death. In such circumstances those who have an ideology either refuse to talk or, if they decide to say something, then it is a proud confession of principle, of the guiding light of their life, for the sake of which they have struggled in life and in death, not sparing others, and they go themselves proudly and boldly to the scaffold.

But what do we find here? The word of these people?—representatives of hundreds and thousands of other such creators of the revolution and collaborators with Soviet rule?

It is, first of all, a *lie*: a lie which nourishes their life, a lie in which their actions are steeped, a lie which gives strength to their last word. An inartistic, coarse, far-fetched lie; a lie involving almost every phase, every statement. A lie of small, nasty boys, playing obnoxious pranks and seeking to deceive their elders. Humiliating, vexing to the point of pain for Russia, for the name of Russia, is the feeling evoked by this lie of Sakovich and Loginov. . . .[108]

General Dieterichs quite obviously felt the same way about those witnesses upon whom his conclusions depend. They had all been employed as guards at the Ipatiev House, and at least two of them, Medvedyev and Letemin, were known to be members of the Bolshevik Party.[109]

Dieterichs certainly did not believe Yakimov because he states, in flat contradiction to what the man himself maintained, that he "was present at the shooting." [110]

Letemin, he calls a "heinous convict" who had been deprived by the Tsar's government of all property and personal rights and sentenced to four years in a corrective prison. He was also a typical "collaborator":

Letemin was typical of those collaborators required by the Soviet leaders and whom they used, not only for the commission of the fanatic crime against the former Tsar and His Family, but also in all of their other activities for the establishment of the so-called peoples' rule in Russia. Letemin was a brilliant representative of just that soviet peoples' rule. He could pity a dog because in essence, by nature, he was a beast himself. And commissar Mrachkovski, who, in selecting volunteers [for the guard] did not accept all who applied, upon making inquiries concerning Letemin's conduct, which, of course, did not reveal wholesome moral qualities, accepted him at once as the type required by the soviet regime.[111]

37

Proskuryakov is described as a "hooligan" [112] who, Dieterichs relates, had become the "blind tool of other people, people of bad will," because of his "youth and stupidity." [113] The blame is placed upon his parents:

> . . . in his 17-year-old eyes, in all his inward make-up, his parents did not have that moral force of authority which, above all other influences, should have and could have stopped him at the edge of the abyss.

Medvedyev, oddly enough, is described by General Dieterichs as the most "cognizant," and his testimony in general, "quite credible." [114] It is hard to explain this attitude since Medvedyev was known to be a member of the Bolshevik party, and his testimony was contradicted in one respect or another by all of the other principal witnesses except, apparently, that "beast" Letemin. Even Medvedyev's wife contradicted him!

General Dieterichs attempts to explain Medvedyev's lies with the rather superfluous assertion that he lied only when it was in his own interest:

> He lied in only one respect—when describing his own role, his own part in the matter. It was quite clear that he was trying in every way to cover up his own participation and unload some of his fault upon others. In the final analysis his explanation is the typical acknowledgment of a murderer with respect to a murder that has been committed by many people with premeditation and according to prearranged conspiracy. Each of the many murderers, admitting the basic fact of the crime and his legal guilt, attempts in every way to exculpate himself at the expense of the others from his real guilt, beclouding his role, minimizing or denying acts which he has himself performed. For this reason Medvedyev stubbornly denied that he took part in the shooting even when confronted by his wife.[115]

It is, of course, axiomatic that no one lies against self-interest. What General Dieterichs seems to overlook, however, is Medvedyev's real interest. As General Dieterichs tells us, Medvedyev was a known member of the Bolshevik party. Therefore, it must be presumed, his sympathies, his loyalties and his obedience lay with the Bolsheviks. He would accordingly say what the Bolsheviks wanted him to say because his own interest lay in that direction. And if the Bolsheviks, therefore, had ordered him to state that the Imperial Family had been murdered when in fact they were not, he could certainly be expected to do so. Naturally the testimony would be so designed as to decrease his personal risk as far as possible, but in general it would be bound to follow the Bolshevik line unless, of course, the interrogators in some way, by compulsion or bribery, made it more in his interest to testify otherwise. But in the latter event his testimony would also be worthless.

The same considerations are true of Letemin, who was likewise a member of the Party.[116] They may also be true—to some lesser extent perhaps—of the other witnesses, Proskuryakov and Yakimov. Even if the latter were not formally Party members, they were, after all, working for the Bolsheviks in a very sensitive position. Their sympathies no doubt therefore also lay with them.

Dieterichs complained that the criminal investigating division was accepting information "without ascertaining who had provided" it, "whence he had come or who he had been in the past." But the conclusions of the judicial investigators were based on something far less reliable. In the case of the guards the judicial investigators *knew* who was providing the information and what their background was. And it was the *worst possible*. Yet the information was accepted. More than that, it formed the basis of their conclusion.

As in the case of the evidence at the mine, one cannot escape the suspicion that the oral evidence was planted—inspired by the planners of Soviet strategy. As Wilton says, there were agents about who "did not know the truth themselves. They merely related what they had been instructed to say." [117]

In the case of the oral testimony, the initial leads were provided under circumstances as suspicious as the appearance of Sheremetevsky. Letemin was apprehended on the very first day, July 25, 1918, because, as Dieterichs relates, the Tsarevich's dog, Joy, was sitting right out in his yard, in plain sight, for everyone to see.[118] The second lead is described by Dieterichs as an act of Providence.[119] Actually it came from Yakimov's sister, through a certain Feodor Nikitich Gorshkov, who related what Yakimov's sister had told someone else—Michael Vladimirovich Tomashevsky. Gorshkov gave this information to the public prosecutor, Kutuzov, on July 29, 1918—two days after Sheremetevsky's appearance.[120]

If this testimony was inspired, it was well planned.

Letemin had a perfect alibi. He was at home on the night of the murder and presumably safe from prosecution. The sources of his information had escaped with the Bolsheviks and were out of reach. Therefore there could be no reprisals or cross-examination.

Yakimov, Medvedyev and Proskuryakov, having also fled, were in the same position.

But the testimony of these other guards could appear, nevertheless. Yakimov's testimony would be given by his sister; Medvedyev's by his wife; and so on. And as Dieterichs tells us, there was actually quite a bit of this kind of second-hand testimony through "innocent", uninvolved intermediaries:

> ... in the first days of the work the criminal investigating division succeeded in tracking down and detaining a whole series of people who were either related to, or friends of, the workers who had served in the guard. Those thus detained included Maria Medvedyeva, wife of Paul Medvedyev, the leader of the guards; Evdokia Starkova, mother of Ivan Starkov, one of the guards; Anna Timofeyeva, an acquaintance of the guard Leonid Labushev; Felix Yakubtsov, a friend of the guard Ivan Kolotov and, finally, Michael Letemin. . . .[121]

In this way, it might be assumed, nobody could get hurt, and nobody could be cross-examined on essential points.

But then, let us suppose, something went wrong. Sergeyev was not sufficiently active. The investigation of the "inspired" theory petered out, and the criminal investigation got hot on the right trail in Perm. A new "plant" was required to stimulate the advocates of the murder theory. So Medvedyev, Yakimov and Proskuryakov were ordered to present themselves. They did not want to be incriminated any more than necessary so Medvedyev denied participation in the shooting [122]—thus contradicting his wife; and Yakimov stated that he was not present [123]—thus contradicting his sister. Proskuryakov, after several denials of all connection with the case, came up with an alibi too—he was in the guard house.

The appearance of Medvedyev certainly conforms to this picture. As indicated above, he defected from the Reds and turned up voluntarily in the Perm area early in 1919. General Dieterichs gives the date of his arrest as February 11, 1919.[124] Proskuryakov also defected from the Reds, page 195, and was arrested on February 21, 1919.[124] Yakimov defected at the same time and place as Medvedyev, in the evacuation of Perm (see page 200), and was arrested on April 2, 1919.[124]

In another context, Dieterichs himself indicates the unreliability of voluntary testimony. Criticizing Sergeyev for inviting such testimony through the press he states:

Of course none of the eye-witnesses would come to testify voluntarily. Who, indeed, could such eye-witnesses be? The participants in the crime, the worker-guards, had hidden themselves. It was necessary to search them out, and they, of course, could not be among the volunteers. Isaac Goloshchekin and Yankel Yurovsky were on the way to Moscow in a parlor-car and Sergeyev could not, of course, count on them. This left only some accidental, poor, forgotten bystander, scared out of his wits by the Bolshevik terror, catching the familiar scent of a returning Kerenshchina in the new regime and even in Sergeyev's announcement. Naturally, none of them could come either, nor did come, fearing that the new leadership might take them for reactionaries.[125]

If we accept this reasoning, there was really only one explanation for the voluntary submissions—for the appearance of those who, like Medvedyev, did voluntarily submit themselves. They were spurious, planted witnesses. And the same might also be said, on the basis of this reasoning, of those who seemed to fall, like ripe fruit, into the investigators' hands.

And if these witnesses were not planted, their testimony was, nevertheless, very weak. Not only were they collaborators, Bolsheviks, liars and persons of poor character, but, upon analysis of their testimony it also becomes apparent that not one of them even claimed to have seen the actual murder of the entire family. Medvedyev alone admits to having seen the bodies, and the coup de grace administered to the Tsarevich. The first volley occurred while he was outside the execution chamber, and by the time he came back the Imperial Family "had already all been shot and were lying on the floor." (Page 208.)

Yakimov asserted that he was not awakened until 4 A.M., long after all the evidence was removed. He did not see the bodies. He did not even see the blood. He repeats the stories of four other guards, who were not available for questioning—Kleshchev, Deryabin, Lesnikov and Brusyanin.

Letemin apparently did not enter the room of execution until two days after the event. And then he could find no blood—and only three bullet holes. He gives the story of Strekotin, who was also not available for questioning.

Proskuryakov first denied ever being in the guard unit. Admitting this, he denied all knowledge of the murder. In all he changed his testimony five times. At the end he gives the stories of Strekotin and Medvedyev. But somewhere in the middle, page 196, he gives the story of Andrei Starkov—"that the family had been taken away

41

from the house". Who could possibly say at which point he was telling the truth?

Such "hearsay" evidence, even at its best, is weak. Here there were no bodies to support it, and the stories themselves are full of inconsistencies.

There was, first of all, the disputed status of Yakimov and Medvedyev. They are the only two witnesses who were said to have actually seen the crime. And they themselves denied it. In the case of Yakimov it is only his sister, Agafonova, who asserts, page 217, that she "understood from him that he . . . had witnessed the entire murder with his own eyes." Medvedyev, on the other hand, is contradicted by three people—his wife, Letemin and Proskuryakov. All of them assert categorically that he did, definitely, take part in the shooting. (See pages 194, 199, 215-216). Proskuryakov flatly asserted: "In this he lies."

Medvedyev's testimony is also contradicted in many other respects. For example:

1- He states, pages 207 and 211, that Yurovsky awakened the Imperial Family. Yet his wife says, page 215, that he told her he was himself ordered to do it, and delegated the duty to Dobrynin.

2- He states, pages 207-208, that he collected the revolvers of all the guards on duty and distributed eleven of them to the "Letts" for use in the execution. Proskuryakov testified that the Letts had their own Nagants.[126] Yakimov's deposition, as reproduced by Wilton,[127] confirms this.

3- He states, page 208, that after the first volley the Tsarevich was "still groaning" and had to be shot again "two or three more times." But Yakimov told Agafonova that the Tsarevich was "killed instantly" in the first volley.[128]

4- He states, pages 207, 211, 214, that the Imperial Family was awakened at midnight, and that by "3 o'clock A.M. everything was finished"—including the clean-up. Yet Tsetsegov heard the truck leave at 3 A.M. (page 193), and Proskuryakov, who helped in the clean-up was not awakened until 3 A.M. (page 197).

There are also additional contradictions of Yakimov's testimony:

1- Yakimov states, page 200, that he and several other guards slept until 4 A.M. when all the clean-up work was done. But Proskuryakov says, pages 197-198, that all of the worker-guards not on duty took part in the clean-up.

2- Yakimov states, page 202, that just prior to the execution Yurovsky spoke to the Tsar as follows:

42

Nicholas Alexandrovich, your relatives have tried to save you, but did not succeed. And we ourselves must shoot you.

But Letemin states, page 194, that Yurovsky read from a piece of paper and said: "Your life is finished."

Medvedyev's wife testified, page 215, that the paper read: "The revolution is dying, and you must die also."

According to Sokolov, page 199, Proskuryakov merely said that Yurovsky began to read "some kind of paper." But Wilton, who concedes that there were "many variations of this utterance",[129] produces Proskuryakov's deposition. It quotes Yurovsky as follows: "Your race must cease to live!" [130]

Some variation in the versions of this utterance would be natural and expected. It would not be expected, however, that no two of them would be alike, or even bear the remotest similarity to each other.

3- Finally, there is Yakimov's description of the people in the chamber of execution. It is, to begin with, much too detailed for belief:

... they were placed as follows: in the center of the room stood the Tsar, next to him, at his right, the Tsarevich sat on a chair, and to the right of the Tsarevich stood Doctor Botkin. . . .. Behind them, against the wall . . . stood the Tsarina with her daughters. . . . To one side of the Tsarina and her daughters, in the corner, stood the cook and the man servant, and on the other side of them, also in a corner, stood Demidova. But on exactly which side, to the right or left, the cook and the man servant stood, and on which Demidova stood, I do not know.

Yurovsky was in the room, to the right of the entrance. Nikulin stood to the left of him, just opposite the door. . . . Next to Nikulin stood those Letts who were also in the room. There were also Letts in the doorway. Behind them stood Medvedyev.[131]

If this description is accurate, the man's memory was photographic. But it could not have been because, as he says, he was describing only what others had seen. Taking into account the fact that these "others" were looking through different windows in different rooms and facing in different directions the result described would seem impossible.

Nor does it seem any more possible if, as Agafonova relates, Yakimov was actually an eye-witness. According to her account, page 216, he was so "shaken" by the scene that he had to leave the room several times, and was still "trembling all over" the next morning. In such a state he would hardly note and recall the precise positions of these 20-odd people.

In any event, if we are to believe Medvedyev, Yakimov misplaced the Tsarina and Dr. Botkin. He also left out two members of the Cheka, including Yermakov. (See page 208.) And according to Bulygin he left out two additional and still more important people, Commissars Voikov and Goloshchekin.[132]

Sokolov does not give the complete text of the testimony of any of the witnesses. Even so, there are puzzling differences between those portions which he quotes and the corresponding portions as reproduced by Wilton and Dieterichs. In each case there are deletions and additions.

There are also indications that much important testimony has not been reported by any of the writers. General Dieterichs, for example, lists a number of people who were questioned in August and September, 1918 and whose testimony is not revealed. These include, among others, the mother of the guard, Ivan Starkov, and the friends of two other guards.[133] Some of this testimony would undoubtedly be significant.

Wilton states that he has purposely omitted the "signed depositions of eye-witnesses" who remained in the power of the Soviets.[134] In this case there is no indication of who they were, except that they could not be Medvedyev and Yakimov, the only eye-witnesses claimed by Sokolov and Dieterichs. The depositions of both of these witnesses are reproduced in full at the end of Wilton's book.

Statements made by Bulygin and Wilton regarding Anastasia's death agony indicate there must have been some other testimony. Wilton, for example, indicates that she "fought desperately" with one of the murderers:

> One of the girls—presumably the youngest Grand Duchess, Anastasia—rolled about and screamed and, when one of the murderers approached, fought desperately with him till he killed her.[135]

Bulygin says that she fainted and at first "escaped the bullets":

> When the smoke of the firing cleared a little and the murderers began to inspect the bodies, they found that the Grand Duchess Anastasia was alive and unhurt. She had fallen in a dead faint when the firing began, and so escaped the bullets.

When the assassins moved her body, the Grand Duchess regained consciousness, saw herself surrounded by pools of blood and the bodies of her family, and screamed. She was killed.[136]

No witnesses are cited for these statements and there is nothing to support them in the testimony reproduced by these writers, or by Sokolov and Dieterichs. The closest one comes is the testimony of Yakimov and his sister, Agafonova:

Yakimov: Of the Imperial Family, as I recall, only Anastasia was mentioned as having been stabbed with bayonets.[137]

Agafonova: The Grand Duchess Anastasia pretended to be dead and they also bayoneted her and struck her with rifle butts.[138]

One is forced to conclude either that important material has been suppressed, or that the writers were taking great liberties in the interpretation of their material.

Finally, although Chemodurov, the Tsar's valet, told several people that the Imperial Family had *not* been killed, we are not provided with his own direct testimony on this question. His testimony is used in the identification of objects found at the mine, and to enumerate the items of clothing brought by the Tsar from Tobolsk, but with respect to the fate of the Imperial Family itself only the following brief passage from his testimony is quoted, by General Dieterichs:

"And where are all these things now?"
The old man was silent, thinking. . . .
"I have no idea," he said finally, "I have no idea what happened to my Tsar and His Family! . . ."[139]

But Chemodurov thought that he knew what did *not* happen to the Imperial Family. He said so to at least three other people, who have reported his statements in their own dispositions:

Colonel Eugene Stepanovich Kobylinsky, commander of the guard at Tsarskoye Selo and Tobolsk: Chemodurov did not believe that the Family had been killed. He said that Botkin, Haritonov, Demidova and Trupp were killed, and that the Family had been taken away; he told me that by killing the aforementioned people the soldiers simulated the murder of the Family, and for the same reason the house was dismantled.[140]

45

Pierre Gilliard: In the latter part of August [1918] I was visited by Chemodurov. His first words were: "Thank God, the Emperor, Her Majesty and the children are alive—but all the others are killed." He told me that he was in Ipatiev's house when "Botkin and the others" were shot.[141]

Sidney Gibbs, English tutor of the Imperial Family: After the Bolsheviks left Ekaterinburg, Chemodurov came to see me. His first words were: "Thank God, the children are safe." I did not understand him. But afterwards in the course of conversation he suddenly asked me: "Do you think they *are* saved?" About ten days before his death he sent me a letter asking if there were any hopes of them being alive.[142]

It is indeed unfortunate that Chemodurov was not questioned more energetically about this by the investigators. But as Dieterichs tells us, Chemodurov died three months later "carrying with him to the grave the mystery of his statement."[143]

The Sverdlov Telegrams

In his account of the murder Sokolov produces a coded telegram, pages 228-231, which, with punctuation added, reads as follows:

Tell Sverdlov entire family suffered same fate as head. Officially family will perish in evacuation.

This telegram was allegedly sent on the day of the murder, July 17, 1918, to the Secretary of the Council of Peoples Commissars in Moscow, Gorbunov, by the Chairman of the Ural Oblast Soviet, Beloborodov. The man for whom the message was intended, Jacob Sverdlov, was Chairman of the All-Russian Central Executive Committee.

If the telegram is genuine, and if it actually refers to the Imperial Family, and if the head of the family—the Tsar—was executed as subsequent public announcements asserted, then the apparent intent of the message was to inform Sverdlov that the family was also executed.

On the other hand, if the Tsar was not executed—if, say, he had been taken to some place less exposed to capture by the White armies—then the telegram conveys quite a different meaning, i.e., the family was not executed either, but *taken to the same place.*

Both interpretations create a problem because they indicate that

Sverdlov did not know in advance what the fate of the Imperial Family would be. And yet, as we are told, it was he who was making the decisions. As Sokolov relates, page 238, the "fate of the Imperial Family was decided between the 4th and the 14th of July, when Shaya Goloshchekin was in Moscow and was living in Sverdlov's apartment." The meaning of this statement is made even clearer by a second statement, page 239, that there were "other people in Moscow who participated in the decision with Sverdlov and Goloshchekin regarding the fate of the Imperial Family."

Sokolov nevertheless interprets the telegram as meaning that the entire Imperial Family was executed. In doing so, however, he must rely for his proof of such execution upon other sources. Considered alone the telegram does not indicate what the fate of the Imperial Family was.

The telegram does reveal that some kind of deception was being practiced. This is the significance of the word "officially". Whatever the real fate of the Tsar and his family, the "official" announcement would not disclose it.

The telegram also indicates that the sender thought the evacuation of Ekaterinburg was imminent. Otherwise no one could say the family would perish "in evacuation".

Finally, one might assume that the sender did not wish the code clerks to know the true intent of the message. Otherwise, under the "execution" theory, the first sentence of the telegram might more simply have read, "Tell Sverdlov whole family executed."

Studied in the light of preceding and subsequent events the telegram can tell us even more. Instead of the two interpretations referred to above, it may have a third, more probable interpretation, which discloses, not the fate of the Imperial Family, but the ruse by which that fate was concealed. To arrive at this third meaning, one must put himself in the position of the acting parties in this drama.

In the first place consider the fact that even the code clerks were kept in the dark. Such a high degree of security does not seem to be warranted, either by the execution of the family, nor by its mere transfer to a "safe place". In the case of execution there was certainly no such need. The Bolsheviks were expected to take some kind of drastic action against the Tsar himself—"bloody Nicholas"—for his "crimes against the people." The murder of the family would not be inconsistent with many other atrocities committed at the time.

Moreover, as already indicated, there were many leaks of information with respect to the supposed "murder" of the entire family.

47

Many of these "leaks" occurred at or before the time the telegram was sent. The guards, of whom there were more than sixty, were all apparently aware of the "execution". And they were passing the details on from one to another. They were also telling their families and friends. The group which destroyed the bodies talked about their work in loud, coarse voices at the communist club. Even the soldiers guarding the mine area knew that "all of them" had been murdered, and would soon be bragging about it to the peasants of Koptyaki. Goloshchekin was to talk about it with people on the train to Moscow.

And yet the code clerks—people normally aware of the most secret communications—could not be trusted with this information? This hardly seems likely.

Furthermore, the wording of the telegram was more calculated to arouse suspicion of an execution or "murder" than of anything else. If this was what it was intended to conceal then the wording was poorly selected.

Finally, within two days *everybody* was to "know" that the Tsar had been executed. The code clerks could then readily interpret the ambiguous phraseology of the telegram. They would "know" that the family had also been executed—"suffered the same fate as its head."

It seems, therefore, far more likely that the real truth was not execution, but something more secret and sensitive. This would be an escape, perhaps, a release, or a transfer to German control. The Bolsheviks could never tell the people that they had allowed the "arch-enemy of the revolution" to escape his "just punishment" —the people's vengeance—and slip through their hands. From a propaganda point of view—and this was all-important to them —an "execution" of some kind was necessary. A release required the greatest security of all.

There was an added reason for secrecy if, as indicated below, the life of the Imperial Family was traded for German assistance against counter-revolutionaries. The provision for such assistance was a part of the "secret protocol" to the supplementary treaties of August 27, 1918, [144] and the reciprocal end of the bargain would, presumably, be deemed equally confidential.

Let us suppose then, as General Dieterichs relates,[145] that the original decision was not to murder the Imperial Family but to remove them all from Ekaterinburg. On the basis of the cryptic wording of the telegram we may assume that their destination was such as to require the highest measure of secrecy, i.e., there was a transfer to German control. Such a decision would be made by the highest authority—by Lenin himself. The only further decision, to be made by people like Sverdlov and Goloshchekin, was how to explain it to the people.

It would be possible, of course, for the Bolsheviks to say that the Imperial Family had been moved to some safe place *in Russia*. But eventually that "safe place" would have to be revealed. People would want to see the Imperial Family. They would demand a "trial" and execution. And since the Imperial Family would be under German control, it would be impossible for the Bolsheviks to produce them.

On the other hand it would be equally dangerous to announce that the Imperial Family were dead—that they had been executed, or died accidentally. The Bolsheviks would not have to "produce" them, but they could never be sure that the Imperial Family would not some day reappear and thus expose them as liars.

There was at least one way out of this dilemma. The "official" announcement could be in the form considered to have the most propaganda appeal if there was a scapegoat to take the blame if the information was ever proved false.

With this idea in mind we can assume that Sverdlov and Goloshchekin decided that the Tsar himself must be "officially" executed. The determination to do this, however, would ostensibly be made, not in Moscow but in Ekaterinburg. It would be made and carried out, in the first instance, by the Ural Oblast Soviet, and then "ratified" by the central authorities in Moscow. In this way, if anything went wrong, the blame could be placed on the bungling or treachery of local authorities. If the Tsar turned up, the local Soviet would be said to have "lied" when it informed Moscow of the "execution". It would have "attempted in this way to cover up its negligence" in allowing the Tsar to escape.

In the case of the family there would be a double deception. The Ural Oblast Soviet would not "admit" or "announce" that it had executed the Tsarina and the children, but would allow this "fact" to be "discovered" by others. If Ekaterinburg were lost (contingency number one), the official announcement would state that the family perished in evacuation. If Ekaterinburg were held (contingency number two) it would be announced that the family was moved to a "safe place".

In the meantime the proper "evidence" of execution would be prepared for "discovery." "Executed" bodies, supplied, perhaps, from the morgues of the Cheka, would be disposed of as though the "executioners" had attempted to conceal their "crime". Under contingency number one they would be "buried" as though the "criminals" wished to simulate "death in evacuation." Under contingency number two they would be destroyed in a manner indicating "crude" (but not completely effective) efforts to conceal the evidence.

This "evidence", when discovered, would conveniently reveal the "fact of execution" without formal admission. The local Soviet would either be exonerated because it acted under the "threat of white guard attack" or thoroughly condemned because it "acted without authority"—all as circumstances might dictate.

The advantage of this complicated procedure was that the central Bolshevik authorities were protected in all events. On the one hand, they would never have to produce the family alive or reveal the "safe place" to which it supposedly had been taken. On the other hand, neither could the central authorities be called "liars" if the Imperial Family should reappear. The local authorities could still be blamed for false "official" reports, and some "rash investigator" of the "execution" would be censured for "too hasty conclusions" based on "flimsy evidence".

The only difficulty in this solution involved the wounded feelings of the local authorities, who might resent their status as scapegoats. But such considerations do not carry weight in the Soviet Union. Furthermore, the local authorities could be taken off the hook by a staged or fictitious trial. Wilton and General Dieterichs report that there actually *was* such a trial in September, 1919,[146] after Perm and Ekaterinburg were retaken. Wilton states that he could not find in the list of "defendants" even one name which resembled any of those implicated by the White investigators' dossier. Nor could he or General Dieterichs find a record anywhere of the names of the "convicted" members of the "Executive Committee".

Having been given his instructions, therefore, we may assume that Goloshchekin returned to Ekaterinburg to give the necessary orders for a simulated execution. The scene of the crime was suitably prepared with bullet marks, and the necessary people were brought in to see the "Imperial Family's blood." They were even made to mop it up.

At the same time diversionary evidence was prepared for contingency number one—simulated death in evacuation. Bodies were obtained, mutilated beyond recognition and buried in the forest to be found by the Whites. Identifying clothing and jewels were placed nearby, and false witnesses coached.

These were the actions which Beloborodov communicated to Sverdlov. He only wanted to tell him that the "evidence" had been prepared, and which contingency was adopted. And so the real meaning of the telegram was not to relate what actually happened to the Imperial Family—whether it had been executed or spared—but to report on the *form of simulation* employed. Its real message was: "Tell Sverdlov entire family suffered same *simulated* fate as its head." In other words, as the sender advised, they would "officially" perish in evacuation.

There was no danger of misunderstanding because this was part of the plan and Sverdlov knew exactly where the Imperial Family were. But there was another kind of hitch. Lenin did not want an evacuation. He was sending reinforcements. (See telegram of July 20, page 235.) Even if the city eventually had to be given up, the announcement could not wait so long. Until the actual evacuation it would be impossible to make the announcement described.

Accordingly, Sverdlov told the Ekaterinburg people they would have to follow contingency number two. The appropriate story was prepared and wired to Ekaterinburg on the 19th. (See pages 227-228.) It announced that the Tsar had been executed by order of the Executive Committee of the Ural Oblast Soviet, and the family had been taken to a safe place. All that had to be done was to change the simulated efforts of the "criminals" to conceal their "crime". Instead of disposing of the bodies as if someone wished to create the appearance of death in evacuation, they would be made to look as though subjected to crude and hasty efforts to destroy them.

Much of this, of course, is pure speculation. There are many possible variations. But any one of them will explain aspects of the case never adequately explained by the investigators.

First of all, this interpretation explains why the official Bolshevik announcement stated that the decision to execute the Tsar was made, in the first instance, by the local Oblast authorities, i.e., the scapegoats.

In the second place, the third interpretation explains the changes in the activity at the mine on July 17. As Sokolov relates, page 174, sulphuric acid was not brought to the mine until *late in the evening of July 17 and during the day on July 18*. It was not even ordered until July 17. Normally one would expect it to have been gotten ready in advance. Moreover, as General Dieterichs relates, the bodies *were* first buried and then, during the night of July 18-19, dug up and destroyed. He relates this in explaining Kostousov's statement,[147] at the communist club, that the bodies were "buried" and "reburied":

July 18 and the night before the 19th presented an entirely different appearance. Those who lived at the grade-crossings and crossroads had never seen such activity, such movement of automobiles, wagons and horses at these points. About 9 o'clock in the morning an auto truck with a supply of gasoline and a large barrel of kerosene, 10-12 pouds [322.43-386.916 English pounds], went past watch house No. 184 into the Koptyaki woods. After several hours another truck passed in the same direction; it carried two or three metal drums. What was in them is unknown. At approximately the same time a carriage also entered the Koptyaki woods, in which Yankel Yurovsky and Nikulin brought several shovels and a considerable amount of sulphuric acid. . . .

During the second half of the day Isaac Goloshchekin came to the Koptyaki woods in a light automobile accompanied by two people. The automobile was left at watch house No. 184 and the passengers went down the Koptyaki road on foot. In about three hours Isaac Goloshchekin's companions returned to the automobile, leaving him in the woods, and went to the city —to the American Hotel. They returned to the woods for Isaac Goloshchekin early in the morning of July 19. They finally returned to the city about nine o'clock in the morning. Accordingly, Isaac Goloshchekin remained in the woods from approximately 5-6 o'clock in the afternoon of July 18 until 7 or 8 o'clock of the morning of July 19. . . .

The significance of all this information is first, that during the period from the early morning of July 17 until the small hours of July 18th, work on the concealment of the bodies was being carried out by Yermakov's group. As Kostousov expressed it, they were at that time "burying". But then, *for reasons which remain unexplained,* Isaac Goloshchekin decided to "rebury" the bodies. During the period from 6 o'clock in the evening of July 18th until 5 o'clock in the morning of the 19th he personally assumed direction of the new concealment of the bodies. For this second work, on "reburial", about 10 pouds of kerosene and 9 pouds [290.187 English pounds] of sulphuric acid were employed, together with whatever liquid was contained in the three iron drums which were brought back to the city in wagons.

Quite without one's wishing it, this picture of the concealment of the bodies brings one back to the picture of the murder of the Imperial Family itself. As in the former, so in the latter, two differing periods of events are observed. In the case of the murder the original plan was to move the Imperial Family to some other place, but then, with Goloshchekin's appearance in Ekaterinburg, coming from Moscow in the capacity of director, all plans were changed. Instead of a transfer of the Most August Family, there burst forth the bloody, bestial drama. At the mine, the Russian human beasts were at first apparently preparing a simple concealment of the bodies, a "burial." Then, with the appearance in the woods of the same beast, Isaac Goloshchekin, an extraordinary procedure was adopted for the concealment of the bodies—a procedure involving the use of kerosene, sulphuric acid and something else "which the world will never know". . . .[148] (Italics added.)

General Dieterichs speculates that the three mysterious drums were used to transport the heads of the Imperial Family.[149] It seems more likely that they were used to bring back those parts of some borrowed and unidentified bodies (including the heads) which the ghoulish workmen did not need or have time to destroy in order to complete their planted "evidence".

One thing, however, still disturbed the Bolsheviks. If they were driven from Ekaterinburg, they would not be around to "discover" the "evidence of execution" themselves. It would have to be found by the Whites. To make sure the Whites did find it, it would be necessary to call the "evidence" to their attention. This was the function of the planted false witnesses. And so it turned out, perhaps, that it was the judicial investigators and not the criminal investigating division who became the unwitting tools of the Bolsheviks, carrying out their wishes, and doing their job.

The third interpretation of the telegram thus also explains why the Soviets delayed formal confirmation of the "execution" of the entire family until after the White investigators had taken their stand. It was necessary to wait and to make sure that they came to the "right" conclusions.

The third interpretation also explains why, in making the first confirmation, the Bolsheviks blamed the murder on fictitious Social Revolutionaries in the Ekaterinburg Soviet.[150] In so doing they absolved the real leaders and agents of the Ural Oblast Soviet of the onus of a crime never committed.

And finally the third interpretation may also explain why pieces of knapsack, overcoat and other travelling equipment were found at the mine, while essential and treasured items, such as medicines and religious articles were left at the Ipatiev House. The former were scattered at the mine as evidence of "death in evacuation" and by oversight never removed. The latter were left in the Imperial Family's living quarters for the benefit of the investigator who would "discover" evidence of execution, and wish to show that

53

there had been no real plan of departure.

One further point. In connection with the telegram of July 19, it should be noted that the *entire* text is part of the public announcement, and therefore a part of the planned deception. Read as an ordinary message, intended only to inform the local authorities in Ekaterinburg of the action taken in Moscow, it would seem to indicate that Sverdlov lied to the All-Russian Central Executive Committee. Under the "escape" theory he would have lied when he spoke of the Tsar's execution, and under the "murder" theory he would have lied when he said that the Tsar's wife and son were sent to a "safe place". Either interpretation would be preposterous. It would mean that while the Ural Oblast Soviet knew the truth, the Central Executive Committee of all the Soviets was not to know!

The telegram, however, is not an ordinary message. It was intended to advise Ekaterinburg of the text of the *public announcement* made in Moscow. This is indicated by Sokolov, page 235, and by the fact that the telegram was sent, not by Sverdlov, but by the official Bolshevik "Press Bureau." (Page 227.) The telegram must therefore be read as indicating, not what Sverdlov actually told the Central Executive Committee, but what the public was supposed to *think* that he told them. Taken by itself there is nothing in the text of this telegram, any more than in the telegram of July 17, to indicate what the actual facts were that it was intended to conceal.

V. Evidence of Escape

Reasons for Its Suppression

As has already been indicated, the accounts of the investigation are selective. The reader's attention is focused constantly upon evidence—clues and extracts from testimony—which seem to support the conclusion that the Imperial Family was "murdered." Evidence to the contrary is either ridiculed, touched upon only briefly, or omitted altogether.

It is quite natural for a writer to emphasize what he considers the most significant material and to deemphasize that which is irrelevant or distracting. In this case, however, there are other reasons for the suppression of such evidence, reasons which may even have influenced the writers in the formation of their conclusions.

The Bolsheviks, as we have seen, could not for propaganda reasons admit or allow the suspicion that they had let the Imperial Family pass from their control. And the White writers also had reasons to exclude this eventuality. Being monarchists, or at least very sympathetic to the Imperial Family, they would not wish to record or perpetuate information which, as it seemed to them, might either discredit the Imperial Family or provide grist for the mill of those who did.

Such information included anything which indicated cooperation with the Germans or Bolsheviks, not excepting, apparently, an *involuntary* transfer to German control. Even though the Imperial Family might have had no choice in the matter, there would always be the suspicion that the transfer was the result of a deal to which the Tsar was a party. Escape presented a similar problem if the circumstances and place of asylum remained unknown.

It should be remembered that World War I was still raging. Russia had sacrificed millions of men for the common struggle, spent great sums of money, and gone deeply into debt to the Western Allies. Under such circumstances anything which might indicate that the Imperial Family was cooperating with Germans was abhorrent. As for involuntary cooperation, one might expect the Tsar to prefer death to capture and imprisonment by the enemy.

The Tsar and the Tsarina had been many times accused of cooperation with Germany. They had been accused of efforts to betray Russia's Allies by negotiating for a "separate peace". And although, as Sokolov points out,[151] investigations made by the revolutionary Provisional Government had disproved such accusations, the suspicion remained. It would only be confirmed by anything which indicated the Imperial Family's ultimate transfer to German control.

The Germans, moreover, were not merely an external enemy. They had helped the Bolsheviks to seize power. As General Dieterichs asserts:

. . . Germany could not overcome her enemies in honest, open battle. At that time, stopping at nothing as a means of struggle, she had thrown the meanest weapons of battle, the most terrible of poisons—political poison, the poison of bolshevism, an injection of anarchy—against our front and rear.[152]

It was, in fact, the Bolsheviks who sued for and made the "separate peace". On December 2, 1917, almost immediately after the Bolsheviks' seizure of power, they made an armistice. This was followed, in March, 1918, by the Treaty of Brest-Litovsk. The Germans were permitted to occupy the Baltic States, parts of Byelorussia, the Crimea and the Ukraine as far as Rostov-on-the-Don. Supplementary treaties were made on August 27, 1918.

As a result Germany was freed of the "two-front" war. She could now mass her entire force against the Allies in the West. It was the Bolsheviks who made this possible.

It was accordingly assumed that the Bolsheviks were under German control. They were considered "puppets" of the Germans, and identified with them. For this reason any link between the Tsar and the Germans was doubly abhorrent.

The Imperial Family was very conscious of all this. They rejected all offers of German assistance for their release and lived, apparently, in constant dread of anything creating the appearance of cooperation.

It is said that the Tsar even opposed efforts to send him anywhere out of Russia. Thus General Dieterichs reports that when loyal troops of the guard at Tobolsk made the suggestion, he replied that "He would never leave Russia and separate Himself from His Family."[153]

Sokolov also states that the Tsar "did not wish to leave Russia" (see page 240). At the time of the Tsar's transfer from Tobolsk, Sokolov says, the tutor, Claudia Mikhailovna Bittner, suggested that they might be taking him out of the country. "Oh, God forbid!" replied the Tsar, "Anything except to be sent abroad!"

The transfer from Tobolsk had aroused fears that the Tsar might be forced to sign the peace treaty. In this connection Sokolov tells us that he asserted:

> Well, they want me to sign the treaty of Brest. But I would rather let them cut off my right hand than do that.[154]

A similar attitude was attributed to the Tsarina. She read in a newspaper that the treaty contained a provision guaranteeing the safety of the Imperial Family. Although of German origin,[155] she exclaimed: "I had rather die in Russia than be saved by the Germans!"[156]

Gilliard, in his testimony, paraphrased the Tsarina's feelings about the transfer from Tobolsk:

> I feel they are taking him [the Tsar] away in order to make an effort to force him to do something evil. They are taking him away alone because they want to separate him from his family in order to attempt to force him to sign something vile out of fear of danger to the lives of all his own whom he has left in Tobolsk, as it was when he signed the abdication at Pskov. I feel that they want to force him to sign the peace in Moscow. The Germans are demanding it because they know that only a peace signed by the Tsar can have any force and effect in Russia. My duty is not to allow this, and not to leave him at such a time. It is easier to struggle together than alone. . . . But at the same time I cannot leave Alexei. He needs me so much. What will happen to him without me? [157]

This abhorrence of anything resembling collaboration is especially noticeable in General Dieterichs' account of the investigation. For him "rumors" of transfer to German control reflected a "shameful" attitude:

> . . . how much these rumors give evidence of the persuasion and conviction, injected by theory into the mind and training, that

the Germans—always the Germans—are a power, a fearsome power. The Germans can give orders to everyone and there can be no question—no disobedience. Our Tsar is, first of all, a brother of the German Tsar. The Russian people can be debased, humiliated, destroyed, but the Russian Tsar has gone off to Germany. . . .

What horror, what shame is concealed in the fabric of all these rumors referred to above; what shame for us all, tolerating and spreading such low thoughts. . . . As if we did not know the spiritual and national power of *our* Tsar.[158]

General Dieterichs complained that the criminal investigating division, which investigated these rumors, not only created doubts in the highest government circles, but "at times provided food for a deliberate continuation of the discrediting of the former Tsar, Tsarina and Their Children as having germanophile tendencies."[159]

Sokolov undoubtedly thought he was combatting this trend. At least that is the impression created by a statement made in his report on the investigation to the Dowager Empress. It is quoted by Bulygin:

> The time will come when a national leader will raise his banner for the honour of the Emperor. He will need all the material collected during the inquiry.[160]

The Tsar was not a mere political ruler. He was a symbol, closely identified with the people of Russia and with their religion. To permit any defacement of this symbol, if not actually sacreligious, was, according to General Dieterichs, at least dangerous, because it would demoralize the people:

> The investigation could in no wise presume to verge upon criticism of the actions of the late former Emperor as Ruler and Tsar. The moral right to pass judgment upon dynastic rulers belongs only to the All-Powerful God, impartial history and the court of national conscience as represented in such institutions as the Zemsky Sobor.[161]
>
> From the civil-political point of view there are, in this world, Tsars who are by nature destined to govern, and there are also Tsars who, by their nature, are called upon to be martyrs to government. The late former Emperor belonged to the second type.
>
> And from the point of view of the ideology of the Russian people, there is still another aspect of this question—the spiritual symbol personified by the figure of the Tsar as Annointed of God. The investigation considered itself obliged to exert every

effort to display the murdered Tsar and Tsarina in as far as possible in this aspect, proceeding from the following considerations: the overthrow of a Tsar who is regarded by the people as merely a Ruler is a crime of "form", a civil-political crime; but the overthrow of a Tsar who is regarded by the people as being also the Annointed of God is a crime of the "Spirit", which strikes at the roots of the whole historic, national and religious outlook of the people, knocking out from under its feet the moral props of its life and existence.[162]

Those who held such views could hardly approach the investigation in an objective manner!

The German Motive

In spite of the apparent selectivity of these writers, their accounts of the investigation, especially the account of General Dieterichs, do indicate the existence of evidence not consistent with their conclusions. And while the brief references which are made do not furnish the information needed to form a definite conclusion as to the fate of the Imperial Family, the evidence of evacuation from Ekaterinburg seems to be of equal if not greater weight than the evidence of "murder". If the conclusions of the investigators are accepted, then it must be with the gravest of reservations.

In the first place it is clear that the Germans were seriously interested in the fate of the Imperial Family. This interest may have been motivated by humanitarian considerations, as is indicated in the diplomatic correspondence quoted by Sokolov, pages 244-245, or it may have been purely political.

General Dieterichs mentions a German offer to assist the Imperial Family some time in August or September of 1917:

> ... in this period there undoubtedly appeared signs of an interest on the part of Emperor Wilhelm in the attitude of the former Tsar and Tsarina. Russian officers of the type that moved in the circles from which the center of the [germanophile] organization was formed appeared in Tobolsk and conveyed to the Imperial Family Wilhelm's proposal for acceptance of his assistance. The answers of the Tsar and the Tsarina were negative.[163]

General Dieterichs also indicates his belief in the story told about Serge Vladimirovich Markov, a former officer in the Empress' Crimean Cavalry. According to this account the Kaiser made an offer of asylum to the Tsarina and the Grand Duchesses, at the urgence of the Tsarina's brother, the Grand Duke Ernest Louis of Hesse-Darmstadt. The offer, reportedly, was rejected and the Tsarina sent a letter to her brother, explaining the rejection, through Markov. Markov, reportedly, displayed the letter to certain people in Kiev. General Dieterichs asserts:

> The letter which Markov brought actually existed. It was seen by others. It was seen by people who could know the Empress' handwriting.[164]

Among possible political considerations there may have been a German desire to prevent the Tsar from falling into the hands of the Allies or of those anti-Bolshevik groups which wanted war with Germany. Sokolov, who believed that the transfer of the Imperial Family from Tobolsk was initiated at the insistence of Germany and begun through a German agent with instructions to escort them to an area under direct German control, assigns this fear as the motive:

> The whole time in Tobolsk the Tsar was under their [German] surveillance. The means employed were old and tested: their spies bore the mark of Rasputin. By this means the Germans fought the Russian patriots, preventing them from carrying off the Tsar.
> When the danger to their interests became real, they carried him off themselves. If the Tsar, even after his abdication from the Throne, had issued an appeal for struggle with the enemy, could the enemy leave him and his son where the threat had arisen anew, the threat of re-creation of a front, of a revival of the former Russian power in the form of the Russian Army upon whose banners the words "Great Russia" were always emblazoned when it was an Empire [monarchy]?
> The purpose of the removal undoubtedly had a political character....[165]

* * *

Where were they taking the Tsar?
The Germans were taking him closer to the disposition of their armed forces on Russian territory. Prince Dolgorukov was with the Tsar to the very last moment. They took him from the door of the Ipatiev House to the prison. There he stated that Yakovlev was taking the Tsar to Riga.[166]

According to Doctor Vladimir Nicholayevich Derevenko, who was the Tsarevich's personal physician, the Tsar himself expressed the opinion that he was being taken to Moscow because the Germans wanted to put him back on the throne. The Tsar declared that he would not accept the throne under such circumstances.[167]

The actual intended destination of the Tsar's transfer from Tobolsk has always remained a mystery because of a sudden change in the route taken. At first his train was directed eastward, towards Omsk. But before reaching Omsk it was intercepted, according to the investigators, and Yakovlev, the commissar in charge, was forced to turn back and go west. The train was finally stopped in Ekaterinburg.

Sokolov explains this change as the result of a Bolshevik effort to deceive the Germans. With one hand, he says, the Bolsheviks issued orders to take the Tsar to the Germans, and with the other gave contrary instructions for his detention in Ekaterinburg. They explained the latter, he says, with the "false pretext of Ekaterinburg's insubordination."[168]

The Germans, however, were in the west, not the east, and the most direct route to Riga was through Ekaterinburg. It seems more logical to assume that Yakovlev was attempting to confuse or avoid some group seeking either to rescue the Tsar, or to assasinate him.

On the other hand, fear that the Tsar might fall into Allied hands, or into those of counter-revolutionaries, would have been a plausible reason for moving the Imperial Family to Ekaterinburg, or even farther west, whether or not there was a deal with the Germans to do so. There were definite signs at this time both of Allied intervention in Siberia, and of growing counter-revolutionary movement. The Japanese, moreover, had just made a landing at Vladivostok.

In addition the Czechoslovak national troops, which had only just been disengaged from battle with the Germans, were at this time being evacuated through Siberia. They were Allied troops, on their way to the Western Front, and with them there were some very anti-Bolshevik, Tsarist officers, including General Dieterichs.

Disputes had already arisen. The Czech movement had been interrupted twice, and within weeks there were to be open hostilities which resulted in the overthrow of Soviet rule, not only in Siberia, but also in the Urals and a large part of the Volga region.

If the transfer were being made at German insistence there were good reasons, too, for holding it up. Among these was the extensive military assistance which the Germans were giving to the counter-revolutionary movement in the South, led by General Peter Nicholayevich Krasnov.

General Dieterichs, however, did not share Sokolov's opinion with respect to the transfer from Tobolsk to Ekaterinburg. The move, he surmised, was motivated either by the Bolsheviks' own fears of an uprising, or by some plan to murder the Tsar in a staged, provocatory "incident".

But General Dieterichs did not intend thus to absolve the Germans of political motivation. On the contrary, he strongly suggests a desire on the part of at least one German faction to wipe out the Bolshevik regime and replace it with a more amenable government in the German Imperial pattern. The reason for the Germans' lack of interest in the transfer from Tobolsk, he says, was that they had their sights set at that time on the Grand Duke Nicholas Nicholayevich and "had absolutely no use for the unfortunate Imperial Family."[169] But when the Germans were repulsed by the Grand Duke, he says they may have determined "to use the name of the former Tsar".[170] General Dieterichs related this story as follows:

The months of April and May, and the beginning of June, 1918, were a period during which the German "military command" in Russia, having become doubtful of the possibility of working with the Bolsheviks, were attracted by a new political fantasy. Having occupied the Ukraine, having secured the position there of the hetman, Skoropadsky, the Germans on the Don made contact with the military organizations united around General Krasnov. He accepted the helping hand of the German command and received from it shells, weapons and bullets. Knowing that the situation of the volunteer groups of General Alexeyev were very serious in all respects, the Germans got the idea of coming to an agreement, through General Krasnov, with Generals Alexeyev and Denikin. Carried away by their blind self-esteem, they fancied that with the help of these generals they could draw out the Grand Duke Nicholas Nicholayevich, who was then living in the Crimea, and who was popular with the mass of the people and also in military circles, and place him on the Russian throne.

Of course the Germans failed to win their newly-conceived political alliance just as definitely as they lost their stake on the Bolsheviks. Generals Alexeyev and Denikin categorically refused to have any conversations with them, and with respect to the Grand Duke Nicholas Nicholayevich it goes without saying that it is impossible to have doubts. These people were all too Russian and national, too aware of where the root of the evil which had overtaken Russia was hidden, to make any compromise with the Germans and sell them their native land.

What could they do further, these short-witted and blind German politician-generals who in their self-esteem acknowledged only force, provocation and dastardliness as means of attaining a goal? Possibly then, roughly at the beginning of

June, they conceived the idea of attaining their political-economic goals by new violence, new dastardliness, this time practiced on the unhappy, overthrown, former Tsar Nicholas Alexandrovich, forgotten by all, physically and morally exhausted, discredited by their agents even in peacetime and now, as they might have supposed, entirely within their power and subject to their will. The hopelessness of their position on the one hand, and brain-befuddling chauvinism on the other, plus the thirst for power of instigators—false Russian nationalists and false patriots—who gave themselves over wholly to the Germans and wandered off to Berlin, could have induced the German command to adopt a base plan: *to use the name of the former Tsar as a threat to the Soviet regime,* and by this means force the latter into complete submission to the German military command and its demands.[171]

General Dieterichs adds a precautionary note—there was no proof:

> Of course, if such a plan existed, it could come only from the bowels of various intriguing departments of the German "military command". It could in no case be the creature of the Ministry of Foreign Affairs in Berlin. At the present time, however, study and investigation of the story of the destruction of the Imperial Family has too little material at its disposal to confirm the existence of such a plan unconditionally. Final clarification of this dark question is in the province of future historical research.[172]

But if the plan to "use the name of the former Tsar" was never adopted, there may nevertheless have been effective German demands for his safety.

In August, 1918, the Germans agreed to give no further support to General Krasnov or any other anti-Bolshevik factions.[173] The German Government promised, in fact, in a secret agreement, "to proceed with all the forces at its disposal against General Alexeyev."[174] What did the Bolsheviks offer in return for these commitments? Resistance to Allied intervention? The use of all means at their disposal, as the secret agreement stated, to put down "the insurrections of General Alexeyev and the Czecho-Slovaks"? The Bolsheviks, as the Germans well knew, had to do this anyway if they wished to survive. The one real trading point which the Bolsheviks had in their chess game with the Germans was the "king" and the "queen"—the Imperial Family in Ekaterinburg.

We can only guess that in return for their commitment to the Bolsheviks—a high price, which meant in effect a continuing support of the "Red", Bolshevik regime, the Imperial German Government at least demanded the safety of the Imperial Family. And we can imagine that, if this was indeed the case, the Bolsheviks held off delivery until the last moment because they knew that once they gave up the "king" and "queen"—their trump cards—their bargaining power was nil. And they needed these trump cards, and all the support they could get, because their regime at this time was ready to collapse.[175]

There were a great many current rumors and reports that the Germans did make such demands for the safety of the Imperial Family. They are very briefly described by General Dieterichs:

> From the beginning of June various Soviet activists began insistently to spread the information that the German command in Moscow was demanding that the Soviet regime hand over the former Tsar and His Family and transfer them to Germany. This was talked about everywhere: in official Soviet organs, in the salons of the ladies of Soviet society, in the underground, white guard organizations of Moscow, among the wide masses of the people in Moscow and Ekaterinburg, and even abroad. And in the ranks of the guards of the Most August Prisoners of the Ipatiev House it was asserted definitely that the Imperial Family would be taken to Germany and that the Emperor Wilhelm had threatened comrade Lenin that "one hair must not fall from the head of the Tsar." This information persisted very stubbornly and insistently, leaving the impression that even if no such definite and categorical demand had been made, there was nevertheless something of that nature.[176]

General Dieterichs also says there was "indirect documentary evidence" of such demands, but he fails, unfortunately, to describe it or identify it:

> And it was not only the reports that forced one to think so; there was also indirect documentary evidence in this direction of "gentle pressure" exerted by the German command upon the official Soviet authorities.[177]

Finally General Dieterichs suggests that some kind of German proposal may have been passed to the Tsar by a certain Ivan Ivanovich Sidorov, who went to Ekaterinburg in June, 1918, from Odessa, passing through the German lines and remaining in the city for some three weeks.[178] But, Dieterichs says, if Sidorov did carry such a proposal, the Tsar rejected it.

General Dieterichs, however, does not know for sure that Sidorov did carry a proposal, or if so, what it was. Obviously, therefore, he cannot prove its rejection or say, even, that it *ought* to have been rejected. The importance of the incident is its demonstration that someone like Sidorov could have come to Ekaterinburg at this time and made contact with the Imperial Family.

General Dieterichs relates that Sidorov carried letters (never delivered) for the Imperial Family "from the Tolstoys, Khitrovo and Ivanov Lutsevin"—trusted friends of the family. Sidorov himself was a former Imperial aide-de-camp. He was a likely person to be chosen to transmit a proposal, or simply to *inform* the Imperial Family in advance of their pending removal.

The tenor of the diplomatic correspondence reproduced by Sokolov, pages 244-245, would appear to indicate that the Germans had no knowledge of the fate of the Imperial Family, but this is hardly conclusive. As General Dieterichs indicates, the German military command and the German foreign office were two hands, one of which did not always know what the other was doing:

> In the second half of 1917 and the first half of 1918 the German politik was almost entirely concentrated in the hands of the "Supreme Command". In the ministry of foreign affairs, sometimes, absolutely nothing was known about the political projects thought up and brought to life by the "Command."[179]

Widespread Disbelief in the "Murders"

The reports of German demands for the surrender of the Imperial Family were followed by equally widespread and persistent reports that the Tsar had been "murdered".[180] They appeared in the newspapers and were widely circulated in high Soviet circles. Nevertheless, when Ekaterinburg was liberated, and the "evidence" of the "real" murders disclosed, there was widespread disbelief.

By August, as Dieterichs relates, the criminal investigating division was following up "rumors, widely circulated at the time, throughout all Siberia, and still not abandoned by many, that the Imperial Family had been saved by Wilhelm and taken somewhere abroad."[181] General Dieterichs further states:

> No one wanted to believe in the possibility of the murder of the entire Imperial Family; no one could accept the existence of a bestiality in man, in human beings, of such unheard of proportions. Rumors, each more fantastic than the others, each

more unbelievable than the others, quickly circulated through the city, and everyone clung to the slightest ray of hope, rejecting the nightmare picture forced upon them by the appearance of the rooms of the Ipatiev House.[182]

Sergeyev complained of a similar disbelief:

The conduct of the investigation was also adversely affected by the widespread conviction of the people, based on various rumors, that the former Emperor and His Family were alive and had been removed from Ekaterinburg, and that all of the information published on this account by the Soviet authorities was provocatory and a lie.[183]

Even those who supported and sympathized with the Bolsheviks were loath to believe their assertion that the Tsar had been "executed". When the announcement was made at a meeting, July 18, in the Ekaterinburg theatre, there were cries from the audience: "Show us the body!" General Dieterichs relates that the Soviet leaders were "greatly confused" as a result:

On the one hand, they were unable to show the body; on the other, the crowd, composed of those whom they had trained, led, created—this crowd which had served them with its efforts in the revolutionary movement—did not believe them and demanded positive confirmation of the oral statement of one of their most important leaders.[184]

Afterwards, Dieterichs relates, when the crowd was dispersing, "almost the entire mass of people, exchanging their impressions, voiced the same thought: 'there is something that is not clear, something foggy, unspoken, in the announcement of the presidium.'"

Doctor Sakovich, the Bolsheviks' Commissar of Public Health, who claims to have heard other Commissars planning to murder the Tsar during his transfer from Tobolsk, stated flatly in this instance: "I do not believe in the shooting of the former Tsar." [185]

The Train From Perm

There was considerable evidence which indicated that the Imperial Family had actually departed from Ekaterinburg some time in June, 1918, at least three weeks before the alleged murders.

Even though General Dieterichs was of the firm belief that the Imperial Family was murdered in Ekaterinburg, he nevertheless

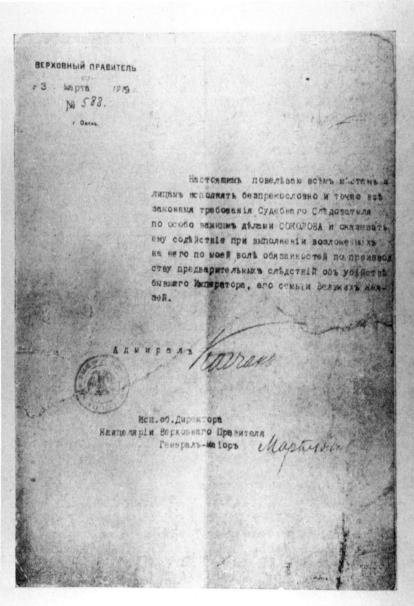

3 . Марта 1919.

№ 588.

г. Омскъ.

Настоящимъ повелѣваю всѣмъ мѣстамъ и лицамъ исполнять безпрекословно и точно всѣ законныя требованія Судебнаго Слѣдователя по особо важнымъ дѣлами СОКОЛОВА и оказывать ему содѣйствіе при выполненіи возложенныхъ на него по моей волѣ обязанностей по производству предварительныхъ слѣдствій объ убійствѣ бывшаго Императора, его семьи Великихъ князей.

Адмиралъ

Исп. об. Директора
Канцеляріи Верховнаго Правителя
Генералъ-Маіоръ

№ 1. Повелѣніе Верховнаго Правителя Адмирала А. В. Колчака.

No. 1.

№ 2 a.

№ 2 b.

№ 2 c.

№№ 2 a, 2 b и 2 c. Тобольскій домъ въ моментъ заключенія въ немъ царской семьи.

Nos. 2a, 2b, and 2c.

№ 3. Кабинетъ Государя въ Тобольскѣ.

№ 4. Комната Государыни
въ Тобольскѣ.

№ 5. Комната Великихъ Княженъ въ Тобольскѣ.

Nos. 3, 4, and 5.

Nos. 6, 7, and 8.

№ 6. Государь съ дѣтьми въ Тобольскѣ.

№ 7. Государь со служителемъ Кирпичниковымъ въ Тобольскѣ.

№ 10. Великія Княжны Ольга Николаевна, Татьяна Николаевна, Анастасія Николаевна и комнатная дѣвушка А. С. Демидова (убита) въ Тобольскѣ. Ольга Николаевна пытается выглянуть черезъ заборъ.

№ 9. Наслѣдникъ Цесаревичъ Алексѣй Николаевичъ въ Тобольскѣ.

Nos. 9, 10, and 11.

№ 12. Знакъ и лита, сдѣ-
ланіе рукой Императрицы
на косякѣ ея комнаты въ
домѣ Ипатьева.

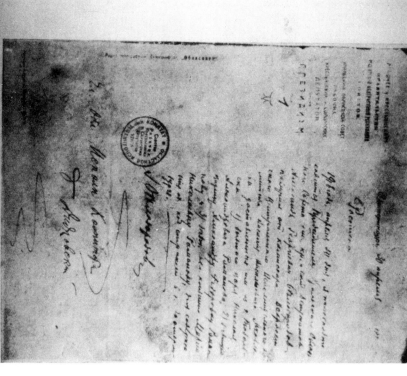

Nos. 12 and 13.

№ 13. Росписка вящшей комиссіи Я̀ковлеву или задержаніи въ Ек...

No. 14.

№ 15.

№ 16.

№ 17.

№ 18.

№№ 15, 16, 17 и 18. Шифръ Государя и Государыни. Найденъ спря-
таннымъ въ трубѣ въ уборной дома Ипатьева.

Nos. 15, 16, 17, and 18.

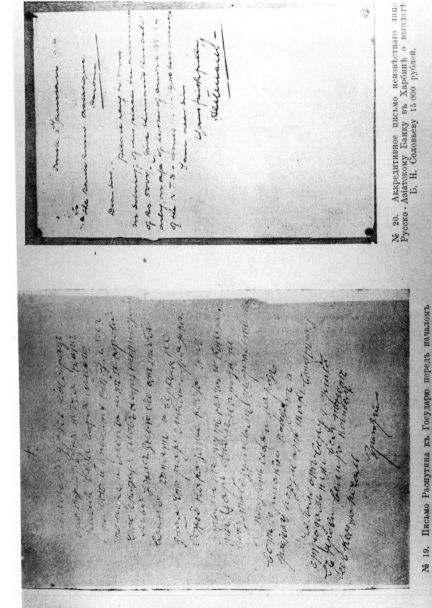

№ 19. Письмо Распутина к Государю передъ началомъ
войны 1914 г.

№ 20. Аккредитивное письмо неизвѣстнаго лица
Русско-Азіатскому Банку въ Харбинѣ о выдачѣ
Б. Н. Соловьеву 15 000 рублей.

Nos. 19 and 20.

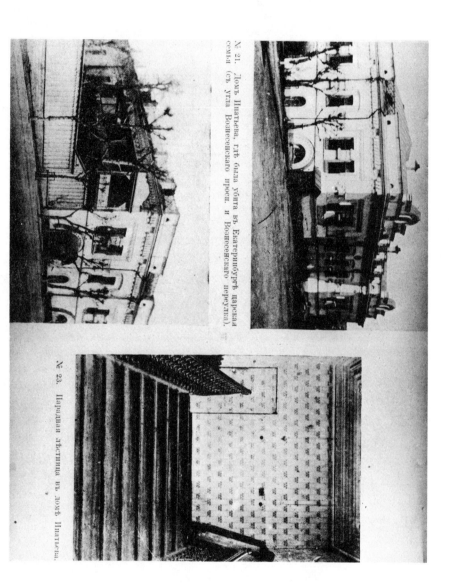

№ 21. Домъ Ипатьева, гдѣ была убита въ Екатеринбургѣ царская семья (съ угла Вознесенскаго просп. и Вознесенскаго переулка).

№ 23. Парадная лѣстница въ домѣ Ипатьева.

Nos. 21, 22, and 23.

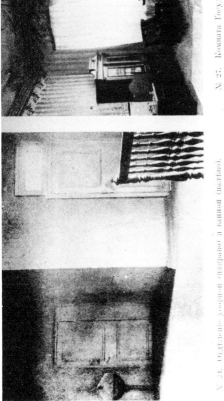

№ 24. Отдѣленіе дворцовъ Спаравои и банной (балвво).

№ 27. Комната Государя, Государыни и Наслѣдника.

Nos. 24, 25, 26, and 27.

№ 28.

№ 28. Комната Великихъ Княженъ послѣ убійства. На полу — извлеченная слѣдственной властью зола и остатки отъ уничтоженныхъ послѣ убійства вещей.

№ 29. Залъ и гостиная, перегороженные аркой. Здѣсь жили докторъ Е. С. Боткинъ и камердинеръ Т. И. Чемодуровъ. Лонгъ-шезъ привезенъ изъ Царскаго.

№ 30. Столовая въ домѣ Ипатьева. Видимая на снимкѣ дверь ведетъ въ комнату Великихъ Княженъ. Около камина видно

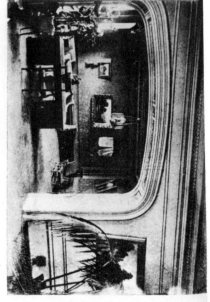

№ 29.

Nos. 28, 29, and 30.

31. Видъ изъ комнаты А. С. Демидовой черезъ столовую, проходную комнату и кухню въ домъ Ипатьева.

№ 32. Домъ Ипатьева со двора. Дверь слѣва ведетъ во дворъ изъ верхняго этажа, дверь справа — изъ нижняго.. Черезъ эти двер... вели царскую семью на убійство.

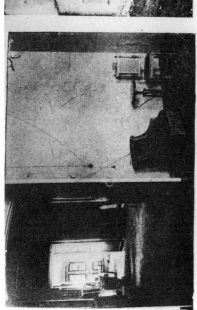

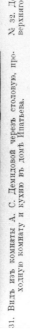

№ 34. Наружный (большой) заборъ, закрывавшій домъ Ипатьева с... стороны Вознесенскаго проспекта. Этотъ снимокъ былъ сдѣланъ... каррыльнымъ, западавшимъ тайно отъ большевиковъ въ моментъ...

№ 35. Внутренній (малый) заборъ, закрывавшій домъ Ипатьева... въ моментъ заключенія царской семьи.

Nos. 31, 32, 33, and 34.

№ 35.

№ 36.

№ 36.

№ 35. Наружный заборъ, со стороны Вознесенскаго переулка.

№ 36. Ворота и калитка при дом Ипатьева.

№ 37. Садъ съ террасой при дом Ипатьева, на снимк видн, а салонъ, Домъ Попова, гд въ моментъ убійства царской семьи жила наружная стража.

Nos. 35, 36, and 37.

№ 39 а.

№ 38.

№ 39.

№№ 38, 39 и 39 а.   Росписки охранниковъ въ домѣ
Ипатьева.

Nos. 38, 39, and 39a.

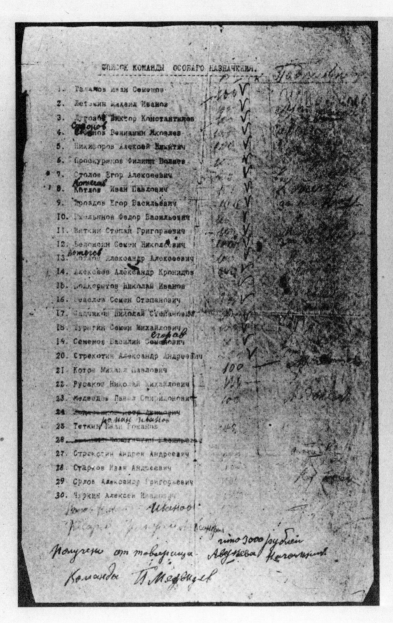

№ 40. Требовательная вѣдомость охранниковъ въ домѣ Ипатьева.

No. 40.

categorically states that the Bolsheviks did originally plan to evacuate them from that city. They were, he relates, to be moved out by rail through Perm—the same route in which the criminal investigating division showed such interest. Thus General Dieterichs states:

> ... at the end of June [1918] the Soviet official authorities in Moscow gave instructions to Ekaterinburg to prepare a train in Perm for the purpose of taking the Imperial Family away somewhere. Whether this was the result of "gentle pressure" from the German command, whether the German command actually, honestly, intended to bring the Tsar out forcibly to the fatherland or was merely using such a demand as a threat to the Soviet regime, are unresolved questions, but the train was prepared by the Soviet authorities in Ekaterinburg, and it was definitely prepared for the Imperial Family.[186]

General Dieterichs further states that this decision was made while Goloshchekin was staying in Moscow at Sverdlov's apartment:

> At the end of June, 1918, and the beginning of July, Isaac Goloshchekin, Ural oblast military commissar, member of the presidium of the oblast soviet and the most influential of the Soviet activists in Ekaterinburg, was in Moscow. He stayed there with his fellow of the same race, Yankel Sverdlov, chairman of the presidium of the central executive committee, who was also a very important activist of the Soviet regime. At this time the question of the further disposition of the Most August Prisoners was being considered in the TsIK [Central Executive Committee] in connection with general conditions on the internal and external fronts, and, apparently, the official central authority gave Ekaterinburg instructions to prepare everything necessary for removing the Imperial Family to some other place, away from the city.[187]

Unfortunately General Dieterichs does not reveal his authority for this statement, nor indicate the nature of the evidence, oral or written, that such a decision was made. Sokolov does not even mention it.

General Dieterichs does, however, categorically state that there was no documentary evidence that the original decision of the Bolsheviks was ever changed:

> In the various documents obtained there is no indication that this original decision of the official Soviet organ of power concerning the removal of the Imperial Family from Ekaterinburg

was changed by it. In the meantime, with Isaac Goloshchekin's return from Yankel Sverdlov's to Ekaterinburg, there was a noticeable change in the idea of how the fate of the Imperial Family should be resolved, and Isaac Goloshchekin begins to assume a leading role in this matter. This new idea was apparently kept in deep secrecy by Isaac Goloshchekin and his closest co-workers, but its influence creeps, nevertheless, into the official orders of Beloborodov with respect to the preparation of the above-mentioned train.[188]

The train referred to was a "special train" that "was being made up in Perm." According to General Dieterichs, it was to have a special guard of "especially trustworthy people" selected from Goloshchekin's own "special" unit.[189]

In so far as Beloborodov's "official orders" are revealed, they appear in the following series of telegrams:

I. Beloborodov to Gorbunov (Moscow), June 26, 1918 (in code):
"We have already stated that entire supply of gold and platinum removed from here two cars are standing in Perm request advise method of preserving in event of overthrow of Soviet power opinion party oblakom and oblast soviet event failure bury entire load in order not to leave to enemies." [190]

II. Beloborodov to Sverdlov and Goloshchekin (Moscow), July 4, 1918:
"Syromolotov has just gone to organize matter in accordance with instructions of center. No cause for alarm. Avdeyev replaced. His assistant Moshkin arrested. In place of Avdeyev Yurovsky. Internal guard entirely changed, replaced by others." [191]

III. Beloborodov to Syromolotov, July 7, 1918:
"If Matveyev's train not yet dispatched, detain it, if dispatched take all measures to detain it enroute so that it will not in any case reach place indicated by us. In event risk at new place of holding, return train to Perm. Await coded telegram." [192]

IV. Beloborodov to Syromolotov, July 8, 1918:
"If possible to replace train guard detachment with unconditionally reliable personnel replace all send back to Ekaterinburg. Matveyev remains commandant of train. Discuss change with Trifonov." [193]

V. Beloborodov to Gorbunov (Moscow), July 8, 1918 (in

code):

"Gusev of Petrograd advised white guard uprising in Yaroslavl we returned train to Perm consult with Goloshchekin how proceed further." [194]

There are some reasons for thinking that General Dieterichs was mistaken, and that the train referred to was not intended for the Imperial Family. For example, Sokolov states in his footnote 52, page 248, that Syromolotov's mission, referred to in telegram No. II, was concerned with "the shipment of money from Ekaterinburg to Perm." He also cites evidence that the Imperial Family was in the Ipatiev House on July 16—more than a week after the train was apparently "returned to Perm". And then there is the "evidence" of the "murder" of the Imperial Family in Ekaterinburg.

The value of the evidence of "murder" has already been discussed, and the evidence that the Imperial Family was still in Ekaterinburg on July 16 is discussed below. As for Syromolotov's mission, Sokolov fails to give any reason or cite evidence for his statement that it concerned the shipment of money. We are left to suppose that he simply inferred this from the mention of "gold and platinum" in telegram No. I.

We have already surmised, however, that ambiguous terms were being deliberately employed, even in coded telegrams, for reasons of extraordinary secrecy. It is not difficult to imagine, therefore, that the terms "gold and platinum" really meant the Imperial Family. If so, the "entire supply of gold and platinum" would mean the "entire Imperial Family" and possibly those people who were with them, such as Doctor Botkin, the servants, or perhaps the Grand Duke Michael Alexandrovich.

On the other hand, it must be noted that General Dieterichs does not refer to the coded telegrams. He may, therefore, have been unaware of their contents and of the reference to "gold and platinum". It might be argued that if he were aware of the reference he might not have thought the train was being prepared for the Imperial Family. There are several reasons, however, why this argument is not convincing.

In the first place, while General Dieterichs also fails to give his reasons, he states categorically that telegrams III and IV *do* relate to a train being prepared for the Imperial Family.[195] There is nothing on the face of these telegrams to indicate this. General Dieterichs would hardly have made a categorical statement so damaging to his conclusions without some sound, independent reason. We can only regret that he did not express it.

In the second place, General Dieterichs likewise categorically states, in contradiction to Sokolov's assertion, that Syromolotov's mission did relate to the Imperial Family.[196] In this case the text of the telegram does indicate a connection because it also mentions the change of guard at the Ipatiev House. Under Sokolov's interpretation the two parts of the telegram are completely unrelated. It seems more natural to conclude that they are related, especially in view of the statement that there was "no cause for alarm." A change of guard at the Ipatiev House would hardly help to ease Goloshchekin's mind with respect to the safety of a shipment of money to Perm. But, as is indicated below, if Syromolotov had been sent to Perm to make some arrangement with respect to the evacuation of the Imperial Family, the change of guard at the Ipatiev House might well have assured him that proper efforts were being made to preserve secrecy—to keep up the appearance that the Imperial Family was still in Ekaterinburg.

There is another aspect of the telegrams which does not conform to Sokolov's interpretation. Sokolov speaks of a shipment of money "from Ekaterinburg to Perm", but the telegrams indicate that the train in question was being dispatched *from* Perm to some destination further west. Telegram No. III instructs Syromolotov, already in Perm, to detain a train "not yet dispatched." Telegram No. V indicates that the train was "returned" to Perm because of the uprising in Yaroslavl, which is west of Perm. Therefore the shipment of money, if there was one, does not seem to be connected with this train.

The telegrams, therefore, seem rather to confirm than to negate General Dieterichs' assertion that the train in question was intended for the Imperial Family. If this is the case the Imperial Family must have left Ekaterinburg by June 26, three weeks before the "murder", travelled westward beyond Perm and then returned to Perm by July 8. There the trail ends.

In addition to the telegrams about the train, there is also other, very significant evidence of the Imperial Family's departure from Ekaterinburg. Some of this is mentioned, but rejected, by General Dieterichs. Thus there were the beliefs and the work of the criminal investigating division. As General Dieterichs relates, the theory "of removal by railroad attracted the criminal investigating division in full degree, captivating its work to the very end of the existence of personnel for this division, i.e., until we abandoned Perm." [197]

General Dieterichs also refers to a mass of oral testimony. He does not analyze it, or even indicate when the departure it describes was supposed to have taken place. He merely summarizes it briefly as follows:

The most varied details of this departure were obtained from the lips of various red army personnel and workers who had left [Ekaterinburg]: some said that the Tsar and the Tsarina were brought from the Ipatiev House to the railroad station "bound in shackles in an automobile of the Red Cross"; others said, on the contrary, that a train of luxurious cars had been formed for the transfer to Perm of the Tsar and His Family; a third group of reports gave it out that one of the workers "had seen with his own eyes" how the Tsar, "in an old worn tunic" was crudely pushed when they put him in the car, but the train itself "was luxurious". Those who passed these reports on surmised "that the Tsar had been taken to Riga in compliance with one of the points of the treaty of Brest." A fourth group had seen the cars that were assigned for the transfer of the Imperial Family, the windows of which were smeared with some kind of black substance. A fifth group had heard from their acquaintances among the red army personnel of the Tsar's former guard that He "was indeed being taken to Germany, because the Bolsheviks were getting a lot of money for him from the German king, and the king was taking him to himself as a surety." They related that the guard Lavushev, or Koryakin, "some one of them", had said "no one could do anything to Him because Lenin had been given strict instructions by the German Tsar that not one hair of our Tsar should be touched.[198]

General Dieterichs pooh-poohs this testimony, but does not explain why it is less credible than the conflicting and dubious testimony of those few guards who said the Imperial Family was murdered.

Bulygin also mentions an incident which indicates an original Bolshevik intention to evacuate the Imperial Family from Ekaterinburg. It is a newspaper article which he saw, some time in June, 1918, in the small town of Kotelnich. This is west of Perm and a short distance west of Vyatka. The article read as follows:

Our little town is about to acquire historical importance as the former Emperor's place of imprisonment: he is about to be transferred here from Ekaterinburg, which is menaced by Czecho-Slovak and White Guard bands. . . .[199]

According to Bulygin, he was himself in command of a White Guard band which planned to rescue the Tsar at Kotelnich. They waited for the Tsar's train but it never arrived. Bulygin finally went on to Ekaterinburg, where he was arrested. Subsequently, he escaped from his guards on a train travelling westward towards Vyatka.[200]

While there are elements in Bulygin's story which raise doubts of its full credibility, the newspaper story which he describes seems to confirm the belief that the train referred to in the telegrams was indeed carrying the Imperial Family. If so, we may assume that the place of its interception was somewhere between Perm and Kotelnich.

Guards of an Empty House

If, as the telegrams seem to indicate, the Imperial Family left Ekaterinburg prior to June 26, how could they have been there for the murder on July 16? The question is: *were they in Ekaterinburg?*

Could the guards keep a secret?

Medvedyev indicated that they could. According to him they were kept on duty at the Ipatiev House for three additional days, just to conceal the "murders" (see page 210):

> The guard of the house remained on duty and was not removed until July 20, in spite of the fact that there was no one left in the house. This was done in order to keep the people from becoming excited and to give the appearance that the Imperial Family was still alive.

How long had this been going on—since July 17, when the Imperial Family was "murdered"; or since sometime prior to June 26, when it was "taken away"?

If the Imperial Family had been taken away from Ekaterinburg, they could, of course, have been brought back—after their return to Perm on July 8. But this hardly seems likely. If the intention was to murder them all—and keep the murder a secret—it would have been much better to do it in Perm than to bring them all back and do it in the very house where everyone knew they had been staying. And if someone happened to see them, the story that the Tsarina and the children were removed to a "safe place" would be disproved.

It seems far more likely that the Imperial Family either left Ekaterinburg for good, or did not leave at all. And the first of these alternatives is not nearly as improbable as it might seem.

There was, first of all, a good reason for removing the Imperial

Family in June. At that time the fall of Ekaterinburg to the Whites was considered a foregone conclusion. This was the military estimate of the situation in Moscow as early as June 15.[201]

And it would not be at all difficult to conceal the prisoners' absence. The prison house was hidden by a high, double, board wall, temporarily constructed for just this purpose—concealment.

It is possible, moreover, that the secret did leak. As General Dieterichs says, many people claimed to have seen the Imperial Family's departure from Ekaterinburg.

It is not without significance, moreover, that on July 4, about a week after his first train telegram, Beloborodov announced a sudden change in the guard personnel. In this change the commander of the guard and his assistant were replaced, as well as the entire interior guard, that is, those who were stationed at posts on the upper floor, where the Imperial Family lived. The assistant commandant, Moshkin, was arrested.[202]

What was the reason for this change? It has never been adequately explained.

The Bolsheviks gave as a reason the alleged theft of a gold cross belonging to the Imperial Family. General Dieterichs rejects this reason,[203] and indeed it is far from convincing, especially since Moshkin is supposed to have been around after the "murder", helping to distribute the loot. (See page 210.)

It has been suggested that the Bolsheviks were dissatisfied with the supposed increasingly lenient attitude of the old guard commander, Avdeyev. But this is pure speculation, and also unconvincing.

Another suggestion was that the purpose of the change was to prepare for the "execution". This would be a plausible reason. A murder might well call for more trusted, "safe" personnel, and greater security. But so would a *simulated* murder and an increased need for secrecy—to prevent a leak of information that the Imperial Family was no longer in Ekaterinburg.

It seems at least equally credible that the change was induced by this need. And there *was* greater secrecy after the change occurred because, as Sokolov related, the ten new guards took over all "internal" duty.[204] Only five of them could speak Russian. Only one was known to be of Russian nationality. And they were all from the Cheka—employees of the Extraordinary Investigating Commission, the forerunner of the G.P.U. and the N.K.V.D.—the secret police. So were the new commander, Yurovsky, and the new assistant commander, Nikulin.[205]

Finally, there is some significance in the fact that Beloborodov reported the change in guard personnel in the same brief telegram in which he reported Syromolotov's controversial mission. As has already been indicated, the most reasonable interpretation of that telegram would connect Syromolotov's mission in some way with the Imperial Family and the change of guard at the Ipatiev House. The most plausible connection would involve an effort to simulate the Imperial Family's continued presence at the Ipatiev House.

Another very significant circumstance is the fact that from sometime before the 26th of June the Imperial Family was held virtually incommunicado. Only a very few people besides guards actually saw or claimed to have seen the Imperial Family during that period.

General Dieterichs states that visitors from among the Soviet leaders were limited to three—Goloshchekin, Beloborodov and Didkovsky.[206] The only exception was the one-time visit on June 21 of the Commander of the 3rd Red Army, Berzins, and a verifying committee. This visit was ostensibly made to disprove the rumors of the Tsar's murder. General Dieterichs records the text of Berzins' telegraphed report, which is dated June 27 and addressed to the Council of People's Commissars, the Commissar of War, the Press Bureau and the Central Executive Committee—all in Moscow:

> In Moscow newspapers which I have received there is an announcement of the murder of Nicholas Romanov by personnel of the Red Army in the course of a patrol from Ekaterinburg. I state officially that on June 21, in the company of members of the V. military inspection, the military commissar of the Urals military region and members of the All-Russian investigating commission I made an inspection of the place of confinement of Nicholas Romanov and family and a check of the guard and watch all members of the family and Nicholas himself are alive and all information concerning their murder, etc. is provocation. 198. 27 June, 1918, 0 hours 5 minutes. Commander in Chief Northern Ural and Siberian Front Berzins.[207]

Although the telegram is dated June 27, the visit was made on June 21, several days prior to Beloborodov's first telegram about the train in Perm.

Among the unofficial visitors, the most important was the Tsarevich's personal physician, Doctor Derevenko. He was the only person who could actually communicate with the Imperial Family. Thus General Dieterichs states that when Sidorov came to Ekaterinburg he had only two possible means of contact with the Imperial

Family.[208] One of these was by concealing a letter among the provisions which were being brought to the Ipatiev House at that time by two nuns, Antonina and Maria. The other was orally, through Doctor Derevenko.

The two nuns were never allowed to see the Imperial Family. They left their provisions at the door.[209]

With respect to Doctor Derevenko, only one visit is unequivocally placed in the period after June 26. General Dieterichs records it as follows:

> After Yankel Yurovsky's appointment as commandant, approximately in the period July 5-8, he invited Doctor Derevenko to the house. After this visit the doctor stopped visiting the Imperial Family altogether. The reason for this was explained by Derevenko himself to interested friends as follows: when he, in response to the invitation referred to, arrived at the house, Yankel Yurovsky brought him, as the story has it, to the Tsarevich, who was prostrate with a sore leg, and asked Derevenko's opinion about the state of His Highness' illness. Derevenko replied that he considered the condition of the Tsarevich's leg to be very serious, and would not permit him to walk under any circumstances. Then, according to the account, Yankel Yurovsky himself took hold of the Tsarevich's leg, began to feel it crudely and knead it, and asserted that it was perfectly well. According to the story, this crude medical treatment of the suffering Tsarevich by Yurovsky so upset the doctor that he decided not to go back to the Ipatiev House at all.[210]

There is something unconvincing about this report. In the first place it does not sound like the probable attitude of a doctor who had attended the Tsarevich continually since 1912, and who had voluntarily shared the Imperial Family's imprisonment in Tsarskoye Selo and Tobolsk.

In the second place General Dieterichs himself does not seem to put much faith in the story. He also seems to have looked upon Derevenko with suspicion, and states that the doctor was never formally questioned:

> . . . . Doctor Derevenko did not offer his testimony. He was questioned by no one, neither by the investigator, Nametkin, nor by the member of the court, Sergeyev, nor by the public prosecutor—by no one. And when the case passed into the hands of the investigator, N. A. Sokolov, who urgently sought out for questioning all of the people of the [Imperial] court who had been with the Imperial Family, Doctor Derevenko was not in Ekaterinburg; he had gone somewhere into the

depths of Siberia, and now remains in Tomsk with the Bolshe-viks.[211]

This leaves the story of Doctor Derevenko's last visit in the category of unofficial, unverified and unverifiable statements obtained at second or third hand through unidentified intermediaries who may or may not be reporting what Doctor Derevenko actually said.

Information with respect to previous visits is extremely indefinite and dates are not given. In fact, as General Dieterichs states, there was very little information about them at all:

> In the beginning, under Avdeyev, Doctor Derevenko visited the Ipatiev House fairly often; he also made an arrangement with that commandant for provisions to be brought to the Imperial Family from outside. But somehow the ordinary people of the city with whom Derevenko associated, and who were certainly not partisans of the Bolsheviks, retained very few recollections of stories told by Derevenko about his visits to the Ipatiev prisoners during this extraordinary period in the life of the Imperial Family.[212]

Doctor Derevenko's situation must also be considered in connection with the report about Sidorov. If Sidorov did bring a communication with respect to the Imperial Family's pending removal from Ekaterinburg, and if as General Dieterichs suggests, Doctor Derevenko transmitted it orally to the Tsar, then Doctor Derevenko knew the truth. Under these circumstances, obviously, he would not tell. The report of his last visit to the Ipatiev House must therefore be considered inconclusive.

Seven other people are mentioned as having seen the Imperial Family in the Ipatiev House during this period. The circumstances are described by Sokolov in a chapter entitled: "The Imperial Family Was In The Ipatiev House Until The Night Of July 17." [213] Three of these people are guards, Proskuryakov, Letemin, and Yakimov, and for reasons already indicated, their testimony carries no weight. For some unexplained reason there is no statement on this point by the principal guard, Medvedyev.

There were thus four witnesses: the priest, Storozhev, and the deacon, Vasili Buimirov, who came to the house on July 14; and two women hired to wash the floors, M. G. Starodumova and V. O. Dryagina, who came on the following day, July 15.

The timing of these visits is in itself suspicious. They were apparently not customary or regular, and it almost seems as if the

Bolsheviks, having tightened the security on July 4, were now, on the eve of the important event, preparing "incontrovertible" testimony that would later "prove" that the Imperial Family was still there.

If such was their intent, however, they did not succeed.

In the first place there is no indication that the two women had ever been in the Ipatiev House, or even seen the Imperial Family, before. They were sent to the Ipatiev House by a labor union. Moreover, during the whole time they were inside they were under the constant surveillance of the guard commandant, Yurovsky. And while the "Grand Duchesses" apparently helped them by moving some furniture, no talking was permitted. The two women, therefore, could have been deceived, as easily as not, by the poorest of actors, in other words, impostors.

In the case of the two clergymen there was a rather startling result. They had each been to the house once before, on June 2. During both visits they merely celebrated religious services and departed. As in the case of the two women, no speaking or other communication with the Imperial Family was allowed.

Moreover, only one of these clergymen testified, apparently. This was Father Storozhev. In his testimony he gives a detailed description of the appearance and conduct of the family. It includes some notable differences between the first and second visits:

. . . . . his [the Tsar's] beard, on my first visit, was longer and wider than on July 1 (14), when, it seemed to me, Nicholas Alexandrovich had shaved around his beard.[214]

He [the Tsarevich] was pale, but not so much so as at the time of my first service. In general he looked more healthy. Alexandra Feodorovna also had a healthier appearance. She wore the same dress as on May 20 [Old Style]. As for Nicholas Alexandrovich, he was wearing the same clothes as the first time. Only I cannot, somehow, picture to myself clearly whether he was on this occasion wearing the St. George cross on his breast.[215]

Father Deacon and I walked in silence to the Art School building, where he suddenly said to me: "Do you know, Father Archpresbyter, something has happened to them there." Since Father Deacon's words somewhat confirmed my own impression I stopped and asked him why he thought so.—"Yes, precisely," the deacon said: "they are all some other people, truly. Why no one even sang." And it must be said that actually, for the first time, no one of the Romanov family sang with us during the service of July 1/14.[216]

What did the deacon mean? That these people whom he had seen were not the Imperial Family? Was he speaking literally or only figuratively? And why don't we have his testimony? We can only speculate about the answer to these questions. But the "proof" that the Imperial Family was in the Ipatiev House is far from convincing, far less convincing, indeed, than the telegrams and the circumstances which seem to indicate that they were not.

"The Diary of Nicholas Romanov"

Sokolov did not have an opportunity to examine what should have been the best evidence of the Imperial Family's continued presence at the Ipatiev House. This was the purported testimony of the Tsar himself—the last pages of "The Diary of Nicholas Romanov"—prompt publication of which was promised in the telegram of the Bolshevik "Press Bureau", July 19, 1918 (see pages 227-228). The last entries of this diary were actually published in 1928,[217] and if they could be accepted as genuine would establish unequivocally the Imperial Family's uninterrupted presence at the Ipatiev House until July 13, 1918, four days prior to the supposed murder.

But these diary entries were even more subject to falsification than the bloody chamber of execution, the questionable "remains" found at the mine and the contradictory testimony of Communist guards. They remained entirely under Soviet control and were published by the Soviet regime. There was never any opportunity for an impartial check of their authenticity. If the Bolsheviks were willing to falsify other evidence, they would not be likely to overlook the opportunity afforded by this diary.

And in spite of the continuous Soviet control of this document, it does indicate, nevertheless, that the Bolsheviks at first planned to move the Imperial Family from Ekaterinburg. The diary thus seems to corroborate General Dieterichs' theory that the train made up in Perm was intended for the removal of the Imperial Family.

There are also entries which indicate a cancellation of this plan of removal, and which ostensibly represent the Tsar's description of subsequent events at the Ipatiev House, the change in the guard, and even an alleged "counter-revolutionary" conspiracy to release the Imperial Family from prison. But these could have been forged as easily as not.

So that the reader may form his own judgment, the entries of this "diary" from June 10, 1918 to the date of its termination on July 13, 1918 are set forth in full below. The dates used by the writer were reckoned according to Old Style, and New Style dates have therefore been included in brackets:

May 28 [June 10]. Monday.
A very warm day. They are constantly opening the boxes in the shed where our trunks are kept and removing various articles and supplies brought from Tobolsk. And without explanation, moreover. All this leads to the suspicion that attractive items can easily be taken home, and thus lost to us forever! Horrible! External attitudes have also changed during recent weeks. The jailers try not to speak to us, as though not in their usual mood, as though feeling a kind of fear and sense of danger in our presence! I can't understand it!

May 29 [June 11]. Tuesday.
Dear Tatiana is 21! A strong wind has been blowing since last night, directly against the window, thanks to which the air in our bedroom has finally become pure and sufficiently cool. We read a great deal. We walked in two shifts again. Kharitonov served a compote for lunch, to the great pleasure of all. In the evening bezique, as usual.

May 31 [June 13]. Ascension Thursday.
In the morning we waited a long time for the priest to conduct services, but in vain. They were all busy in the churches. In the afternoon, for some reason, we were not allowed to go out in the garden. Avdeyev came and talked for a long time with Eug. Serg. [Botkin]. He [Avdeyev] stated that he and the Regional Soviet feared an outbreak of anarchists and that we could therefore, perhaps, anticipate an early departure, probably for Moscow! He asked us to get ready to leave. We began to pack right away, but quietly at Avdeyev's special request, so as not to attract the attention of the rank of the guard.

He [Avdeyev] returned about 11 o'clock in the evening and said that we would remain several days longer. And so, until *June 1 [14]*, we lived as in camp, unpacking nothing.

The weather remained fine. There were walks, as usual, in two shifts. Finally, after supper, Avdeyev, slightly tipsy, explained to Botkin that the anarchists had been seized, the danger passed and our departure cancelled! After all the preparations it was quite a blow! In the evening we played a little bezique.

June 3 [16]. Sunday.
Again we had no service. I read the whole week and today

finished the history "Emperor Paul I" by Shilder—very interesting.

We are all waiting for Sednev and Nagorny, whom they promised to return to us today.

June 5 [18]. Tuesday.
Dear Anastasia is already 17. The heat was very great both outside and in. I am still reading Saltikov, volume III—interesting and intelligent.

The whole family took a walk before tea. Kharitonov has been preparing our food since yesterday. Provisions are brought every other day. He is teaching the girls to prepare food. In the evening they make dough and in the morning they bake bread! Not bad!

June 9 [22]. Saturday.
In the last few days the weather has been magnificent, but very hot. It was very stuffy in our rooms. Especially at night. At Botkin's written request we were allowed to walk for an hour and a half. Today six men came during tea, probably from the Regional Soviet, to see which windows to open. The determination of this question has dragged on for approximately two weeks! Various characters have come at frequent intervals and, in our presence, stared at the windows in silence.

The aroma from all the gardens in the city is extraordinary.

June 10 [23]. Trinity Sunday.
The day was notable for several events. In the morning one window was opened for us. Eug. Serg. had trouble with his kidneys and suffered a great deal. At 11:30 we had a real Mass and vespers. At the end of the day Alix and Alexei had supper with us in the dining room. In addition we walked for two hours! The day was wonderful. It turns out that yesterday's visitors were commissars from Petrograd. The air in the room has become pure, even cooler toward evening.

June 12 [25]. Tuesday.
It was extraordinarily hot yesterday and today. Also in the rooms, even though the window was open all the time! We walked for two hours in the afternoon. During dinner there were two severe storms which freshened the air! Eug. Serg. is much better, but still in bed.

June 14 [27]. Thursday.
Our dear Maria is 19. The weather is still tropical, 26° [C.] in the shade and 24° [C.] in the rooms. It is very difficult to endure! We passed a night of alarm and sat up in our clothes
. . . .

All this was due to our having recently received two letters, one after the other, in which we were advised to get ready to be carried off by some loyal people!

But the days passed and nothing happened. The waiting and the uncertainty were very upsetting.

June 21 [July 4]. Thursday.
There was a change of commandants today. At dinner time Beloborodov came with some others and explained that the man we took for a doctor, Yurovsky, had been appointed to the place of Avdeyev.[218] In the afternoon, before tea, he [Yurovsky] and his assistant prepared an inventory of the gold objects —ours and the children's. They took most of these away with them (rings, bracelets, etc.). They explained that an unpleasant incident had occurred in our house, referring to the disappearance of our things. Thus the belief of which I wrote on May 28 [June 10] was confirmed. I'm sorry for Avdeyev but it was his own fault since he did not keep his people from stealing things out of the trunks in the shed.

June 23 [July 6]. Saturday.
Yesterday, the commandant, Yu[rovsky], brought a box with all the confiscated valuables, asked us to check the contents, sealed it in our presence, and left it with us for safekeeping. The weather became cooler and it was not so oppressive in the bedroom. Yu[rovsky] and his assistant are beginning to understand what sort of people surrounded us, guarded us and robbed us.

Not to mention our things—they even kept for themselves most of the supplies brought from the convent. Only now, after the change, have we learned of this, because all of the provisions have begun to go to the kitchen.

During all these days I have, as usual, done a lot of reading. Today I started volume VII of Saltikov. I greatly enjoy his tales, stories and articles.

It was a rainy day. We walked for an hour and a half and came back to the house dry.

June 25 [July 8]. Monday.
Our life has not changed a bit under Yu[rovsky]. He comes into the bedroom to make sure the seal on the box is unbroken and looks out the open window. All morning today, and up until 4 o'clock they were testing and fixing the electric lights. Inside the house there are new guards, Letts, but outside they are the same—part soldier, part worker! According to rumors several of Avdeyev's guards have already been arrested!

The door to the shed containing our baggage has been sealed. If only that had been done a month ago!

At night there was a storm and it has become even cooler.

June 28 [July 11]. Thursday.
About 10:30 in the morning three workers came to the open window, raised a heavy grating and fastened it from the out-

side—without any warning from Yu[rovsky]. We like this type less and less!
I began to read volume VIII of Saltikov.

June 30 [July 13]. Saturday.
Alexei took his first bath since Tobolsk. His knee is getting better, but he cannot straighten it out completely. The weather is warm and pleasant. We have no news whatever from outside.

Here the diary ends.

It will be noted that the entry for May 31 (June 13) indicates that the Imperial Family was forewarned of an impending departure. It thus corroborates General Dieterichs' belief in such a plan.

It should be noted, however, that General Dieterichs' belief was based on telegrams dated July 4, 7 and 8, three weeks after Avdeyev supposedly informed the Imperial Family that the planned departure had been "cancelled". And the telegram purportedly referring to the shipment of "gold and platinum" was dated June 26, twelve days after this supposed cancellation. If any of these telegrams referred to preparations for the removal of the Imperial Family, there must have been a further change of plan of which the Imperial Family was apparently not informed.

If any of these telegrams referred to an actual removal of the Imperial Family, at least some of the diary entries made subsequent to May 31 (June 13) must be forgeries.

In the light of what has already been said about the telegrams, the latter conclusion seems the most probable.

The second part of the entry for May 31 (June 13), beginning with the words "And so, until *June 1*. . . . . ." is certainly open to great suspicion. The method of transition to another day's entry is unique. It is an unusual insertion, very much out of character with other portions of the diary.

There was, moreover, no real reason for a change in departure plans at the time indicated. The reports of the investigators indicate that the decision to do away with the Imperial Family was not made (if made at all) until some time in July. Avdeyev's reference to an uprising of "anarchists" must be discounted as an effort to keep the Imperial Family in ignorance of the real reason for the planned departure. The real threat to the Bolsheviks in Ekaterinburg on June 13—and the only known reason for the Imperial Family's removal—was the advance on Ekaterinburg of Czechoslovak and White forces. And this reason was not being alleviated, it was becoming more urgent. As has already been stated, the fall of Ekaterinburg was considered in Moscow, on June 15, to be inevitable. Military movements might have necessitated *postponement* of the Imperial Family's planned departure, but certainly not *cancellation*.

Many subsequent entries in this diary are also suspect, since they contain declarations which are of value only to the Bolsheviks and which corroborate official Soviet statements that are generally regarded as fabrications. Thus we find entries from June 21 (July 4) supporting the Bolshevik explanation of the change in the guard—that this change was made because of alleged thefts from the Imperial Family. And on June 14 (27) there is the very uncredible reference to a loyalist conspiracy to carry off the Imperial Family. Surely the Tsar would not jeopardize the safety of loyal supporters by confirming their activities in writing, or permit his family to sit up clothed all night and thus leave the plan open to discovery by guards who might enter their rooms at any moment! More probably this entry is an insertion made by some other person to support the reference to a "counter-revolutionary" conspiracy made in the official announcement of the Tsar's "execution".

There is nothing, moreover, in the later diary entries which could not have been written by anyone who wished to "continue" the diary to the desired date. These entries are less frequent than earlier ones and even omit significant events which one would expect to be mentioned.

It seems most extraordinary, for example, that the diary should end on July 13, with no mention of the visit made the following day by Father Storozhev and the deacon. The diary customarily mentions religious services held at the house, and often, when this is the case, even describes the occasions when services were *not* held. In the light of this, one would certainly expect to find an explanation of the Imperial Family's inability to sing in the customary manner during the service of July 14!

It seems reasonable, therefore, to consider the "diary" as better evidence of the Imperial Family's escape than proof of its execution. The entry of May 31 (June 13) confirms the other evidence of the Imperial Family's departure, and subsequent entries must be read with great reservations. The Imperial Family may well have been on a train somewhere near Perm when the final entries are supposed to have been written!

83

German Diplomatic Correspondence

Serge Petrovich Mel'gunov, in his study of the Tsar's fate, describes German diplomatic correspondence published in 1935 by Gottlieb von Jagow, former State Secretary of the German Foreign Ministry.[219] On the basis of this correspondence Mel'gunov relates that on June 21, 1918, Count Mirbach, the German Ambassador in Moscow, suggested to the Soviet Commissar of Foreign Affairs, Georgi V. Chicherin, that rumors of harm to the Imperial Family during the siege of Ekaterinburg should be dispelled. Expressions of concern were also made to the Soviet Ambassador in Berlin, A.A. Joffe, who advised that the Soviet Government had determined to move the Imperial Family out of Ekaterinburg, but was prevented from doing so by an interruption in rail communications and the actions of the Czechs.

Several days later, according to Mel'gunov's summary, Chicherin told Count Mirbach that counter-revolutionary efforts in Ekaterinburg had been liquidated, and that, while the telegraph was not working properly, "according to information reaching bourgeois circles, the Imperial Family was on a train near Perm."

If the "information reaching bourgeois circles" was accurate, then the Imperial Family may have left Ekaterinburg sometime between June 21, when Berzins made his inspection, and June 27, when he sent his wired report (see page 74 above) after telegraph communication was, presumably, reestablished. The "information reaching bourgeois circles" would also substantiate the belief that Beloborodov's telegram of June 26 with respect to the shipment of "gold and platinum" actually referred to the movement of the Imperial Family.

In his description of this German correspondence, Mel'gunov also indicates a substantial inaccuracy in Sokolov's version (page 244) of Riezler's report to Moscow of July 20. According to the source quoted by Mel'gunov this communication, made three days after the Tsar's reported execution, contained the suggestion that the Germans give up their demand for a battalion in Moscow in exchange for the release of the Tsarevich and his mother. The pertinent part of the text should read as follows:

> If, at the time of the conversations with respect to the battalion, Joffe actually suggests that the Entente powers also have a military force in Moscow for defense against unexpected eventualities on our side, perhaps it would be possible to obtain the

release of the Tsarina and the Tsarevich (on the premise of their inseparability) putting forth humanitarian motives. For the final development of counter-revolution it is extremely important to wrest the Tsarevich from the hands of the bolsheviks so as to prevent the Entente powers from using him and in the event it is not possible to oppose him with Michael Alexandrovich.[220]

This suggestion indicates (a) that the "humanitarian" interest of the Germans in the fate of the Imperial Family was actually motivated by political considerations, and (b) that Riezler believed the published announcement of the Tsar's execution. On the other hand, it also indicates that the German Embassy in Moscow was not kept fully informed of the progress of the negotiations then going on between Moscow and Berlin. If we accept as accurate the information contained in the tape of the conversation between Sverdlov and the unknown correspondent in Ekaterinburg, which took place on the same day, July 20, that Riezler's report was made, then we must assume that the German demand for a battalion in Moscow had already been withdrawn, and that the most crucial phase of the negotiations had been passed. (See pages 235-236.) If the fate of the Imperial Family was involved, it may have already been decided. If Riezler's suggestion had any relevance at all, or if it was anticipated, the safety of at least two members, the Tsarina and the Tsarevich, was perhaps, at this time, assured.

Subsequent Reports From German Sources

If the Imperial Family did get to Perm, where did they go after that? Where did the trail lead from Perm?

In a "Translator's Commentary" there is hardly room for an evaluation of the many later day reports of those claiming to have seen, or be, members of the Imperial Family in exile. But it is interesting to note that the German Ministry of Foreign Affairs went on dickering with the Bolsheviks over the release of the "widowed" Tsarina and her children until the middle of September, 1918.[221]

There are also two accounts, reported by Sokolov, which deserve mention. The first is that of Serge Markov, the man who allegedly bore the Tsarina's letter of explanation to the Grand Duke Ernest Louis of Hesse-Darmstadt.

Sokolov first quotes the statement of an unidentified General

"N", who met Markov in Kiev. General "N" was questioned by Sokolov on September 2, 1919 in Omsk. His statement was as follows:

In Kiev, in the German kommandatura, I met a gentleman whom I did not know. He said that he was a cornet of the Crimean Horse Regiment, the Empress Alexandra Feodorovna's Own. He said he was the step-son of Governor General Dumbadze and that his last name was Markov. His mother's maiden name was Krauze. Markov was a confirmed monarchist of clearly-expressed German crease. Markov related that he followed closely on the heels of the Imperial Family and was at Tsarskoye when they were imprisoned there. Then, as he stated, he commanded a Red squadron somewhere and wound up in Tobolsk. . . . After leaving Tobolsk, he said, he learned, while in Moscow, that they [the Imperial Family] were being taken to Ekaterinburg. Everyone who listened to him told him that the Imperial Family had been killed. . . . Markov assured us that the whole Imperial Family was alive and in hiding somewhere. He said that he knew where they were, but that he did not want to say exactly where. . . . In Kiev this same Markov enjoyed a very special position with the Germans. He was in communication by telegraph with the German command in Berlin. The Germans paid a great deal of attention to him. He did not leave Kiev with our echelon, but with the German command. When he went to the city he was accompanied by two German corporals. He said that he had been everywhere and that in Soviet Russia he had access everywhere to the Bolsheviks through the Germans.[222]

Sokolov then quotes the statement of Markov himself, which was delivered to Sokolov's agent [223] in March-April, 1921:

During the period from July 19 to August 15 [1918] (when I left Petersburg for Kiev), according to all the information which I had obtained from the Germans at that time in contact with Smolny (one was an employee of the German general consulate in Petersburg, Herman Shill; the others I do not remember)— the family was still alive. The Germans repeatedly said: "Yes, the Tsar was probably shot, but the family is alive." Yes, I spoke with Shill. I do not remember the others with whom I spoke . . . . Magener came to Kiev in the middle of October. He turned out to be an employee of the German Ministry of Foreign Affairs. About 53 years old. He spoke excellent Russian, having lived in Odessa for 23 years before the war. He had some kind of a commercial business. He went to Germany before the war. Magener categorically stated that the Imperial Family was alive, that he knew nothing about the Tsar, but that in any event the Tsar was not with his family. He had learned this from German intelligence in the Perm guberniya. He had spoken with Joffe and Radek. They both categorically stated that the Imperial Family was alive.

At the end of 1918 I made the acquaintance of a German spy, whose last name I do not remember, but I do know that he worked for two and a half years during the war on the radio-telegraph in Moscow. He told me that his nephew had recently been working in the Perm guberniya and had told him that the Imperial Family was unquestionably alive and was constantly moving about in the Perm guberniya.[224]

This is what the German Foreign Ministry apparently believed. They too had lost the trail in Perm.

The other significant report mentioned by Sokolov appears in the first—French—edition of his account of the investigation. It does not appear in the Russian edition. It relates to the prediction of the Tsar's simulated execution which was made by Count Hans-Bodo von Alvensleben, the Kaiser's personal contact with Hetman Skoropadsky. Sokolov tells of it as follows:

In the summer of 1918, while the Ukraine was occupied by the Germans, there was a certain Count Alvensleben in Kiev. This personage was a member of the German diplomatic service, at first attached to Marshal Eichorn and then, after his assassination, to Mirbach. During the regime of Hetman Skoropadsky Alvensleben played one of the most important political roles in the Ukraine. He was considered a russophile and a monarchist and was very popular in Russian aristocratic circles. He was, in particular, on excellent terms with M. Bezak and the General Prince Dolgorukov who was commander of the anti-Bolshevik forces in the Ukraine.

Prince Dolgorukov testified as follows: "I recall very well that on the 5th or 6th of July, 1918, Bezak informed me by telephone that Alvensleben had just come to visit him to give him some important news. I went to Bezak's. . . . Alvensleben told us that the Emperor Wilhelm wished to rescue the Emperor Nicholas II at all costs, and had taken measures to that end. . . . He forewarned us that between the 16th and the 20th of July we would learn that the Emperor had been put to death. He forewarned us that like the rumors current in June concerning the death of the Emperor, this news would be false, but it was necessary to disseminate it in the interests of the Emperor himself. He asked us to keep this conversation secret, and to let others believe, when the moment came, that we were convinced of the Emperor's death. On the 18th or 19th of July the newspapers in Kiev announced that the Emperor had been put to death in Ekaterinburg and that the Imperial Family had been removed to a safe place. I was astounded I assure you by the manner in which Alvensleben proved to have such advance information."

There were prayers for the late Emperor in the churches of Kiev. "There was no delay in the spread of the news," Prince Dolgorukov adds, "that Alvensleben had *wept* during the funeral service. Bezak and I were amazed to see *the facility with which this man played his role.*" [225]

VI. Conclusion

One cannot, of course, come to a conclusion after reading the accounts of only one side, and unfortunately we do not have the record, the "dossier", or the reports of the criminal investigating division.

One could reach the conclusion that the theory of rescue by the Germans was suppressed. General Dieterichs asserts that it "was finally dropped when, with the collapse of German power, it became known that the Imperial Family was not in Germany and had not been there." [226] But to whom was this "known"? Who "knew" that the Imperial Family had not been heard from? General Dieterichs presents no evidence.

Perhaps, indeed, the Imperial Family *had* been heard from in a most unexpected way. If, indeed, they were in Germany with the family of the Tsarina, or in the Crimea with the family of the Tsar, or even still in Perm when, in January, 1919, it was captured by the Whites, the Imperial Family may well have expressed a desire to remain "officially dead," thereby inspiring the sudden changes in the investigating personnel and the renewed search for "remains" which was soon to take place.

It was in December, 1918 that the Tsar's mother, the Dowager Tsarina Maria Feodorovna, and his sisters, the Grand Duchesses Xenia and Olga Alexandrovny, suggested that Bulygin go from the Crimea to Omsk for "another attempt to find out what had become of the Imperial Family." [227] It was in the next month, January, 1919, that General Dieterichs, an army man, was given supervision over the *judicial* phase of the investigation. In the next month, February, Sokolov was appointed, and not long after that the activities

89

of the criminal investigating division were terminated.

And then, as Bulygin relates, Sokolov, upon his arrival in Europe, was given 1,000 pounds by the Emperor's mother, the Dowager Empress Maria Feodorovna, presumably to continue his work.[228] Yet, as her biographer relates, she never ceased to feel and state that the Imperial Family were alive.[229]

But in spite of all this, it would be rash to conclude that these investigators expressed conclusions in which they did not believe. Nor would it be precise to say that they were "duped" by flimsy, planted evidence. It would probably be most correct to say that even if some selected few were made aware of the real truth—of the correct answer to the greatest riddle of a land of riddles, mysteries and enigmas—there were others who found it easy to believe what they were supposed to believe and wanted to believe, and thus accepted without question what they found.

They wanted to do honor to their Tsar—for whom, they thought, there were only two honorable courses, to remain a prisoner or die a martyr. As General Dieterichs said, some Tsars are born to rule, others to die as martyrs—martyrs to government, martyrs to the concept of God-anointed spiritual and temporal authority.

To confirm that Nicholas II so died, I am sure, was one of the intended purposes of the investigation. Sokolov indicated as much in his report to the Dowager Empress. "The time will come," he wrote, "when a national leader will raise his banner for the honour of the Emperor. He will need all the material collected during the inquiry." [230]

Nevertheless the investigators seemed puzzled by the fact that the Tsar did not come walking back, after the defeat of the Germans, present himself to his loyal followers and say: "Look, I am alive after all." If the Tsar had really escaped, if he was a prisoner of the Germans, why did he not come back to claim his throne?

Merely to spell out such a course is to answer the question. If the Imperial Family owed their lives to German demands, and if the price was German support of the Bolshevik regime—it would mean that survival of one family had been obtained at the cost of the welfare of a whole people, their own, Russian people. This would not be an easy thing for the Tsar to admit, even though he was not responsible for the decision.

But there was another reason also that the Tsar could not appear. It was a less personal reason, and one his followers could not admit.

Russia was no place in which a ransomed king could return and be recrowned with greater glory than before. The days of Richard the Lion-Hearted had passed.

For eight months prior to the Bolshevik seizure of power, Russia had a democratic government. For all its faults and weaknesses —whatever they may have been—that government was democratic, perhaps too democratic. People like General Dieterichs might speak with contempt of the "Kerenshchina". They might ridicule the popular fascination with "words, speeches, politics, meetings, democratic principles and *other poison*", but they could not deny that this "poison" was popular. It was the overwhelming trend of the times.

The Tsar had abdicated and the termination of the monarchy was generally accepted. When he gave up the throne Russia did not go into mourning. People paraded and danced in the streets, and sang the "Marseillaise". The day of autocracy was ended. The Tsar could not fail to see this.

Nor could the Tsar help in the fight against the Bolsheviks. The White governments were all committed to some form of constitutional government, and even if they wanted to support a monarchy they could not. If a few loyal monarchists raised their heads, or if some officers, after a few vodkas, sang "God Save the Tsar", there would be storms of protest. If the White governments even appeared to support monarchy they would lose followers at home and all possibility of assistance from the Allied governments abroad.

Bulygin and Wilton both relate this. Bulygin says, for example, that General Denikin could not even openly supply a bodyguard for the Dowager Empress.[231] And as Wilton says, it was a "cardinal maxim of the Kolchak Government that it wielded supreme authority over the Russian dominions pending the convocation of a 'Constituent Assembly' ". This formula, he said, had been "adopted as a *sine qua non* by the powers of the Entente." [232]

Under such circumstances, if the Tsar were alive, it must certainly have appeared to him that the best way he could help his countrymen was to "remain dead". And perhaps he succeeded in convincing others that this was so. Perhaps his persistence in this fictitious death was a greater martyrdom, and more to his "honor", than death in Ekaterinburg or the "materials" so laboriously gathered there by the investigators. He was greater, perhaps, than they knew, and more of a martyr than they could suspect.

If this is true then he became, not a martyr to "government", as General Dieterichs would have it, but a martyr to democracy—a martyrdom that was all the more difficult because its goal, in his

91

lifetime, whenever that was or will be ended, has not yet been realized.

But this is all speculation . . .

Nevertheless let it be considered by all who proclaim their loyalty to the Tsar!

FOOTNOTES
FOR
TRANSLATOR'S COMMENTARY
1 – 232

[1] The translation is from the Russian edition, which was published posthumously: *Ubiistvo tsarskoi sem'i*, Berlin, Slovo, 1925. There is also a French edition, *Enquête judiciaire sur l'assassinat de la famille impériale russe*, Paris, Payot, 1924, and a German edition, *Der Todesweg des Zaren; Dargestellt von dem Untersuchungsrichter*, Berlin, Stollberg, 1925. An abridged German version was also published in 1936 under the title *So begann der Bolschewismus, Leidensweg und Ermordung der Zarenfamilie*, Berlin, Deutsche Verlagsgesellschafft.

[2] See the Table of Contents of the complete work which appears on pages 105–108.

[3] Unless otherwise indicated, all dates are given in western style ("New Style"; "N.S.") and therefore thirteen days later than dates reckoned according to the system ("Old Style"; "O.S.") used in Russia prior to February 14, 1918. Some non-Soviet writers continued to employ Old Style dates even after this change.

[4] Now Sverdlovsk.

[5] The revolution in Russia occurred during World War I, when Russia was allied with the western powers against the Central Powers—Germany, Austria-Hungary and the Ottoman Empire. The first revolutionary Russian government (the "Provisional Government"), which was anti-Bolshevik, continued the war effort and launched a new offensive against Germany's eastern front. Peace with Germany was made by the Bolsheviks at Brest-Litovsk on March 3, 1918, while the Imperial Family was imprisoned at Tobolsk.

[6] *Ma Mission en Sibérie*, Paris, Payot, 1933, 301–305.

[7] Paul Petrovich Bulygin, *The Murder of the Romanovs*, New York, McBride, 1935, 272–273.

[8] *Id.*, 273–274.

93

9 *Id.*, 157–158, 240, 252–253.

9a Related by Prince G. Sidamon-Eristov in the "Annex" to his French translation of a Soviet version of the Imperial Family's last days. Paul Mikhailovich Bykov, *Les derniers jours des Romanov*, Paris, Payot, 1931, "Annexe", pp. 169–176.

10 *The Last Days of the Romanovs*, London, Butterworth, 1920. There was also an American edition, published in 1920 in New York, by George H. Doran Company; a French edition, *Les derniers jours des Romanof*, Paris, Grès & Co., 1920; and a Russian edition, *Posledniye dni Romanovykh*, Berlin, 1923.

11 *Op. cit.*, (London ed.) 13–16.

12 Bulygin makes the following contradictory assertion, *op. cit.*, 158: "Sokolov was still working very hard [in 1921], now attending to the duplication of the records of his investigation, *only one copy of which was brought from Siberia*, now unravelling the complex and subtle knot of personal relations and intrigues which hampered his work in Europe." (Italics added.) Possibly Bulygin had forgotten about the copy entrusted to Wilton, to whom he refers as "our good friend." (*Op. cit.*, 269.) Sidamon- Eristov, on the other hand, indicates that Sokolov never recovered any of the copies! *Op. cit.*, 171: "Sokoloff, dès son arrivée en France, se mit en quête de ses dossiers, ce fut en vain. Il voulut, des moins, savoir ce qu'étaient devenues les caisses confiées au général Janin. Il n'y réussit pas non plus."

13 Wilton, *op. cit.*, 16.

14 *Le tragique destin de Nicolas II et de sa famille*, Paris, Payot, 1921. There is an English edition, *Thirteen Years at the Russian Court*, London, Hutchinson & Co., 1921; and a Russian edition, *Tragicheskaya sud'ba Russkoi imperatorskoi familii*, Revel, EPK, 1921.

15 *Ubiistvo tsarskoi sem'i i chlenov doma Romanovykh na Urale* [The Murder of the Imperial Family and Members of the House of Romanov in the Urals], 2 vols., Vladivostok, Mil. Acad., 1922.

15a Except where reference is made specifically to the Russian or French editions, all page references to Sokolov's work are to pages of the partial translation which appears on pages 102–250, below.

16 Dieterichs, *op. cit.*, I, 16.

17 Bulygin, *op. cit.*, 155.

18 Wilton gives the text of the announcement, *op. cit.*, 102–103. Both he and General Dieterichs considered that it was an effort to lay the blame for the murders on the Social Revolutionary Party. See Dieterichs, *op. cit.*, I, 318–319. With the exception of Beloborodov, none of the named accused, three of whom were described as members of the Ekaterinburg Soviet, had been mentioned in the reports of the investigation made by the White authorities.

19 There were two soviets in Ekaterinburg, the "local", city, Soviet, and the Ural Oblast (Regional) Soviet. At the time of the Imperial Family's disappearance the chairman of the Oblast Soviet was Beloborodov. Bykov was listed as a member. Prince Sidamon-Eristov states, *op. cit.*, p. 10, that Bykov succeeded Beloborodov as President of the Ekaterinburg "Conseil des Soviets", and describes him on the title page of his translation as "President of the Ural Soviet in Ekaterinburg." Wilton indicates,

op. cit., 139, that the local, city, Soviet "knew nothing, at the time, of the execution."

[20] *Rabochaya revolyutsiya na Urale*, Ekaterinburg, 1921. The article was later published in Berlin, *Arkhiv Russkoy Revolyutsii* [*Archives of the Russian Revolution*], XVII. Kerensky gives an "abridged" form in Bulygin, *op. cit.*, 140–152.

[21] *Posledniye dni Romanovykh*, Sverdlovsk, Uralkniga, 1926; Moscow, State Publ., 1930. An English translation was published in New York by International Publishers as *The Last Days of Tsar Nicholas*, and in London by Martin Lawrence, Ltd. as *The Last Days of Tsardom*, both in 1934. The French translation, *Les derniers jours des Romanov, supra*, was published in 1931.

[22] *Op. cit.*, (London ed.), 81.

[23] Dieterichs, *op. cit., I*, 82.

[24] *Ibid.*, 92.

[25] Sverdlov was President of the All-Russian Central Executive Committee. This organ, described in the Constitution as the "supreme legislative, administrative and controlling body of the Russian Socialist Federal Soviet Republic," was elected by the All-Russian Congress of Soviets. It in turn appointed the Council of People's Commissars. It was of course subordinate to the Party organization.

[26] Dieterichs, *op. cit.*, I, 94.

[27] *Ibid.*

[28] Sometimes simply referred to as the criminal investigating division.

[29] Dieterichs, *op. cit.*, I, 95.

[30] *Id.*, I, 96–97.

[31] *Id.*, I, 98.

[32] *Ibid.*

[33] *Id.*, I, 111.

[34] *Id.*, I, 113–114.

[35] *Id.*, I, 114.

[36] *Id.*, I, 115.

[37] *Id.*, I, 114.

[38] *Id.*, I, 120.

[39] *Id.*, I, 160.

[40] Prior to the coup d'état engineered on November 17, 1918 by supporters of Admiral Alexander Vasil'yevich Kolchak.

[41] Victor M. Chernov was the leader of the Social Revolutionary Party, which won the majority of the votes for the Constituent Assembly in November, 1917. His personal influence upon the Ural Oblast Government must have been very small since he did not arrive in Ekaterinburg until October 11, 1918, long after the investigation began and hardly more than a month before the Kolchak coup, following which he was arrested.

[42] Dieterichs, *op. cit.*, I, 123–125.

[43] *Id.*, I, 126.

[44] *Id.*, I, 127.

[45] *Id.*, I, 127–128.

[46] *Id.*, I, 129.

[47] Sokolov, pages 153–156, also gives Sergeyev credit for having some

pieces of the floor of the chamber of execution tested for the presence of human blood.

[48] Dieterichs, *op. cit.*, I, 130–131.

[49] Wilton, *op. cit.*, 134–135.

[50] Dieterichs, *op. cit.*, I, 161.

[51] *Id.*, I, 146.

[52] *Id.*, I, 177.

[53] Sokolov declines to identify the "expert artilleryman" who examined the bullet holes, the "chemist N." who made the blood tests, or the "University of N." which is described as one of the sources of serum used for the Uhlenhuth test. The other writers make very little reference to these tests at all.

[54] Sokolov omits this passage of Letemin's testimony. It appears in Dieterichs, *op. cit.*, I, 139.

[55] Wilton, *op. cit.*, 97.

[56] Dieterichs, *op. cit.*, I, 29.

[57] Wilton, *op. cit.*, 239.

[58] Gilliard, *op. cit.*, (N.Y. ed.) 274; (Paris ed.) 231.

[59] See pp. 259–264 of the Russian edition. The victims in that case were the Grand Duke Serge Mikhailovich, a grandson of Tsar Nicholas I; the Grand Duchess Elizabeth Feodorovna, sister of the Tsarina; the Princes Ivan, Constantine, and Igor Constantinovichi and Prince Vladimir Pavlovich Paley, cousins of the Tsar; Feodor Remez, the Grand Duke's secretary; and a nun, Barbara Yakovleva.

[60] Russ. ed., 264.

[61] Russ. ed., 260.

[62] Dieterichs, *op. cit.*, I, 11.

[63] Dieterichs, *op. cit.*, I, 268.

[64] *Id.*, I, 267.

[65] *Id.*, I, 272.

[66] Proskuryakov and Yakimov are quoted to the effect that the Imperial Family was told to come downstairs because there was danger of an attack, or street firing, and that to remain upstairs would be dangerous. Medvedyev testified that the Tsarina and her daughters wore no outer clothing, that their heads were uncovered, and that the Tsar and the Tsarevich wore field shirts. See pages 199, 206, and 212.

[67] Bykov claims that the purpose of the destruction was to forestall any attempt to stir up the people with "holy relics" of a "martyred" Imperial Family. Under this hypothesis there would have been no purpose in destroying the bodies of Dr. Botkin and the three servants.

[68] Dieterichs, *op. cit.*, I, 196–198.

[69] Dieterichs, *op. cit.*, I, 267–271.

[70] This could be the brilliant shown in Photograph No. 111 and listed by Sokolov in Item 47, page 184, as weighing "10 karats". It could also, less probably, be one of the two brilliants lumped together without description or identification in Item 55, pages 186–187.

[71] Presumably Item 46, shown in Photograph 111.

[72] Presumably Item 13, shown in Photograph 89.

[73] Presumably Item 12, shown in Photograph 88.

[74] Presumably Item 31, shown in Photograph 108.

[75] Dieterichs, *op. cit.*, I, 229.
[76] Wilton, *op. cit.*, 115.
[77] Dieterichs, *op. cit.*, I. 154–155, 243–244.
[78] Dieterichs, *op. cit.*, I, 231, 259.
[79] *Id.*, I, 27.
[80] *Id.*, I, 260.
[81] Wilton, *op. cit.*, 96. Cf. 20.
[82] Dieterichs, *op. cit.*, I, 97.
[83] *Id.*, I, 86–87.
[84] Dieterichs, *op. cit.*, I, 87.
[85] *Id.*, I, 87–88.
[86] Dieterichs, *op. cit.*, I, 240–241.
[87] General Dieterichs briefly refers to, and rejects, a report that the Bolsheviks were trading the Tsar in exchange, or as surety, for some kind of a German grant or loan. *Op. cit.*, I, 117. It seems more probable that a German ransom would consist in the reduction of war indemnities and support of the Bolshevik regime, including assistance in the suppression of "counter-revolutionary" movements. See *infra*.
[88] *Id.*, I, 197.
[89] Wilton, *op. cit.*, 117.
[90] Bulygin, *op. cit.*, 252–253.
[91] *Ibid.*
[92] Dieterichs, *op. cit.*, I, 93.
[93] *Id.*, I, 44.
[94] Bulygin, *op. cit.*, 158, 252.
[95] Dieterichs, *op. cit.*, I, 269.
[96] *Id.*, I, 207.
[97] Dieterichs, *op. cit.*, I, 266–267.
[98] Bulygin, *op. cit.*, 238; Wilton, *op. cit.*, 90.
[99] Wilton, *op. cit.*, 292.
[100] Dieterichs, *op. cit.*, I, 257.
[101] *Id.*, I, 247. Cf. 86, 263.
[102] Dieterichs, *op. cit.*, I, 406–407.
[103] *Id.*, I, 407.
[104] *Id.*, I, 409–415.
[105] *Id.*, I, 287.
[106] *Id.*, I, 413–414.
[107] *Id.*, I, 36n.
[108] *Id.*, I, 414–415.
[109] *Id.*, I, 291. Sokolov also mentions Medvedyev's Party membership, page 206.
[110] Dieterichs, *op. cit.*, I, 162.
[111] *Id.*, I, 105.
[112] *Id.*, I, 417, 418.
[113] *Id.*, I, 400.
[114] *Id.*, I, 295, 396 [by typographical error 296 in volume as published].
[115] *Id.*, I, 396. [By typographical error 296.]
[116] *Id.*, I, 291. According to Dieterichs, Strekotin, the source of Letemin's information, and, with Medvedyev, the source of Proskuryakov's, was also a member of the Party. *Ibid.*
[117] Wilton, *op. cit.*, 20.

[118] Dieterichs, *op. cit.*, I, 36–38.

[119] *Id.*, I, 126.

[120] *Id.*, I, 126, 157.

[121] *Id.*, I, 100.

[122] See pages 209 and 213.

[123] Yakimov asserts, page 200, that he went to bed at 11 o'clock the night before the murder and did not know anything about it until he was awakened and told by some of the guards at "about 4 o'clock" the following morning.

[124] These dates of arrest are given in Dieterichs, *op. cit.*, I, 161–162.

[125] *Id.*, I, 130.

[126] Dieterichs, *op. cit.*, I, 424. This passage from Proskuryakov's testimony is omitted by Sokolov.

[127] Wilton, *op. cit.*, 281.

[128] Dieterichs, *op. cit.*, I, 158. This passage, from Agafonova's testimony is omitted by Sokolov.

[129] Wilton, *op. cit.*, 89.

[130] *Id.*, 305.

[131] See pages 201–202.

[132] Bulygin, *op. cit.*, 238.

[133] Dieterichs, *op. cit.*, I, 100, 140.

[134] Wilton, *op. cit.*, 13.

[135] *Id.*, 90.

[136] Bulygin, *op. cit.*, 238.

[137] See page 203.

[138] Dieterichs, *op. cit.*, I, 158. This passage from Agafonova's testimony is omitted by Sokolov.

[139] *Id.*, I, 41.

[140] Wilton, *op. cit.*, 217.

[141] *Id.*, 238.

[142] *Id.*, 253.

[143] Dieterichs, *op. cit.*, I, 42.

[144] *Soviet Documents on Foreign Policy*, Jane Degras, ed., London, 1951, vol. I, 97.

[145] See *infra*, pages 66–67.

[146] Dieterichs, *op. cit.*, I, 10–11, 318–319; Wilton, *op. cit.*, 102–103.

[147] Dieterichs, *op. cit.*, I, 243–244.

[148] *Id.*, I, 247–248.

[149] *Id.*, I, 273.

[150] Wilton, *op. cit.*, 102–103.

[151] Russ. ed., 68–70.

[152] Dieterichs, *op. cit.*, I, 18.

[153] *Id.*, I, 72.

[154] Russ. ed., 45.

[155] The Tsarina was the fourth daughter of the Grand Duke Louis IV of Hesse-Darmstadt (as well as a granddaughter, through her mother, the Grand Duchess Alice, of Queen Victoria).

[156] Wilton, *op. cit.*, 70.

[157] Rus. ed., 46.

[158] Dieterichs, *op. cit.*, I, 118.

[159] *Id.*, I, 113–114.
[160] Bulygin, *op. cit.*, 155.
[161] The Zemsky Sobor [Assembly of the Land] was a loose, medieval type of nationwide convocation of the clergy, nobles and townsmen. It was summoned in earlier centuries to put a seal of approval on decisions of great national import.
[162] Dieterichs, *op. cit.*, I, 19.
[163] *Id.*, I, 72.
[164] *Id.*, I, 78. Markov himself, in his memoirs, makes no reference to such an offer or letter, and seems, in fact, by assertions not compatible with their existence, to indirectly deny the existence of such an offer or letter. See Serge Vladimirovich Markov, *How We Tried To Save The Tsaritsa.* Putnam's, New York, London, 1929.
[165] Russ. ed., 108.
[166] *Id.*, 109.
[167] Serge Petrovich Mel'gunov, *Sud'ba Imperatora Nikolaya II poslye otrecheniya* [The Fate of the Emperor Nicholas II after Abdication]. Paris, La Renaissance, 1951, 282.
[168] Russ. ed., 109.
[169] Dieterichs, *op. cit.*, I, 364.
[170] *Id.*, I, 375.
[171] *Id.*, I, 373–375.
[172] *Id.*, I, 375.
[173] See statement of the Duke of Leuchtenberg to DeWitt Poole, *Papers Relating to the Foreign Relations of the United States, 1918, Russia,* Washington, D.C., 1931, vol. II, 643.
[174] Secret Protocol to the German-Soviet Supplementary Treaties of 27 August, 1918, *Soviet Documents on Foreign Policy,* Jane Degras, ed., London, 1951, vol. I, 97.
[175] See for example, George F. Kennan, *The Decision to Intervene,* Princeton, 1958, 437–438, and Beloborodov's telegram of June 26, 1918 reproduced by Sokolov, page 233.
[176] Dieterichs, *op. cit.*, I, 375.
[177] *Ibid.*
[178] *Id.*, I, 376–377.
[179] *Id.*, I, 373.
[180] *Id.*, I, 46–48, 378.
[181] *Id.*, I, 114.
[182] *Id.*, I, 45.
[183] Report dated January 31, 1919 as quoted by Dieterichs, *op. cit.*, I, 136.
[184] Dieterichs, *op. cit.*, I, 408.
[185] *Id.*, I, 390. See also 99.
[186] *Id.*, I, 379.
[187] *Id.*, I, 210.
[188] *Id.*, I, 211–212. Parts of this statement seem to indicate that Goloshchekin was acting contrary to the decision of the TsIK—a conclusion that would be flatly contradictory to assertions of both Dieterichs and Sokolov that Ekaterinburg was acting under orders from the central authorities. The only explanation of this apparent inconsistency would appear to be that the "new idea" involved, as indicated previously, not

the actual disposition of the Imperial Family, but a subsequent decision to simulate its execution.

[189] *Id.*, I, 211.

[190] See page 233.

[191] Dieterichs, *op. cit.*, I, 31. Sokolov includes only part of this telegram in his text, page 226, although the complete text appears in Photograph No. 129.

[192] Dieterichs, *op. cit.*, I, 212.

[193] *Ibid.*

[194] See page 234.

[195] Dieterichs, *op. cit.*, I, 212.

[196] *Id.*, I, 179.

[197] *Id.*, I, 116.

[198] *Id.*, I, 117.

[199] Bulygin, *op. cit.*, 163.

[200] Bulygin states, *op. cit.*, 177, that his escape occurred shortly before the Yaroslavl uprising, which began July 6. But at another point, *id.*, 173, he asserts "it was during the days of my imprisonment that the Emperor and the entire Imperial Family were executed." The "execution" was supposed to have occurred on July 16–17. One more inconsistency in this contradiction-laden case!

[201] See Kennan, *op. cit.*, 448 n24.

[202] Sokolov, Russ. ed., 132.

[203] Dieterichs, *op. cit.*, I, 50.

[204] Russ. ed., 132.

[205] *Id.*, 138.

[206] Dieterichs, *op. cit.*, I, 299. Didkovsky was apparently an influential member of the Oblast Soviet during part of the time that the Imperial Family was in Ekaterinburg. *Id.*, I, 317.

[207] *Id.*, I, 48.

[208] *Id.*, I, 377.

[209] Sokolov, Russ. ed., 139–140.

[210] Dieterichs, *op. cit.*, I, 299–300.

[211] *Id.*, I, 44–45. Sokolov states (Russ. ed., 135n) that Doctor Derevenko was questioned by military authorities in Tomsk on September 11, 1919, and Bulygin indicates (*op. cit.*, 260–261) that in October, 1919 Derevenko erroneously identified one of some "Yurovsky brothers" as the "Tsar's murderer". General Dieterichs further states that Derevenko did cooperate with the investigators for a short time after the liberation of Ekaterinburg, expressing his opinion about some matters such as "Doctor Botkin's finger". But there is no mention of any testimony concerning the doctor's alleged last visit.

[212] Dieterichs, *op. cit.*, I, 299.

[213] See pages 117–125.

[214] See page 120.

[215] See page 123.

[216] See page 124.

[217] *Dnevnik Nikolaya Romanova* [The Diary of Nicholas Romanov], *Krasny Arkhiv* [Red Archive], XXVII, 1928, 110–138. This installment included entries from January 1 (14), 1918 to June 30 (July 13), 1918,

inclusive. An earlier installment containing entries for 1917 was published in vol. XXII, 71–91.

[218] Yurovsky had accompanied Dr. Derevenko on one of his visits to the Tsarevich, on May 13 [26], 1918.

[219] See Mel'gunov, *op cit.*, 330 ff. He refers to Jagow, *Documents from the Prussian Archives of the Ministry of Foreign Affairs*, Berlin Monatshefte, May, 1935.

[220] See Mel'gunov, *op. cit.*, 332. It is, of course, impossible to tell which version of this communication is correct, or whether either of them are. Sokolov obtained his from Riezler, Mel'gunov's is from Jagow. If the German government still wished to preserve secrecy, it is unlikely that either Riezler or Jagow would reveal the actual or complete text of any documents affected.

[221] See Mel'gunov, *op. cit.*, 408.

[222] Sokolov, Russ. ed., 100. It is not clear whether, by the term "whole Imperial Family", General "N" and Markov meant to include the Tsar. Markov's own account, set forth below, would indicate that he, at least, did not. In his memoirs, referred to above, he claims no personal knowledge of the fate or whereabouts of the Imperial Family.

[223] Apparently the agent was Bulygin. See Bulygin, *op. cit.*, 200.

[224] Sokolov, Russ. ed., 100–101. Smolny was the Soviet govt. headquarters in Petersburg. A. A. Joffe was Soviet Ambassador to Germany. Karl Radek was Chief of the Central European Department of Narkomindel (Commissariat of Foreign Affairs).

[225] Sokolov, Fr. ed., 310–311.

[226] Dieterichs, *op. cit.*, I, 115.

[227] Bulygin, *op cit.*, 179–180.

[228] *Id.*, 237.

[229] Tisdall, Evelyn Ernest P., *Marie Fedorovna, Empress of Russia*, New York, John Day, 1957, 311.

[230] Bulygin, *op. cit.*, 155.

[231] *Id.*, 178.

[232] Wilton, *op. cit.*, 135.

A TRANSLATION OF SECTIONS
OF
NICHOLAS A. SOKOLOV'S
THE MURDER OF THE IMPERIAL FAMILY

TRANSLATOR'S NOTE

For the convenience of the reader the identity of certain people mentioned in the text, especially in Chapter Twenty-Two, is given below:

Count Kotsebue: Second-Captain of cavalry, an officer of Her Majesty's Regiment of Uhlans, first commander of the palace guards at Tsarskoye Selo after the revolution of March, 1917. He was relieved because of his sympathy with the Imperial Family.

Colonel Eugene Stepanovich Kobylinsky: an officer of the Petrograd Life Guards Regiment, commander of the guards at Tsarskoye Selo and Tobolsk. Although likewise sympathetic to the Imperial Family, he retained this position until the Imperial Family was transferred to Ekaterinburg.

Magdalena Frantsevna Zanotti: lady of the bedchamber.

Maria Gustavovna Tutelberg: lady of the bedchamber.

Sidney Ivanovich Gibbs: English Tutor.

Claudia Mikhailovna Bittner: tutor.

Pierre Andreyevich Gilliard: French tutor.

Alexandra Alexandrovna Tegleva: nana; subsequently wife of Pierre Andreyevich Gilliard.

Elizabeth Nicholayevna Ersberg: Tegleva's assistant.

Alexei Andreyevich Volkov: the Tsarina's valet de chambre.

Serge Ivanovich Ivanov: servant of the Tsarevich.

All of the above-mentioned people except Count Kotsebue were with the Imperial Family in Tobolsk, Zanotti in a different house. Tutelberg, Gibbs, Tegleva, Ersberg, Volkov and Ivanov travelled to Ekaterinburg with the second echelon of the Imperial Family—the Tsarevich, Olga, Tatiana and Anastasia—and, with the exception of Volkov, were there released. Volkov was imprisoned in Ekaterinburg with the other followers of the Imperial Family who were not held in the Ipatiev House.

TABLE OF CONTENTS*

*Translator's Note: Chapters 1-15, 26, and Sec. 1 of Chapter 17 as well as the Supplement to Chapter 19 are not included in this translation because they do not deal directly with the evidence of murder of the Imperial Family.

*Translator's Note: Chapters 1-15, 26, and Sec. 1 of Chapter 17 as well as the Supplement to Chapter 19 are not included in this translation because they do not deal directly with the evidence of murder of the Imperial Family.

*Translator's Note: Chapters 1-15, 26, and Sec. 1 of Chapter 17 as well as the
Supplement to Chapter 19 are not included in this translation because they do
not deal directly with the evidence of murder of the Imperial Family.

108

*Translator's Note: Chapters 1-15, 26, and Sec. 1 of Chapter 17 as well as the
Supplement to Chapter 19 are not included in this translation because they do
not deal directly with the evidence of murder of the Imperial Family.

N. SOKOLOV

(1882-1924)

Nicholas Alexeyevich Sokolov was born in 1882, in Mokshan, Penza Guberniya. He attended the boys' gymnasium in Penza and then completed the course of law at Kharkov University. He served in the Department of Justice for the most part in his own Penza Guberniya. Close to the common people by birth, Sokolov served among the peasants whom he knew and whose psychology he so well understood, learning it in his struggle with the crimes of the peasant world—sometimes characterized by comic incidents, at other times passing over to dark, terrible, bloody drama. Sokolov won renown as an outstanding investigator by virtue of his work and talents, not only in government circles but also among the common people who knew and loved him.

The revolution found him serving as Court Investigator for Major Cases. After the Bolshevik seizure of power Sokolov disguised himself as a peasant, left Penza and merged into the peasant community. He was so close to this world that he enjoyed its life and, as he often said, could have remained there. But duty called. In Siberia the flag of national struggle with the usurpers of power was raised. Sokolov went there on foot. Serious work awaited him. He was appointed to the post of Court Investigator for Especially Important Cases of the Omsk Regional Court and was soon entrusted with the investigation of the murder of the Imperial Family. He gave himself up to this work heart and soul. Complicated and difficult in itself, his task was still further complicated by the circumstances of civil war. A tireless worker, Sokolov continued to wrest the frightful secret from the mine at the "Four

Brothers" until the very last minute—when Red patrols were literally approaching the mine itself. And then—a long, difficult journey across the whole of Siberia to preserve the materials of the investigation. After the execution of Admiral Kolchak, Sokolov went to Europe.

Here another series of disappointments and difficult experiences awaited him. Alone, supported by no one, deeply convinced of the extraordinary importance of the truth of the murder of the Tsar and His Family, believing that this truth properly belonged to the future National Russia, that it must be preserved for the Russian people— Sokolov had to wage a long and painful struggle for its defense against those who tried to use it in their personal interests. Some insisted upon silence at all costs because the truth—death—was not to their liking. Others, on the contrary, wanted to use this truth for the benefit of their own personal interests.

Nicholas Alexeyevich did not falter. "The truth of the Tsar's death is the truth of the sufferings of Russia," he said. And he guarded this truth for future generations, guarding it from every encroachment of political intrigue. He determined to proclaim the truth himself— on his own, and not under the banner of any political party whatsoever. And perhaps the time will come when the future Russia will express its great gratitude to him, and venerate his memory as a shining, pure fighter for the Truth.

Death overtook him in the middle of his work. The great difficulties through which he passed had taken their toll—his heart had been seriously ailing for a long time. The doctors ordered absolute rest—physical and spiritual. But Nicholas Alexeyevich could not rest. He lived through his difficult struggle in the ugly circumstances of emigration.

Nicholas Alexeyevich died suddenly on the 23rd of November of a heart attack in the locality of Salbris, in France, where he was buried.

Over his modest grave in a French country graveyard his friends placed a cross with this inscription:
"Your Truth is Truth eternal."

Prince N. Orlov

FROM THE AUTHOR

It was my lot to conduct the investigation of the murder of the Emperor Nicholas II and his family.

Within the limits of truth I endeavored to do everything possible to find out the facts and preserve them for future generations.

I did not think that I would have to proclaim them myself, as I had hoped a Russian national government would make them known upon its own authority. But stern reality indicates that favorable circumstances for this will not arise in the near future. Inexorable time will obscure the facts in oblivion.

I do not in any way pretend to know all the facts, and through them the whole truth. But up until now I have known them better than anyone else.

The mournful pages of the sufferings of the Tsar speak the sufferings of Russia. Having determined to break my vow of professional silence, I have assumed the whole weight of responsibility, knowing that service of the law means service of the people's welfare.

I know that the inquisitive mind of man will find many questions unanswered by this investigation: it is necessarily limited because its principal subject is murder.

But the victim of the crime was the bearer of supreme authority, governing for many years one of the most powerful peoples.

Like every fact, the crime occurred in time and space and, in particular, under conditions of a great struggle for the determination of national destiny.

Both of these factors, the personality of the victim and the actual

111

conditions in which the crime was committed, give it a special character. It is a phenomenon of history.

"One of the characteristics of a great people is its ability to get back upon its feet after a fall. No matter how great its debasement, when the hour strikes it will gather its confused moral forces together and incarnate them in one great man, or in several great men, who will lead it back to the straight, historical road which it has temporarily abandoned." [1]

No historical movement can be conceived separately from its past. In our past there is a terrible, evil deed: the murder of the Tsar and his family.

I have proposed to serve my countrymen with a truthful account.

Therefore, keeping in mind the words of the great Russian historian, no matter how blindingly bright my own personal recollections of events may at times have been, I have tried to set forth facts based exclusively upon the data of the strict, judicial investigation.

First, then, it is necessary to understand how the investigation was set up.

Organization of the Investigation

On July 25, 1918 [2] the city of Ekaterinburg, in which the Imperial Family was held in confinement, was captured from the Bolsheviks by troops of the Siberian army and by Czechs.

On July 30 of the same year a judicial investigation was begun. It was begun by the court investigator for major cases of the Ekaterinburg Regional [Okruzhny] Court, Nametkin,[3] in the customary manner prescribed by law: by virtue of resolution No. 131 of the court prosecutor, dated July 30.

On August 7, 1918 the Ekaterinburg Regional Court in a plenary session of its divisions resolved to relieve Nametkin from further work on the case and to entrust it to a member of the court, Sergeyev.

This transfer was induced, on the one hand, by the conduct of Nametkin himself, and on the other hand, by the situation prevailing at that time.

In the face of facts which indicated a murder, if not of the entire Imperial Family then at least of the Emperor himself, the military authority, which in the first days after the capture of Ekaterinburg was the only authority guaranteeing order, made a firm demand upon Nametkin, as investigator for major cases, to commence an investigation without delay.

Relying upon the letter of the law, Nametkin told the military authority that he did not have the right to begin an investigation, and would not begin one, until he had received a resolution of the court prosecutor, who was not present in Ekaterinburg during the first days following its liberation.

Nametkin's conduct evoked great displeasure against him both on the part of military circles and of the public. They felt that his extreme regard for the law was not without ulterior motive. They accused him of cowardice in the face of the Bolsheviks, who continued to threaten Ekaterinburg. Some even went further in their suspicions.

The natural result of the situation thus created would have been a transfer of the case to the court investigator for especially important cases for the district in which Ekaterinburg was located, but Kazan, where this investigator was residing, was cut off from Ekaterinburg by the Bolsheviks.

At the proposal of the court prosecutor the case was transferred to a member of the court, Sergeyev, a course which was authorized in some circumstances by special law.

During the first months in which Sergeyev was carrying on his work, there was a conglomerate of governments in the territory of Russia that was free of Bolsheviks, from the Volga to the ocean. These governments were not yet united. Such a union took place on September 23, 1918 in Ufa, where a single government for the whole territory was created in the form of a directorate of five men.

On November 18, 1918 supreme authority was concentrated in the hands of the Supreme Ruler, Admiral Kolchak.

On January 17, 1919, by order No. 36, the Admiral instructed General Dieterichs, former commander-in-chief of the front, to turn over to him all of the effects of the Imperial Family that had been found, together with all materials of the investigation.

By resolution of January 25, 1919, the member of the court, Sergeyev, by virtue of the Supreme Ruler's order, which had the force of a special law, turned over to Dieterichs the actual results of the investigation and all material evidence.

The transfer was effected in strict juridical manner in the presence of the court prosecutor, V.F. Iordansky.

During the first days of February, General Dieterichs brought all of the materials to Omsk and put them at the disposal of the

Supreme Ruler.

It seemed dangerous to the higher authorities to leave the case in the general category of local, Ekaterinburg cases, if only for one strategic consideration. It seemed necessary to take special measures for the preservation of historic documents.

In addition, to leave the case any longer in the hands of a member of the court was not now justified in view of the scope of the work: it had become apparent that a great many people, scattered throughout the whole territory of Siberia and even further, would have to be interrogated, whereas a member of the court could not leave it.

Finally, the transfer of the case to Sergeyev, in itself a compromise, contradicted the basic law, which vested conduct of preliminary investigations in the special, technical staff of court investigators.

On February 5 I was summoned by Admiral Kolchak. He called upon me as investigator of especially important cases for the Omsk Regional Court. He ordered me to acquaint myself with the material of the investigation and to give him my ideas concerning the manner of further investigation.

On February 6 I gave the Admiral my reasons for the following proposed procedure:

1. The investigation must be based upon the principles of the law, as this has been established up to the present time: the code of criminal procedure;

2. A sufficient number of court investigators must be assigned as it is physically impossible for one person to do the work;

3. The direction of the investigation must be vested in a single, rather than joint, authority. For this I had in mind a senator with experience in investigating technique.

But stern reality was harsh with us. Such senators were not to be found in distant Siberia. In addition there were no rank and file technical people, since the institution of court investigators was virtually unknown in Siberia. Some were afraid to become involved · in a dangerous case.

On February 7 I received the proposal of the Minister of Justice for the conduct of a preliminary investigation, and on the same day accepted from General Dieterichs all reports of the investigation and material evidence.

On March 3, prior to my departure for the front, the Admiral found it necessary to limit my freedom of action by a special order.

He took a personal interest in the case and indicated in the order that the investigation, entrusted to me by law, was being made in accordance with his wishes. He manifested this interest to the very end.

After his death I arrived in Europe, where my work consisted in the interrogation of several witnesses.

I have indicated in its main outline the basis upon which the judicial investigation was set up, having in mind the mistaken notion which has become rooted in the public mind concerning this aspect of the case, and particularly the role of General Dieterichs.

To my regret, he has not himself remained at the highest level of historical impartiality, describing himself in his work as a superior "director" of the investigation.[4]

This is not correct. General Dieterichs, who enjoys esteem and authority in military circles, has defended the work of the court investigator more than any one has. It is to him, more than anyone, that we are indebted for the truth. The truth, however, was ferreted out, not by military, but by judicial authority, set up in accordance with the desires of the Supreme Ruler. And, of course, General Dieterichs never directed the work of the court investigator, and could not direct it, if only for the simple reason that the work of an investigator, as it has been so correctly defined by the great Dostoyevsky, is free creation.

Photographic plate No. 1 sets forth those plenary powers with which the judicial investigator was invested by the Supreme Ruler.

I here set forth the results of a successive judicial investigation. At its basis lies the law, the conscience of a judge, and the demands of the search for truth.

Supreme Ruler
3 March 1919
No. 588
Omsk

By these presents I order all places and persons to fulfill, absolutely and precisely, all lawful demands of Court Investigator for specially important cases SOKOLOV, and to assist him in the fulfillment of the duties imposed upon him by my command in connection with the conduct of a preliminary investigation of the murder of the former Emperor, his family, and of the Grand Dukes.

Admiral Kolchak

Seal

Acting Director
of the Chancellery of the Supreme Ruler
Major General Martianov

No. 1. Order of the Supreme Ruler, Admiral A. V. Kolchak

CHAPTER SIXTEEN

[pp. 142-148]

The Imperial Family Was in the Ipatiev House
until the Night before July 17.

IT HAPPENED sometime during the night of the 16th-17th of July. How do we know that the Imperial Family was in the Ipatiev House until that fateful night?

The priest, Storozhev,[5] testified: "On Sunday, May 20 (June 2), I had finished the regular service—the early morning liturgy—in the Ekaterinburg Cathedral. I returned home about 10 o'clock in the morning, and had just gotten ready to have tea when there was a knock at the front door of my apartment. I opened the door myself and saw a soldier before me. He had an unsightly appearance, a pock-marked face and small, fugitive eyes. He had on an old, padded khaki jacket and a worn-out military cap. He had no epaulettes, of course, or cockade. When I asked him what he wanted the soldier replied: 'They need you for a service for the Romanovs.' I did not know what he was talking about and asked: 'What Romanovs?'—'Well, the former Tsar,' the caller explained. From the ensuing conversation I gathered that Nicholas Alexandrovich Romanov had asked for Mass to be said. 'He wrote a note asking that Mass be said,' the caller advised me. I expressed my readiness to perform the requested service and said I would have to bring along a deacon. The soldier made long and strenuous objections to inviting Father Deacon, stating that the 'commandant' had ordered him to bring only a priest. But I insisted, and the soldier and I went to the Cathedral. There I obtained everything necessary for the service and asked Father Deacon Buimirov to

117

come with me. The three of us then went to the Ipatiev House. This house had been surrounded with a double, planked enclosure since the Romanov Family was imprisoned there. The carriage stopped near the first, outer, wooden enclosure. The soldier accompanying us went in front, the deacon and I followed. The outer guard admitted us. After being detained for a short time at the small inner gate, which was locked and which faced in the direction of the house formerly belonging to Solomirsky, we went inside the second enclosure and came to the gate of the Ipatiev House itself. Here there were many young men in civilian clothes, armed with rifles and with hand grenades on their belts. These armed men were obviously the guard. We were led through the gate to the yard and from there through a side door into the lower floor of the Ipatiev House. Mounting the stairs, we came up to the interior main door and then, through a passage-way, into the study (on the left) where the commandant had established himself. There were guards everywhere, on the stairs, on the landings and also in the ante-room—the same young men in civilian clothes armed with rifles and hand grenades. In the commandant's room there were two men of middle age, as I recall, wearing field shirts. One of them was lying on the bed and seemed to be asleep. The other was smoking cigarettes in silence. There was a table in the middle of the room—with a samovar and bread and butter on it. There was a piano in the room, on which lay rifles, hand grenades and something else. The room was a mess—dirty and disorderly. The commandant was not in the room when we arrived. A young man soon appeared in a field shirt, Khaki pants and a wide, leather belt on which hung a large revolver in a holster. He had the appearance of the average 'informed' worker. I found nothing brilliant, outstanding or appealing in this fellow's external appearance or in his subsequent conduct. I rather guessed than understood that he was the 'commandant' of the house of special appointment as the Bolsheviks called the Ipatiev House while the Romanov Family was held there. The commandant looked at me without greeting us or saying a word. (I was seeing him for the first time and did not even know his name, and have now forgotten it.) When I asked what service we should perform, the commandant replied: 'They asked for Mass (*obednitsa*).' Neither the deacon nor I had any conversation with the commandant. I only asked if we were permitted, after the service, to give Romanov the host which I showed him. The commandant looked at the host briefly. After a moment's thought he handed it back to the deacon and said: 'You can give it to him, but I must warn you that there can be no unnecessary conversation.' I could no longer restrain myself and replied that it was not my intention to engage in conversation. My answer apparently annoyed the commandant somewhat and he said, quite curtly: 'Yes, none outside of the requirements of the service.' The deacon and I put on our vestments in the commandant's room. At the same time one of the servants of the Romanovs brought a censor with burning coals into the commandant's room. (It was not Chemodurov—I never saw him in the Ipatiev House and only became acquainted with him later, after the surrender of Ekaterinburg by the Bolsheviks.) The servant, as I recall, was tall and wore a grey suit with metal buttons. . . . . . And so, having put on the holy vestments and taking with us everything necessary for the service, we went from the commandant's room into the passageway. The commandant opened the door himself—the door leading to the living room—pushing me ahead. The deacon came with me and the commandant entered last. The living room into which we came was joined by an archway to a smaller room —a drawing room, in which I saw a table prepared for the service near the front corner.[6] But at this time I was distracted from my observation of the appointments of the living room and drawing room. I had scarcely crossed the threshold of the living room when I saw three people turn away from the window—they were Nicholas Alexandrovich, Tatiana Nicholayevna and another older daughter. I did not have time to notice exactly which one. In the other room, which was separated from the living room, as I have said, by an archway, were Alexandra Feodorovna, the two younger daughters and Alexei Nicholayevich. The latter was lying on a travelling (folding) cot and I was shocked by his appearance. He was pale to such a degree that he seemed transparent. He was gaunt and so very tall I was astounded. In general his appearance was of one extremely sick. Only his eyes were alive and bright, looking at me, a new person, with noticeable interest. He had on a white shirt and was covered to the waist with a blanket. His bed was to the right of the entrance wall, just beyond the archway. Near the bed was a chair in which sat Alexandra Feodorovna. She had on a loose dress, as I recall, of dark bluish color. I did not see any jewelled ornaments on either Alexandra Feodorovna or her daughters. Alexandra Feodorovna attracted attention with her great height and bearing, a bearing

119

which can only be described as 'stately'. She was sitting in the chair, but got up (with energy and firmness) when we entered and left the room and whenever during the service I said 'Peace be to all', when I read the gospel, and when we sang the more important prayers. Next to Alexandra Feodorovna's chair and further along the right wall stood both younger daughters, and then Nicholas Alexandrovich himself. The older daughters stood in the archway. Standing apart from them, in the living room beyond the archway, were a tall, old gentleman and a woman. (I was later told they were Doctor Botkin and Alexandra Feodorovna's maid.) Still further to the rear stood two servants: the one who brought us the censor, and another whose external appearance I did not see and do not recall. The whole time the commandant stood in a corner of the living room, near the farthest window. He occupied, in this fashion, a most proper distance from the worshippers. There was definitely no one else in the living room or in the room beyond the archway.

Nicholas Alexandrovich wore a khaki field shirt, khaki pants and high boots. On his breast, he wore an officer's cross of St. George. He had no epaulettes. All four daughters, as I recall, wore dark skirts and simple, white jackets. All had their hair cut fairly short at the back. They had a lively appearance and, I would say, almost happy.

Nicholas Alexandrovich impressed me with his firm bearing, his calm, and particularly his manner of looking straight at one, firmly, in the eyes. I did not see in him any signs of fatigue or spiritual depression. It seemed to me that there were slight traces of grey in his beard (his beard, on my first visit, was longer and wider than on July 1 (14) when, it seemed to me, Nicholas Alexandrovich had shaved around his beard.)

As for Alexandra Feodorovna, she was the only one who had an appearance of fatigue, or rather, illness. I forgot to mention something that particularly attracted my attention—that extraordinary, I say it outright—deference to my holy office, with which all the members of the Romanov Family each time bowed in reply to my silent greeting when I entered the living room, and also upon completion of the service.

Taking our places in front of the table with the icons, we began the service. The deacon spoke the prayer of petition and I sang. Two feminine voices accompanied me (I imagine it was Tatiana Nicholayevna and one of the others). At times I was also accompanied by the low bass of Nicholas Alexandrovich (he sang, for example, the 'Our Father' and other hymns). The service went lively and well, they prayed very earnestly. At the end of the service I gave the usual blessing with the Holy Cross and then paused for a moment, not knowing whether I should approach the worshippers with the Cross so they could kiss it, or whether this was forbidden and I, with my false move, might create future difficulties for the Romanov Family when they sought permission for attention to their spiritual needs. I glanced at the commandant to see what he was doing and how he was reacting to my desire to approach with the Cross. It seemed to me that Nicholas Alexandrovich also threw a quick glance in the direction of the commandant. The latter was standing in his place in the far corner and looking at me quietly. Then I took a step forward and at the same time Nicholas Alexandrovich, with firm, direct steps, not turning his direct gaze from me, approached the Cross first and kissed it. Behind him came Alexandra Feodorovna and all four daughters. I went over to Alexei Nicholayevich who was lying on the bed. He looked at me with such lively eyes that I thought: 'Now he will surely say something.' But Alexei Nicholayevich kissed the Cross in silence. The deacon gave him the host and also gave it to Alexandra Feodorovna. Then Doctor Botkin approached the Cross and the named servants—the girl and the two man-servants.

On June 30 (July 13) I learned that on the following day, July 1 (14), Sunday, Father Meledin was going to perform the liturgy at the Ipatiev House, and that he had already been advised of this by the commandant. At this time the commandant was a certain Yurovsky, known for his cruelty. He was a former military medical attendant.

I expected to take Father Meledin's place in the Cathedral and perform the services for him on July 1 (14).

At 8 o'clock in the morning of July 1 (14) someone knocked on the door of my apartment. I got up at once and went to unlock it. It turned out to be the same soldier who had come the first time to summon me to perform services at the Ipatiev House. In answer to my question: 'What can I do for you?' the soldier replied that the commandant 'required' me at the Ipatiev House to say Mass. I remarked that Father Meledin had already been asked, but the soldier replied: 'Meledin is replaced. They want you.' I did not question him further and said I would take Father Deacon Buimirov with me—the soldier made no objection—and that I would be there at 10 o'clock. The soldier took his leave and went off, while I, getting dressed, went to the Cathedral and obtained all the things required for the service. At 10 o'clock A.M. I was already at the Ipatiev House with Father Deacon Buimirov. We had hardly passed through the gate when I saw Yurovsky watching us from the window of the commandant's room. (I did not know Yurovsky, I had only seen him some time before making a speech in the square.)

When we entered the commandant's room we found the same disorder, dust and desolation as before. Yurovsky was sitting behind a table drinking tea and eating bread and butter. Some other man was sleeping in his clothes on the bed. Upon entering the room I said to Yurovsky: 'Some one asked for clergy here. Here we are. What must we do?' Yurovsky did not greet us but only stared at me, and said: 'Wait here a bit and then you will say Mass.' I asked him: 'Which liturgy am I to celebrate—*obednya* or *obednitsa?*' Yurovsky said, 'He wrote *obednitsa.*'

The deacon and I began to prepare the books, vestments and other things. Yurovsky drank up his tea and watched us in silence. Finally he asked: 'So your name is S -s-s' and dragged out the initial letter of my last name. Then I said, 'My name is Storozhev.'—'So, yes,' took up Yurovsky.—'So you have already performed services here.'—'Yes,' I replied, 'I have.'—'Well, so you will be performing again.'

At this time the deacon, turning to me, began to insist for some reason that we must not celebrate the liturgy of *obednya* but *obednitsa.* I noticed that this disturbed Yurovsky and he began to eye the deacon. I hastened to put an end to this, telling the deacon that it was necessary to do as they asked everywhere and that here, in this house, it was necessary to do as they said. Yurovsky was apparently placated. Seeing that I was rubbing my hands as though cold, Yurovsky asked me, with the trace of a smile, what the matter was. In answered that I had recently been ill with pleurisy and was afraid the illness might return. Yurovsky began to give his ideas on methods of curing pleurisy and said that he himself had an operation on his lungs. We exchanged a few more words. Yurovsky conducted himself without reproach and in general was correct with us. . . . . . When we had vested and the censor was brought with burning coals (some soldier brought it), Yurovsky asked us to pass into the living room for the service. I went into the living room first, then the deacon and Yurovsky. At the same time Nicholas Alexandrovich entered through the doors leading into the inner room. Two of his daughters were with him, I did not have a chance to see exactly which ones. I believe Yurovsky asked Nicholas Alexandrovich: 'Well, are you all here?' Nicholas Alexandrovich answered firmly: 'Yes, all of us.'

Ahead, beyond the archway, Alexandra Feodorovna was already in place with two daughters and Alexei Nicholayevich. He was sitting in a wheel-chair and wore a jacket, as it seemed to me, with a sailor's collar. He was pale, but not so much so as at the time of my first service. In general he looked more healthy. Alexandra Feodorovna also had a healthier appearance. She wore the same dress as on May 20 [Old Style]. As for Nicholas Alexandrovich, he was wearing the same clothes as the first time. Only I cannot, somehow, picture to myself clearly whether he was on this occasion wearing the St. George cross on his breast. Tatiana Nicholayevna, Olga Nicholayevna, Anastasia Nicholayevna, and Maria Nicholayevna were wearing black skirts and white blouses. Their hair (as I recall they were all the same) had grown and now came to the level of their shoulders at the back.

It seemed to me that on this occasion Nicholas Alexandrovich and all of his daughters were—I won't say in depressed spirits— but they gave the impression, just the same, of being exhausted. On this occasion the members of the Romanov Family took exactly the same positions during the service as they had on May 20 (O.S.). Only now Alexandra Feodorovna's chair stood next to that of Alexei Nicholayevich—further from the archway and a little behind it. Behind Alexei Nicholayevich stood Tatiana Nicholayevna (she pushed his wheel chair when they kissed the Cross after the service), Olga Nicholayevna and, I think (I don't remember exactly), Maria Nicholayevna. Anastasia Nicholayevna stood next to Nicholas Alexandrovich, who stood in his usual place by the wall to the right of the archway.

Beyond the archway, in the living room, stood Doctor Botkin, a girl and three servants: one tall, another short and stocky, and the third a young boy. Yurovsky stood in the living room at the same far, corner window. There was no one else in these rooms during the service.

According to the liturgy of the service it is customary at a certain point to read the prayer 'Who Resteth with the Saints'. On this occasion for some reason the deacon, instead of reading this prayer, began to sing it, and I as well, somewhat embarrassed by this departure from the ritual. But we had scarcely begun to sing when I heard the members of the Romanov Family, standing behind me, fall on their knees. . . . .

After the service everyone kissed the Holy Cross. Father Deacon gave the host to Nicholas Alexandrovich and Alexandra Feodorovna. (Yurovsky's agreement had been obtained beforehand.)

As I went out I passed very close to the former Grand Duchesses and heard the scarcely audible word: 'Thank you'—I don't think I just imagined this. . . . . .

Father Deacon and I walked in silence to the Art School building, where he suddenly said to me: 'Do you know, Father Archpresbyter, something has happened to them there.' Since Father Deacon's words somewhat confirmed my own impression, I stopped and asked him why he thought so.—'Yes, precisely,' the deacon said: 'they are all some other people, truly. Why no one even sang.' And it must be said that actually, for the first time, no one of the Romanov Family sang with us during the service of July 1/14."

On Monday, July 15, some women were sent from the labor union to wash the floors in the Ipatiev House. It was possible to question two: Starodumova and Dryagina. They testified:

Starodumova: [7] "If I am not mistaken, on Monday, July 15 of this year, four women were sent from the union to wash floors in the house where the Tsar and his family were living. . . . From the Ipatiev House they sent us to the Popov House where the Imperial guard was living. There the chief of the guards, Medvedyev, ordered us to wash the floor in the command quarters and then took us to the Ipatiev House which was called the house of special appointment. They took us into the yard and up the stairs leading from the lower to the upper floor. They let us into the upper floor where the Tsar was living with his family. I personally washed floors in almost every room set aside for the Imperial Family. We did not wash the floor in the commandant's room. When we went into the house the Tsar, the Tsarina and all the children were in the dining room. . . . . The Grand Duchesses helped us straighten up and move the beds in their bedroom and talked gaily among themselves. We ourselves did not speak with anyone of the Imperial Family. The commandant, Yurovsky, was watching us almost the whole time. I saw him sitting in the dining room talking with the Tsarevich, asking him about his health."

Dryagina: "I also washed floors in the Ipatiev House with Maria Starodumova and the other women. As far as I can remember it was on Monday, July 15 of this year. The chief of the guards,

Medvedyev, took us into the house. In the house I saw the Tsar, the Tsarina, the Tsarevich, the four Grand Duchesses, the doctor, and some old woman. The Tsarevich was sitting in a wheelchair. The Grand Duchesses were happy and helped us to move the beds in their room."

The guards, Proskuryakov, Letemin, and Yakimov, explained:

Proskuryakov: "I saw the whole Imperial Family, except the Tsarina, the last time several days before their murder. At that time they were all walking in the garden. They were definitely all of them out walking, except for the Tsarina. That is the Tsar was there himself, his son, and his daughters: Olga, Tatiana, Maria, and Anastasia. The doctor was also there, the servant, the cook, the maid, and the boy. . . . . I can't recall exactly what day it was, but it was not long before their death."

Letemin: "On July 16 I was on duty at post No. 3 (in the courtyard by the small gate) from four o'clock in the afternoon until eight o'clock in the evening and I recall that as soon as I went on duty, the former Tsar and his family returned from a walk. I did not notice anything of special significance at this time."

Yakimov: "The last time I saw the Tsar and his daughters was on July 16. They were walking in the garden at 4 o'clock in the afternoon. I don't recall if I saw the Tsarevich at that time. I did not see the Tsarina. She was not walking then."

CHAPTER SEVENTEEN

Sec. 2 [pp. 167-173]

The Lower Floor of the Ipatiev House as Described
by the Member of the Court, Sergeyev

The inspection of the lower floor was made by the member of the court, Sergeyev.

The room designated number I (the entrance hall) aroused his suspicion. Here he noticed that the floor had been washed, and the presence of blood. In his report he states: "The floor of this room is of wood, covered with yellow paint. It bears clear traces of washing, in the form of wavy and zigzag bands of sand particles and of whitening, which have firmly adhered to it in drying; in the cornices there are thicker layers of the same dried mixture of sand and whitening; stains of a reddish hue are visible on the surface of the floor. During the inspection this part of the floor was marked off with special markings and protected from external influences."

The neighboring room, designated number II, gave a clear picture of the crime.

Its floor also proved to have been washed: "The floor is covered with yellow paint and bears, on the left half, coming in from the entrance hall, the same traces of having been washed; in the cornices of the floor, accumulations of a dried mixture of sand and whitening are also observed."

An extremely great amount of damage was found in this room.

In order to more clearly understand the language of the reports in which it is described it is necessary to look not only at the draw-

126

ings but also at the photographic snapshots.

When one comes into the room numbered II from the entrance hall (number I), he sees the view shown in photograph No. 46.

Looking at this photograph one sees the eastern wall of the room with a door into the adjoining room designated number III (a store-room).

This eastern wall is of wood, its surface covered with plaster and wallpaper.

In the picture are seen two arches, upon which the vaulted ceiling of the room rests. They are both of stone, covered with plaster and wallpaper, but the lower part of the arch to the right of the viewer is trimmed with planks of wood, covered with wallpaper.

The south wall, shown in photograph No. 47, is contiguous to this right arch.

The south wall is of stone, plastered and covered with wallpaper. As in the case of the arch contiguous to it, its lower part is trimmed with planks of wood, covered with wallpaper.

There is a window in the south wall, which looks out on Voznesensky alley. It is the only window in the room.

The door from room number II, leading into room number I (the entrance hall), opens outward into the latter.

Photograph No. 48 shows a view of this door, closed, from the west wall of the room.

In the door shown in photograph No. 46, Sergeyev found two bullet holes: "In the right fold of this door, at a height of 173.3 centimeters from the floor there is a trans-piercing hole of circular form; there is a similar hole in the left fold of the door at a height of 97.7 centimeters from the floor; the thickness of the folds of the door is 5.5 centimeters; the diameter of the trans-piercing holes, measured on the outside of the door (the side in room number II) is 6.8 millimeters and the diameter of these holes on the side of the store-room (room number III) is 8.2 millimeters."

Corresponding exactly with these two holes through the door, Sergeyev found two points at which the surface of the wall of the store-room had been damaged.

It was obvious that the two bullets striking this door had come from room number II while the door to the store-room was closed.

In the door shown in photograph No. 48, Sergeyev found one bullet hole: "In the door-post (to the right as one looks at the picture), at a height of 111 centimeters from the floor, there is a trans-piercing hole, round in form; there is a similar hole in the corresponding fold of the door; if this fold is opened and pushed back

127

to the door-post, the hole in the door coincides with the hole in the door-post; the channel of the hole becomes wider as it penetrates from within the room in the direction of the door, folded back, and ends in a wide hole in the door with splintered pieces of wood around its circumference."

It was obvious that the bullet striking this door had come from room number II, while the door to the entrance hall was open.

In the eastern wall (photograph No. 46) Sergeyev found 16 defacements: "In the eastern wall there are sixteen cavities similar to the marks of penetrating bullets or marks made by blows with some type of hard weapon. Upon examination of these cavities with a probe it proved impossible to determine the direction and length of the channels, in view of the fact that the probe, in the course of its penetration into the channels of the cavities, encountered crumbling pieces of plaster. For the sake of convenience in describing the arrangement of the cavities, they have all been numbered in the present examination in the order of their distance from the corner of the left arch, working towards the door-post contiguous to the right arch; the height of each cavity from the floor was also measured. In accordance with this plan the results of the measurements can be shown in the following table: [8]

Nos. in order	Distance from arch (in centimeters)	Distance from floor (in centimeters)
1	17	51
2	31	142
3	40	62.2
4	48.8	66.6
5	57.7	75.5
6	60	71.1
7	73.3	60
8	80	55.5
9	91.1	124.4
10	97.7	88.8
11	102.2	22.2
12	106.6	64.4
13	115.5	168.8
14	144.4	31
15	155.5	35.5
16	164.4	55.5

In the area of these defacements Sergeyev found clear traces of washing of the wallpaper: "In the vicinity of the cavities numbered 3, 6, 7, 8, 11, 12, 14, 15 and 16 the wallpaper bears traces of having been washed: in places the plaster is visible beneath the effaced paper, and in several parts of the washed area only the top layer of paper has been effaced so that the design of the wallpaper has been obliterated."

The damage to the east wall did not penetrate its entire thickness; there was none on the side of the store-room.

In the floor (photograph No. 46) Sergeyev found 6 places where it has been damaged: "In that part of the floor to the left of the entrance (from the entrance hall), in the vicinity of that area which bears the traces of having been washed, six cavities are found with slightly splintered edges; upon examination of the channels of the cavities with a probe it is found difficult to determine their depth because the probe, in the course of its movement, encounters particles of splintered wood. In the interests of convenience in describing these cavities they have all been numbered in the present examination in the order of their distance from the east wall on which the above-described sixteen cavities were distributed. In accordance with this plan the results of the measurements thus made are set forth in the following table:

Nos. in order	Distance from east wall (in centimeters)
1	35.5
2	93.3
3	95.5
4	137.3
5	222.2
6	382.2

In the south wall (photograph No. 47) Sergeyev found two defacements: "On the south wall, below the windowsill and to the left of it, if one stands facing the window, there is a trans-piercing hole of circular form, in the wood trimming, at a distance of 86.6 centimeters from the pillar of the arch and a distance of 80 centimeters from the floor. Below it there is a hole of the same form and appearance at a distance of 46.4 centimeters from the floor and somewhat to the left of the first hole."

The impact of bullets in both doors was obvious. It was more difficult to establish the nature of the defacements of the walls and the floor. For this purpose Sergeyev removed pieces of wood from them.

As soon as these excisions had been made it was clear that the defacements had been caused by bullets.

In Sergeyev's report it is stated: with respect to the *east wall:* "The presence of revolver bullets was discovered in the excised pieces of the wooden part of the wall"; with respect to the *south wall:* "The upper piece was cut from the wall first; upon removal of the section thus cut away a revolver bullet fell out. It had been lodged in the space between the trim and the stone wall. When the second (lower) portion was cut away a revolver bullet was found in it, stuck in the upper layer of the trim."

In the floor, besides bullets, there were also found in the bullet channels and in the crevices between the boards, running stains having the appearance of blood: "All of the cavities in the floor are bullet channels; in several of them the bullets had stuck in the thickness of the wood; on the sides of the excised pieces reddish stains were discovered, going downwards across the entire thickness of the boards in the form of running stains."

Unfortunately Sergeyev did not photograph room number II in the condition in which he found it. Photographs Nos. 46-48, which I made, show its appearance after the cuts from the walls and the floor had already been made.

Photograph No. 49 shows several pieces of wood from the east wall, with bullets lodged in them; photograph No. 50 a piece of the floor with a bullet and a bloody running stain; photograph No. 51 a piece of the floor with two bullet marks.

While examining room number II I found that Sergeyev had not noticed several other bullet marks here. I discovered them in both arches (photograph No. 46).

In the left arch there were two marks: "The upper defacement of the arch, on the front side (facing the viewer), is at a height of 1 meter 37 centimeters from the floor; it has the form of a slender cone; its depth in the thickness of plaster is 2 centimeters; its diameter at the edges is 4 centimeters; the edge of the wallpaper around this cavity is sharply torn, its shreds hang around the whole cavity. This cavity is unquestionably a bullet mark, the bullet striking this front face of the arch at a slightly upward angle, the direction of penetration. The second cavity, in the side wall of the arch (towards the east wall), is at a distance of 70 centimeters from the floor; it has an elongated form and is quite clearly a bullet mark, 3.5 centimeters in length and 2 centimeters deep in the thickness of plaster. The direction of both described marks is the same: the shots which made these marks were fired by persons standing to the left of the door leading into this room from the entrance hall (number I)."

In addition, the second strike against the left arch also ricocheted against the east wall. In photograph 46 this ricochet mark is the nearest to the arch and to the floor.

The right arch especially attracted my attention (photograph No. 46). Part of its trim had been removed, as is apparent in the picture. This was done by Sergeyev because there were drawings of a pornographic character on the wallpaper.

Immediately beneath the removed trim I found a sharp bullet mark in the plaster of the arch: "Under this cutting of the wood trim there is a cavity in the thickness of plaster, cone-shaped in form, undoubtedly made by a bullet; it is 2.5 centimeters in depth; its diameter from the edges is 1 centimeter; it is at a distance of 1 meter 6 centimeters from the floor."

The eye is caught by several rips in the wallpaper of the arch, near the cutting of the trim: apparently a bayonet, coming loose, struck with glancing blows against the wall at this point.

Examination of the trim removed by Sergeyev was especially interesting.

My report of this examination states: "On the board (its thickness is 3 centimeters) there is a perfectly defined bullet hole, penetrating the entire thickness of the wood. The entrance was made on the side which is covered with wallpaper and is 1 centimeter in diameter; the exit is on the back side of the board and has the same round form; on this side, around the hole, the wood has been chipped off; its diameter is somewhat greater than that of the entrance: about 1.5 centimeters. At a point immediately beneath this bullet channel in the board there is a bullet channel in the plaster of the arch. On the front side of the board four bayonet blows are clearly visible. Three of them penetrate the thickness of the wood one centimeter, and one, superficial, blow penetrates the layer of wallpaper and pasteboard and barely enters the layer of wood; the depth of this last blow is three millimeters. The three deep holes have equal measurements: 4 millimeters in length and width; the superficial one is 5 millimeters in length. All of these bayonet blows are below the bullet hole and 6.75 centimeters away from it. They are all quite close to each other. For a precise determination of the origin of these holes, the point of a bayonet of a three-line Russian rifle was carefully inserted in them. The shape of the holes coincided exactly with the shape of the bayonet.

Sergeyev also failed to notice the spatters of blood on the wallpaper. I found them on the east and south walls; (they are circled and marked with arrows on photographs Nos. 46-47).

131

My report states: "On the wallpaper on the east wall, quite close to the excisions made by the member of the court, Sergeyev, in the direction of the door-post of the door leading to the store-room (number III), there are many spatters of blood which have already blackened with time; but several of them still retain the characteristic coloring of blood: reddish-yellow: they all run upwards and to the left, from the excisions towards the door. On the wallpaper of the south wall, quite close to where the pieces of wood were removed, many similar blood spatters are observed; their direction is from the excisions upwards and to the right, downward and to the left."

Photograph No. 52 shows this wallpaper with the blood spatters.

In this room number II Sergeyev found an inscription in the German language on the south wall:

Belsatzar ward in selbiger Nacht
Von seinen Knechten umgebracht.[9]

This is the 21st stanza of a well-known work of the German poet, Heine, "Belshazzar". It differs from the original stanza of Heine in the omission of a very small word: "aber," i.e. "but nevertheless."

When one reads this work in the original it becomes clear why this word was omitted. Heine's 21st stanza is in contrast with the preceding 20th stanza. It follows the preceding one and is connected with it by the word "aber." Here the inscription expresses an independent thought. The word "aber" is here out of place.

Only one conclusion is possible: the person who made the inscription knows this work of Heine by heart.

Photograph No. 53 shows a view of this inscription.

On this same south wall I discovered a symbol consisting of four marks.

Photograph No. 54 shows their appearance.

On this same lower floor, in the room designated number X, Sergeyev found a pencil inscription on the door: "Rudolph Lacher Y.T.K. Jäger. Trient."

A captured soldier of the Austrian army by the name of Rudolph lived in this room. He was a servant for Yurovsky and his executioners from the Cheka.

CHAPTER EIGHTEEN

1. [pp. 173-179]

Scientific Examination of Parts of the Walls
and Floor of the Ipatiev House to Determine
the Nature of the Damage to Them.

The pieces of wood removed by Sergeyev from the Ipatiev House were subjected to two types of examination.

It was necessary to determine precisely the number of times they had been struck and the type of the weapons.

It was necessary to establish scientifically whether there was human blood on them.

I here set forth the results of the first type of examination in the language of the original reports.[10]

1. *A piece of wood from the east wall of room number II.*
"One side has obvious remains of plaster and the lath work to which it is affixed. Two indentations are clearly seen on this plastered side of the wood. Both are cone-shaped, and the edges of the wood near these indentations are depressed in the direction of their course. The diameter of one of them is 1 centimeter, the depth of the second is 2.2 centimeters. On the bottom of the second indentation, the one with a depth of 2.2 centimeters, the bottom of a bullet can be felt beneath the layer of plaster. The bullet has not been removed."

Conclusion of the expert 26 February 1918: [11]

"Having examined this piece of wood, the expert came to the definite conclusion that the first cavity in this piece is the mark of a bullet. It is most probable that this mark was made by a bullet from a revolver of the Nagant type. The bullet found in the other cavity was removed from it with the aid of a chisel, so that it was necessary to break the piece apart. The bullet's shape had not changed. From its measurements the expert came to the definite conclusion that this bullet belongs to an automatic pistol of the Browning type. The expert declined at the present moment to specify the type of weapon precisely, considering it necessary for this to weigh the bullet specially."

Conclusion of the expert 27 February 1919:

"Upon weighing the bullet its weight is found to be 4½ grams. Taking into account its weight and external appearance (of circular mould), it must be accepted that it belongs to a three-line automatic pistol of American manufacture."

2. The second piece of wood from the same wall.

"One side of the piece also has remains of plaster and of the lath work to which it is affixed. This piece has a trans-piercing hole passing through the entire thickness of the piece. The entrance is on that side which is covered with a layer of plaster; the exit is on the opposite side. The hole is round in form; its diameter 6 millimeters. The edges of the hole are depressed from the side of entrance toward the side of emergence."

Conclusion of the expert 26 February 1918: [11]

"The expert came to the conclusion that the hole in this piece of wood was made by a bullet passing through its thickness. This bullet belongs to a three-line revolver, most probably of the Nagant type."

3. The third piece of wood from the same wall.

"One side of the piece also has remains of plaster and lath work. On the side of the piece which is covered with a layer of plaster there is a hole which passes through the entire thickness and comes out in the opposite side of the piece. It is round in form; its diameter is 6 millimeters. The edges of the hole are depressed from the side covered with plaster, along the course of the hole. It is plain to see that this hole is the channel of a bullet striking through the piece of wood. Sergeyev has written on it with a black pencil: 'Bullet removed.' "

Conclusion of the expert 26 February 1919:
"The expert came to the conclusion that the hole in this piece was made by a bullet passing through its thickness. The bullet is three-line, from a revolver, but it is not possible to determine the type."

4. *The fourth piece of wood from the same wall.*
"One of its sides is also covered with a layer of plaster and has remains of lath work. On this side there is an indentation in the wood, round in form, with a diameter and depth each of 1 centimeter. The edges of the wood around the indentation are depressed inwards. The bottom of the indentation is also covered with a light layer of plaster."

Conclusion of the expert 26 February 1919:
"Upon examination of this piece the expert came to the conclusion that the indentation in the piece is the mark of a bullet belonging to a three-line revolver or automatic pistol."

5. *The fifth piece of wood from the same wall.*
"The piece is also covered with a layer of plaster and has remains of lath work. On this side there is a hole in the wood, round in form, having a diameter of about 1 centimeter. A probe inserted into this hole penetrates into the thickness of the wood 8 centimeters and does not go further, striking some hard object which gives the sound of metal when struck by the probe."

Conclusion of the expert 26 February 1919:
"The bullet was removed from it, also with the aid of a chisel, and for this purpose it was necessary to break this piece apart. The external appearance of the bullet had not changed. Upon measuring it the expert came to the definite conclusion that this bullet belongs to a three-line Nagant revolver."

6. *The sixth piece of wood from the same wall.*

"One side of it is covered with a layer of plaster and has pieces of lath work. On one side there are two indentations in the wood. One of them has a diameter of 1 centimeter and a depth of 5 millimeters. The other indentation has a diameter of 8 millimeters. The edges of the wood around it are flattened and depressed inwards along the course of the indentation. Its depth is 2.8 centimeters. The probe does not go further and strikes against the bottom of a bullet seated in the thickness of the wood and visible to the naked eye."

Conclusion of the expert 26 February 1919:

"Having examined this piece the expert came to the conclusion that the indentation [sic. (singular)] found upon examination of this piece is a bullet mark. Its appearance corresponds most closely with the bullet of a three-line Nagant. The bullet found upon examination of this piece was removed with the aid of the same chisel, so that this piece was broken apart. The external appearance of the bullet was little changed. Upon measuring it, the expert came to the conclusion that this bullet also belongs to a three-line automatic pistol (of round mould)."

7. *The seventh piece of wood from the same wall.*

"One side of this piece is also covered with a layer of plaster and has pieces of lath work. On two side-walls of this piece of wood two indentations of round form are plainly seen; their diameter is about 1 centimeter. Obviously these indentations are the marks of two bullets striking this piece from the sides."

Conclusion of the expert 26 February 1919:

"Having examined this piece the expert came to the conclusion that on this piece there are the marks of two bullets striking against it. One belongs to a three-line, the other to a four-line revolver."

8. *The eighth piece of wood from the same wall.*

"One side of this is covered with a layer of plaster. On one of its side walls there is an indentation of round form, running along the side wall, having a diameter of about 8 millimeters."

Conclusion of the expert 26 February 1919:

"The indentation in this piece is the mark of a bullet belonging to a three-line revolver. No other conclusions concerning this bullet are possible."

9. *The ninth piece of wood from the same wall.*

"An indentation of round form, with a diameter of 1.1 centimeters, runs along one of the side walls. One side of the piece has a layer of plaster and pieces of lath work. The direction of the indentation which runs along the side wall is from the side covered with the layer of plaster."

Conclusion of the expert 26 February 1919:

"Having examined this piece of wood the expert came to the conclusion that the hole in this piece is the mark of a bullet belonging to a three-line revolver. It is caused by a ricochet. Because of this it is not possible to make any other conclusions."

10. *The tenth piece of wood from the same wall.*

"One of its sides is covered with a layer of plaster. On this side there is an indentation in the wood, round in form, having a diameter of 1 centimeter. A probe inserted in the hole passes through the entire thickness of the wood and strikes against the bottom of a bullet which is stuck in the wood and the end of which sticks out a distance of 1 centimeter."

Conclusion of the expert 26 February 1919:

"The bullet found upon examination of this piece was removed from it with the aid of the same chisel, for which purpose it was necessary to break the piece apart. The external appearance of the bullet was almost unchanged. Upon measuring it the expert came to the conclusion that this bullet belongs to a three-line revolver of the Nagant type."

11. *The eleventh piece of wood from the same wall.*

"On one of its sidewalls there is a hole, round in form, having a diameter of 8 millimeters. A probe inserted into this hole penetrates the entire thickness of the wood and strikes against the bottom of a bullet, which sticks out with a small end."

Conclusion of the expert 26 February 1919:
"The bullet found upon examination of this piece was also removed from it with the aid of a chisel, for which purpose it was
necessary to break the piece apart. The external appearance of the
bullet was little changed. Upon measuring it the expert came to
the conclusion that this bullet belongs to a three-line revolver
of the Nagant type."

12. *The twelfth piece of wood from the same wall.*
"A bullet is seated in the center of the chip."

Conclusion of the expert 26 February 1919:
"The bullet was readily removed from the chip, which broke in
two parts. Its external appearance was little changed. Upon
measuring it the expert came to the conclusion that this bullet belongs to a three-line revolver of the Nagant type."

13. *The thirteenth piece of wood from the same wall.*
"From the side, in this chip there is a bullet adhering to one of
the outer walls of the chip, lodged in its seat. It is barely clinging
to the chip and almost all of its sides are clearly visible. The bullet
is in a jacket. Its end is truncated or compressed from the blow."

Conclusion of the expert 26 February 1919:
"The bullet was readily removed from this piece by hand. Its
external appearance was little changed. But the jacket was somewhat torn off. Upon measuring the bullet the expert came to the
conclusion that this bullet belongs to a three-line revolver of the
Nagant type."

14. *The piece of wood from the south wall.*
"In the center of the piece, on the same side to which wallpaper
has been pasted, there is a bullet channel of round form, 6 millimeters in diameter. The channel runs towards one of the side walls
of the piece, near which the bullet, clearly visible with the naked
eye, has stuck."

Conclusion of the expert 26 February 1919:
"The external appearance of the bullet is little changed. Upon

measuring it the expert came to the conclusion that this bullet belongs to a three-line revolver of the Nagant type."

15. *The second piece of wood from the same wall.*

"In the center of the piece, on the side covered with wallpaper, there is a hole, round in form, with a diameter of about 1 centimeter. This hole is trans-piercing. It passes diagonally through the entire thickness of the piece and emerges on the opposite side, nearer the side wall."

Conclusion of the expert 26 February 1919:

"Upon examination of this piece the expert came to the conclusion that the hole in this piece was made by a bullet belonging to a three-line revolver."

16. *A piece of floor.*

"One side of the board is painted with yellow paint. On this side two rectangles had been drawn in black pencil.[12] In the center of one of these a hole, oval in form, is seen, having a length of 1.5 centimeters, 1.1 centimeters in width. The edges of the wood around this hole have been flattened and depressed in the direction of the depth of the hole as it goes into the wood. It is quite plain to see that this hole was made by a bullet striking the wood from the painted side. A probe, inserted into this hole, passes through the entire thickness of the wood and emerges from the opposite side. Thus this hole is trans-piercing. The exit side of the hole is oval in form; its length is 1 centimeter and its width 9 millimeters; but it is difficult to give precise measurement since this side of the board is chipped, changing the precise form and size of the hole. The edges of this hole on the painted side of the board have, as it were, still another coloring: a darkish red color. But without a scientific examination it is not possible to determine the nature of this, since it is possible that this coloring in distinction from the color of the paint which covers the board, comes from the prime coat on which the paint lay, the latter having been chipped off around the hole by the blow, apparently, of the bullet. It the center of the other rectangle a hole is observed, of the same form as that just described, having a length of 2.3 centimeters and width of 1½ centimeters. A probe, inserted in this hole, penetrates 2½ centimeters and does not go farther: it strikes against the bottom of a bullet which is clearly seen with the naked eye. The edges of the wood around this hole, which was made by the bullet, are also flattened and depressed along the course of the hole in the direction of the bullet. Around this hole, on the painted side of the board, a coloring of some other kind is seen, also darkish red. Upon careful examination of the course of the bullet channel several strands of wool were found in the small splinters of wood which lay in the channel quite close to the bullet. Some of the strands of wool are of cream color, the others red. These strands of wool were carefully removed from the channel with the aid of a probe and placed in a special package. The bullet was not removed prior to the making of a scientific investigation of the colorings seen near the entrance channels of the bullets.

17. *The second piece of floor.*

"One side of the board is also colored with the same paint. In the center of the piece on the painted side there is a hole, almost round in form, with a diameter of 1 centimeter. The edges of the wood around this hole are flattened and compressed along the course of the hole into the wood. The hole is trans-piercing. It penetrates the entire thickness of the wood. It is impossible to take its measurements on the opposite side because of the chips in the board. The surface of the board on the painted side, on which is the entrance of the hole, and on the opposite side, where its exit is, has, as it were, a certain darkish red coloring. But it is not possible to determine the nature of this by external examination. The hole is undoubtedly a bullet channel."

18. *The third piece of floor.*

"On one side the piece has been painted with the same paint as the preceding ones, and it also has on this side the traces of a pencil outline. On this painted side a hole of semi-circular form is observed. It passes through the entire thickness of the piece and emerges, not on the opposite side, but, passing through the piece diagonally, emerges in one of the side walls. It is difficult to determine its measurement in the side wall due to the fact that the walls of the hole in the wood have somewhat come together. The edges of the wood on the painted side are also flattened and depressed into the wood along the course of the hole. No coloring is noted around the hole on either the entrance or exit side."

19. *The fourth piece of floor.*

"One side is painted with the same paint as the preceding pieces. Near the very edge of the piece a speck of darkish red color is observed, round in form, having a diameter of 5 millimeters. It is on the side of the piece that is covered with paint, and also near the edge. A part of the wood at the very edge near the speck has either been removed with the aid of a chisel or has chipped off. The side wall of the piece, beginning right at the edge where the speck and the chipping off are located, has a coloring suggesting blood. It extends to a length of 7 centimeters and a width of 2.5 centimeters."

20. *The fifth piece of floor.*

"On the painted side, at the very edge of the piece, there is an indentation in the wood, round in form, 2 centimeters in diameter, with a depth of ½ centimeter. In the center of the indentation a bullet is plainly visible, fixed in the wood and flattened. The bottom of the indentation around the bullet, and its edges, have what appear to be traces of blood. The side wall of the piece has a clearly visible running blood stain, extending along this side wall right from the edge of the depression in which the bullet is located. The length of the stain is 7 centimeters; in width it takes up the width of the board."

Conclusion of the expert 26-27 February 1919:

a) with respect to the bullet in the piece of floor in item 16:

"When the bullet was weighed, its weight was found to be about 15 grams. For a more precise determination of the nature of the weapon to which it belongs an exact measurement of it was made with a venier caliper; its exact diameter was 11.43 millimeters, i.e., 4½ lines. This bullet belongs to an automatic pistol of the Colt type, 45 caliber."

b) with respect to the bullet in the piece of floor in item 20:

"This bullet had been very much flattened. Because of this it was not measured. Its weight is 5½ grams. It most probably must be accepted that this bullet belongs to an automatic pistol of the Browning type, made in Europe (but not in Russia)."

There was no doubt that there were six bullet channels in the five pieces of floor. It was necessary to preserve these pieces for investigation of blood. Therefore I sacrificed clarification of the question as to the type of weapon by which the remaining channels were made, limiting myself to the submission of two bullets to the expert.

Photograph No. 55 shows several of the bullets found in the Ipatiev House.[12a]

2.   [179-191]

Scientific Analysis of Pieces of the Floor for Blood.

Five pieces of the floor were submitted to scientific analysis for blood: one from room number I and four from room number II.

They were conducted by two different institutions. One made an analysis of all of the pieces on which I noticed blood.[13] The other, at the request of Sergeyev, analysed a part of the last of the above-mentioned pieces.

I here set forth the results of the analyses in the language of the original reports:

A) *Chemical-Microscopic Analysis.*

"The suspected stains on board No. 297 were so small, particularly the stain in the area of the pencil outline at the edge of the board, that it was doubtful whether they would give a positive reaction to tincture of guaiac.

On the other hand, if the reaction should be only mildly positive, a doubt would arise whether this had not been produced by a substance scraped from the board under examination, and forming a component part of the paint, wood, caulking, etc.

Therefore it was necessary to determine in advance whether a positive reaction to tincture of guaiac would not be produced by a substance from the board itself, with its layer of floor paint. For this purpose, with a previously cleaned, semi-circular chisel, I scraped off part of the painted surface of board No. 297 in that area where no suspected stains were observed. A quantity of scrapings exceeding the quantity which would have been furnished by the suspected stain was treated with one percent ammonia in a china cup (which I had personally washed by previously treating the cup with a mixture of chrome). The ammonia was a 25% solution from the firm of Kahlbaum in Berlin, accurately diluted with the purest distilled water, which I had myself prepared by

142

distilling pharmaceutical distilled water to which sulphuric acid and potassium manganate had been added (the later reagents being the purest—the H_2SO_4 from the Tentelevsky plant in Petrograd).

Two cc. of the one percent ammonia were added. After steeping for six hours the fluid was filtered through a very fine filter (the funnel having been previously washed with a mixture of chrome, and distilled water). The filter and scrapings were washed with 5 cc. of purest distilled water. The filter was placed in a previously washed and annealed platinum cup. The filtrate was evaporated by a slow heating of the cup, accomplished by allowing the cup to stand in a copper air chamber in which the temperature was maintained at not more than 80° C. After evaporation of the water, there were added to the dried residue 0.2 cc. of 60% acetic acid, 2 cc. of 97° rectified spirits, 1 cc. of a freshly-prepared alcoholic tincture of guaiac and 1 cc. of ozonized turpentine. The yellowish color of the mixture did not change in the course of 50 minutes.

Parallel with this test a test of the reagents was made, that is, a mixture was made of the following: 1 cc. of 60% acetic acid, 3 cc. of 97° spirits, 3 cc. of tincture of guaiac—freshly made 1% —and 3 cc. of ozonized turpentine. The yellowish color of the mixture did not change in the course of 60 minutes.

(By ozonized turpentine is understood yellowed French turpentine which has stood in the light for a long time in an open vessel.)

In addition to this, at the same time and parallel with the above-described test of scrapings from board No. 297, tests of the same character were made, with the observance of all of the same conditions, except that human blood diluted 1:1000 (prepared 3-4 days beforehand) was added to the scrapings in quantities of 0.1 cc.; 0.3 cc.; 0.5 cc.; and 1.0 cc. The following result was obtained:

The extract from the scrapings to which 0.1 cc. of diluted blood had been added produced a very weak, green coloring of the guaiacic reagent mixture after 15 minutes; the extract from the scrapings with 0.3 cc. of diluted blood immediately produced a clear (distinct) green coloring of the guaiacic reagent mixture. The green coloring of the reagent mixture appeared even clearer with the extract from the scrapings to which 0.5 cc. of diluted blood had been added, and finally the extract from the scrapings to which 1.0 cc. of diluted blood had been added immediately produced a dark, blue-green coloring of the guaiacic reagent mixture.

In this manner I determined that the scrapings from floor board No. 297, with its painted surface, did not of themselves show a reaction to tincture of guaiac, and that an unquestionably positive reaction was obtained when there were added to the scrapings 0.3 cc. of human blood diluted 1:1000.

After this the test of the suspected stains on the material evidence was begun.

"Section of board" No. 297 has two stains on its painted surface, in the region of the pencil outlines. One, which we call stain 297-A, is near the center of the board and the other, 297-B, is at the edge of the board.

"Section of board" No. 298 has a bloody running stain, with no clots of dried blood, along the channel of the bullet which was lodged in the board and which was removed the 24th of February.[14] This stain we call No. 298-A. The other suspected stain on board 298 is at the entrance of the trans-piercing bullet channel. Since this stain is very insignificant, I broke the board apart along the course of the bullet channel. A suspected running stain was found along its concealed channel, the continuation of the suspected stain found at the entrance of the bullet channel and extending along one half of the channel. No clots of dried blood were observed in the running stain. We call this running stain No. 298-B.

"Section of board" No. 299 has a trans-piercing bullet hole. Because the suspected stains at the edges of this hole were very small the board was broken apart along the course of the bullet channel. When it was broken apart, however, the entire bullet channel was not exposed, but only the lower part thereof, equal, approximately, to one half of the entire channel. A suspected running stain is observed along the course of the entire channel, the continuation of the suspected stains at the entrance of the channel. No dried clots of blood were exposed in the running stain.

"Section of board" No. 300. In order to test for the presence of blood a scraping was taken from that surface of the board which forms a crevice in the floor, and in which a part of the bullet channel is seen. On this surface of the board a suspected running stain is observed with very small clots of dried blood.

"Section of board" No. 301 is the edge of a board. Not far from the surface of the edge, which forms a crevice in the floor, is the seat of a bullet which was removed on the 24th of February, 1919. The area of the seat of the bullet is colored with a suspected running stain which extends continuously to and along the board surface which forms the floor crevice. In the removal of the bullet a fragment of the board was split off and it is necessary to restore it to its place in order to see that the stain at the seat of the bullet and the running stains on the crevice surface of the board run together continuously, the one into the other. The running stains on the crevice surface become, in places, very thin, dried clots.

In this manner suspected stains 297-A, 297-B, 298-A, 298-B, 299, 300, 301 were subjected to tests with tincture of guaiac and for the production of hemin crystals (Teichmann crystals).

Stains No. 297-A and No. 297-B were scraped off in their entirety, but only partial scrapings were made from the others, that is from Nos. 298-A, 298-B, 299, 300 and 301, in view of their great size and in order to leave material for testing by the Uhlenhuth method.

The scrapings, each in a separate china cup (well washed beforehand, after having been treated with a mixture of chrome), were moistened with several drops of purest distilled water and then with two cubic centimeters of one percent ammonia. After standing for six hours the liquid was passed through a filter (filter No. 589—a black sheet having a diameter of 5 centimeters manufactured by Schleicher and Schüle) (the funnel having been well washed after treatment with a mixture of chrome). The filtrates from the extracts were received into previously washed and annealed platinum cups. The filters and the scrapings were washed twice with a small quantity of purest distilled water. The wash waters were collected in the same platinum cups in which the respective filtrates were received. In this fashion, from 5 to 8 cc. of liquid (extract) collected in each platinum cup. In order to conduct further tests it was necessary to concentrate the extracts thus obtained, and this was done by evaporating the water (and other volatile substances, for example, ammonia) by heating. The heating was done by placing the platinum cups with the extracts, uncovered, on the upper surface of a copper air chamber, the internal temperature of which did not exceed 80° C. When the contents of the cups was reduced, approximately, to 2 cc. in Nos. 297-A and 297-B and to 3-4 cc. in Nos. 298-A, 298-B, 299, 300 and 301, the heating was discontinued.

To conduct the tests with tincture of guaiac the following procedure was adopted: approximately 0.5 cc. of each tested extract was poured from each platinum cup into moistened, absolutely clean test tubes. To each test tube there was then added 0.3 cc. of 60% acetic acid. The mixtures were each tested with blue litmus paper (prepared from azolitmin). The reactions in each case were sharply acid. There were then added to each extract 2 cc. of freshly-prepared, one percent tincture of guaiac (1 dram resinae geraici [guaiaci?] + 99 grams of 95° ethyl alcohol with subsequent filtering) and 2 cc. of ozonized turpentine.

Nos. 298-A, 298-B, 299, 300 and 301 gave sharply positive reactions, manifested in the immediate assumption by the reactive mixture of a dark blue coloring.

A clearly distinct reaction was produced by No. 297-A. There appeared immediately a distinct, light blue coloring of the reactive mixture.

No. 297-B (about 0.5 cc. of extract, as indicated above) produced an indistinct change in color of the guaiacic mixture. Therefore the entire contents of the platinum cup, i.e., the entire extract from the suspected stain, was subjected to the test with tincture of guaiac. It was done in this manner: to the entire extract there was added 0.5 cc. of glacial acetic acid (after which the liquid showed a sharply acid reaction to litmus paper), 2 cc. of 1% tincture of guaiac and 2 cc. of ozonized turpentine. There immediately appeared a weak blue coloring of the reaction mixture, seen distinctly in comparison with the control mixture of 0.5 cm. of acetic acid + 2 cm. of tincture of guaiac + 2 cm. of ozonized turpentine.

The result of the described tests with tincture of guaiac was to establish the presence of blood in the suspected stains of the material evidence, Nos. 297-A, 297-B, 298-A, 298-B, 299, 300, 301.

In order that the results obtained might be more readily visualized I have provided a table (see p. 183 [147]) in which the above-described results are shown together with the numbers of the respective china cups in which the extracts of blood were produced from the suspected stains, the number of the platinum cups in which the extracts and wash waters were received, and the colors of the extracts.

In the manner indicated, the test of suspected stains No. 297-B was completed by using up all of the substance of the stains.

Further investigation of the other extracts was directed to obtaining hemin crystals (Teichmann's reaction).

For this purpose the contents of platinum cup No. 8, i.e., the extract from suspected stain No. 297-A, in view of its small quantity and complete transparency, was subjected to a test without any kind of additional treatment in the following manner: the entire extract was transferred to a slide (carefully washed after treatment with chromic mixture); the transfer of the extract to the slide was accomplished in this manner: 2-3 drops of the extract were deposited on the center of the slide with a special, small pipette, and then evaporated until dry; on the spot thus formed there were

№ 45. Надпись на русскомъ и мадьярскомъ языкахъ, сдѣланная въ домѣ Ипатьева чекистомъ-мадьяромъ за сутки до убійства.

№ 43. Чекистъ. Я. М. Юровскій.

№ 42. Чекистъ. Ш. И.Голощекинъ.

№ 41. Охранникъ П. И. Клещовъ.

№ 44. Семья Я. М. Юровскаго: отецъ, мать, жена и сынъ.

Nos. 41, 42, 43, 44, and 45.

№ 46. Комната, гдѣ была убита царская семья. Вост. стѣна.

№ 47. Та же комната. Южная стѣна.

№ 48. Та же комната. Западная стѣна.

№ 49. Куски дерева съ пулями изъ вост. стѣны.

Nos. 46, 47, 48, and 49.

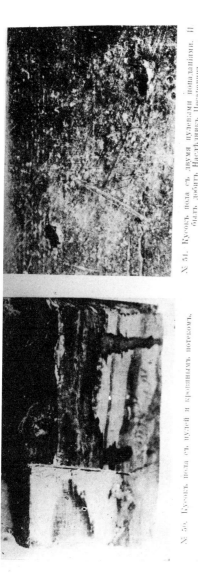

№ 50. Кусокъ пола съ двумя пулевыми повалданіами. И бать добить. Насѣкалинъ. Цесаревичъ.

№ 51. Надпись на нѣмецкомъ языкѣ, обнаруженная въ комнатѣ (съ ...

№ 50. Кусокъ пола съ пулей и кровяными потеками.

№ 52. Куски обоевъ съ кровяными брызгами.

Nos. 50, 51, 52, and 53.

№ 54. Обозначеніе изъ четырехъ знаковъ, обнаруженное въ комнатѣ убійства (на южной стѣнѣ).

№ 55. Нѣкоторыя изъ пуль, извлеченныя изъ стѣнъ и пола въ комнатѣ убійства.

№ 56. Дневникъ Наслѣдника Цесаревича. Найденъ у охран-

Nos. 54, 55, and 56.

№ 57. Книга Великой Княжны Ольги Николаевны съ надписью на ней Государыни. Въ ней обнаруженъ листъ бумаги съ текстомъ стихотворенія «Молитва», писаннаго рукою Ольги Николаевны (см. стр. 282).

№ 58. Иконы царской семьи, найденныя въ домѣ Ипатьева послѣ убійства.

Nos. 57 and 58.

№ 59. Предметы, обнаруженные въ Екатеринбургѣ послѣ убійства царской семьи. Слѣва въ верхнемъ ряду — икона Спасителя. Она была обнаружена на груди Великой Княгини Елизаветы Федоровны, трупъ коей былъ найденъ на днѣ шахты вблизи г. Алапаевска.

60. Иконы царской семьи, подаренныя ея Распутинымъ.

№ 61. Оборотная сторона этихъ иконъ съ надписями Распутина (см. стр. 280).

Nos. 59, 60, and 61.

№ 62. Вещи царской семьи и убитыхъ съ нею лицъ, найденныя
въ Екатеринбургѣ послѣ убійства.

№ 63. Вещи царской семьи, найденныя въ Екатеринбургѣ послѣ
убійства. На снимкѣ видны игрушки Наслѣдника Цесаревича и
зонтъ Государыни.

Nos. 62 and 63.

№ 64. Перевалъ № 184. Здѣсь везли трупы царской семьи.

№ 65. Коптяковская дорога, по которой везли трупы царской семьи. Два сосновыхъ пня: остатки четырехъ сосенъ. Четыре Братьевъ».

Nos. 64, 65, 66, and 67.

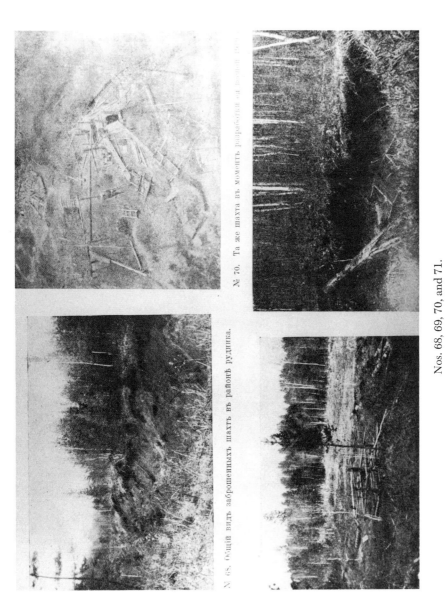

№ 68. Общій видъ заброшенныхъ шахтъ въ районѣ рудника.

№ 70. Та же шахта въ моментъ разработки ея весной 19...

Nos. 68, 69, 70, and 71.

№ 72. Мѣсто вблизи переѣзда № 184, гдѣ находилась большевистская застава.

№ 73. Раскопки въ районѣ рудника весной и лѣтомъ 1919 года.

№ 74. Раскопки въ районѣ рудника весной и лѣтомъ

№ 75. Веревка и части сосновой доски, найденная на рудникѣ.

Nos. 72, 73, 74, and 75.

№ 77. Малый костеръ для курени отъ комаровъ, возлѣ котораго были найдены останки семейства.

№ 76. Мостикъ, набросанный сослуживцами по контяковской дорогѣ, затѣмъ грузовой автомобиль, доставившій трупы парской семьи къ руднику.

Nos. 76, 77, and 78.

№ 79. Костеръ влизи открытой шахты, гдѣ уничтожались трупы царской семьи.

№ 80. Костеръ у старой березы.

№ 81.

№ 82.

№ 83.

Nos. 79, 80, 81, 82, 83, 84, and 85.

№ 91. Фонарь съ солнца, найденный на рудникѣ.

№ 92. Стекло отъ фонаря, найденное на рудникѣ.

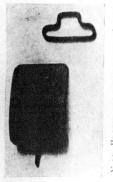

№ 88. Пряжка отъ пояса, малаго образца, найденная на рудникѣ.

№ 89. Пряжки отъ туфель съ лазами, найденныя на рудникѣ.

№ 90. Пряжка отъ туфель, найденная на рудникѣ.

№ 86. Пряжка отъ пояса офицерскаго образца.

№ 87. Портретъ Государя. (Пряжка

Nos. 86, 87, 88, 89, 90, 91, and 92.

№ 93. Оправа-держатель
отъ пенснэ, найденная
на рудникѣ.

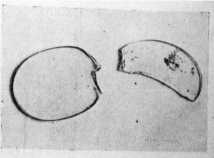

№ 94. Стекла отъ пенснэ, найденныя на рудникѣ.

№ 95. Искусственная челюсть, найденная на рудникѣ.

№ 96. Остатки щеточки малаго формата (для
усовъ), найденные на рудникѣ.

№ 97. Запонка и машинка для галстука, найденная на
рудникѣ.

Nos. 93, 94, 95, 96, and 97.

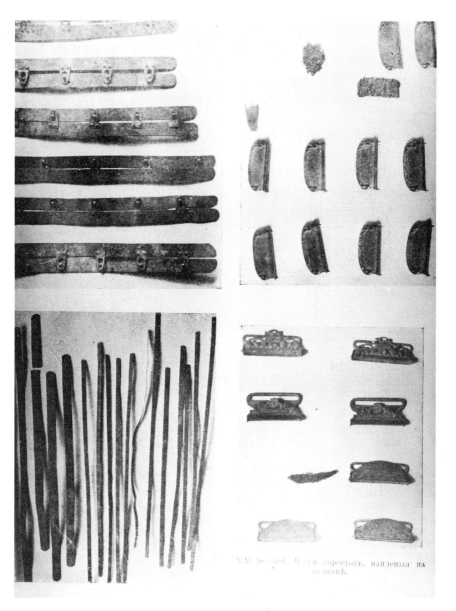

Nos. 98, 99, 100, and 101.

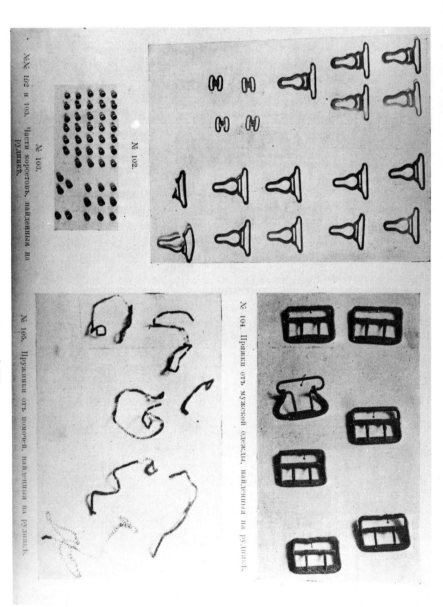

№ 102.

№ 103.

№№ 102 и 103. Части корестовъ, найденныя на рудникъ.

№ 104. Пряжки отъ мужской одежды, найденныя на рудникъ.

№ 105. Пружины отъ помочей, найденныя отъ рудникъ.

Nos. 102, 103, 104, and 105.

[Table appearing on page 183]

esignations of e points and cord of proedings of the urt investiator in which e material vidence is escribed.	Corresponding numbers of the present record of proceedings.	Nos. of the china cups in which the extracts of blood were produced.	Nos. of the platinum cups in which the filtered extracts and wash waters were received.	Color of the extracts after filtering and washing of the filters.	Results of test with tincture of guaiac.
Section of board" escribed in point of record of proeedings 17-18 'ebruary 1919.	297-A.	I.	8.	Very weak rose.	Positive reaction: immediate appearance of distinct blue coloring with part of extract.
	297-B.	II.	9.	Colorless.	Positive reaction: immediate appearance of weak blue coloring on application of entire extract.
Section of board" escribed in 2d oint of record of roceedings 17-18 'ebruary 1919.	298-A.	VI.	7.	Reddish.	
	298-B.	VII.	I.	Red.	
Section of board" escribed in point of record of proeedings 17-18 'ebruary 1919.	299.	IV.	4.	Red.	Sharply positive reaction: immediate appearance of dark blue coloring of reactive mixture with part of extract.
Section of board" escribed in point of record of proeedings 17-18 'ebruary 1919.	300.	III.	1.	Red.	
Section of board" escribed in point of record of proeedings 17-18 'ebruary 1919.	301.	V.	6.	Red.	

again deposited 2-3 drops of extract which were again evaporated, and so on until the entire extract was on the slide; the evaporation of the liquid was accomplished by heating the slide on the upper surface of a copper air chamber, within which the temperature was maintained at not more than 40° C. When the entire extract had been transferred to the slide, several particles of finely powdered, chemically purified, sodium chloride were added to the last drop; when only a very small amount of moisture remained on the slide, the evaporation (the drying of the preparation) was completed at room temperature. The spot was then moistened by rubbing it with the end of a glass rod which had been slightly dampened with purest distilled water; the spot was covered with a cover-glass in such a way that the latter was slightly raised; this was accomplished by depositing upon the object-glass several absolutely clean grains of sea sand; beneath the cover-glass there was placed, with a glass rod, a quantity of glacial acetic acid sufficient to completely fill the space between the slide and the cover-glass; this was heated carefully over a very small flame—the flame of a wick alcohol lamp—until a bubble of steam began to appear; after this a slow evaporation of the acetic acid was produced by placing the slide upon a copper chamber within which a temperature of not more than 40° C. was maintained. The color of the liquid between the glasses was light brownish. Examination under the microscope for the appearance of hemin crystals was made every 5-10-15 minutes; however, such crystals were not observed, not only up to the moment when very little fluid remained between the glasses, but even when additional glacial acetic acid placed between the glasses had almost completely evaporated.

Thus it was not possible to demonstrate that the light, suspected stain, No. 297-A, was a stain of human blood; it is only established that this stain, and similarly stain No. 297-B, are blood stains.

Before producing a Teichmann's reaction with the principal portions of the extracts derived from stains Nos. 198-A, 198-B, 299, 300 and 301 and remaining after the test with tincture of guaiac, the following operation was performed with them, with the purpose of cleaning, in as far as possible, the blood pigment from admixtures which might, for example, be component substances of the wood that had been extracted in the weak ammonia. To each extract there was first separately added a small quantity of a weak solution of the purest tannin (Gerbsäure I, from the Kahlbaum plant in Berlin); then there was added one percent acetic acid, one drop at a time, with the subsequent immersion in the mixed liquid of very thin, blue litmus paper; the addition of acetic acid was discontinued when a weakly acid reaction was obtained in all of the extracts. At this moment crumbly, cottony precipitates, colored with a reddish-brown color, fell from the solutions; the intensity and shade of the coloring of the precipitates were not the same in the various platinum cups. The precipitates which were smallest in volume, but most purely colored with a reddish color, formed in cups I and 1 (No. 298-B and 300), the other three precipitates (No. 298-A, 299 and 301) were large in volume, but had a duller shade of color. All of the precipitates were washed three times with the purest distilled water, to which the smallest quantities of a solution of tannin and acetic acid had been previously added. The washing of the precipitates was accomplished in the following manner: the contents of the platinum cups were poured, for treatment in a centrifuge, into test tubes which had been marked with the numbers of the cups; after the precipitates had settled in the test tubes, the transparent, colorless liquid standing above them was decanted; water was again added to the precipitates, after which the test tubes were shaken and left standing at rest until precipitates had again settled. When, following a third addition of water, the latter was poured off, the precipitates were subjected to the Teichmann test.

By means of special pipettes, which I had prepared for each test tube separately, the precipitates, which still contained considerable water, were transferred drop by drop to absolutely clean slides which had been marked, with a diamond, with the numbers of the platinum cups; the slides were then placed upon a copper air chamber, within which the temperature was maintained at not more than 40°C. When one drop dried, a new one was deposited on the same place until there was a sufficient quantity of the substance on the slide. Further treatment of the preparations and observation for the appearance of hemin crystals were conducted in precisely the same manner as has been described above with regard to the testing of stain 297-A.

When this was done all tested extracts, i.e., No. 298-A, 298-B, 299, 300 and 301 produced Teichmann hemin crystals.

The formation (falling from solution) of hemin crystals did not occur with equal readiness in each case. While extracts No. 298-B and 300 (especially 300) produced the indicated crystals quite quickly, the others, Nos. 298-A, 299 and 301 (especially 298-A) formed them with greater difficulty. It was observed that the hemin crystals were formed with particular difficulty (not quickly, or **not** from the first prepared material) in those extracts which contained many microscopic, fatty-like (or fatty) drops in the treated microscopic preparations; the color of the evaporating liquids between the slides and the object glasses was brown, and after evaporation to a small volume the consistency was thick and viscous. Evidently a resinous substance had been drawn from the pine wood of the boards along with the substance of the blood.

It must be noted that the hemin crystals obtained in each case were of rhombic form, of varying size, sometimes long, sometimes short, sometimes very large, most often very small; at the beginning of their formation they had an absolutely regular form; but in almost every case, as soon as the formation of the crystals had begun, then, by the following day, the beautiful, regular hemin crystals seen in the old preparations the day before were no longer seen, and instead there were: either enlarged crystals which had lost their sharp distinctness at the ends, or nodules of crystals, most often having the shape of sheafs; these nodules consisted most often of regular, rhombic shaped discs, i.e., they were the same hemin crystals, but fused together.

The examination of the microscopic preparations was made with a Zeiss microscope, without extension of the tube, with a Hügens eyepiece No. 4 and objective D.

In this manner it was established by the present analysis that the blood-like stains and running stains on material evidence Nos. 298, 299, 300 and 301 were formed by blood and that it was human blood.

B) *Serological Analysis According to Uhlenhuth's Method.*

A careful inspection of the material evidence made by myself and (chemist N.) [15] indicated that there was absolutely insufficient material for an analysis according to Uhlenhuth's method on the painted side of the floor board described in point 1 of the record of proceedings 17-18 February 1919 made by the court investigator (No. 297).

The following material evidence was sufficient for both chemical-microscopic analysis and serodiagnostic analysis according to Uhlenhuth's method:

1. Section of board described in pt. 2 of the record of proceedings, with two bullet holes—one deep and the other trans-piercing (No. 198).

2. The section of board described in pt. 3 of the record of proceedings (No. 299).

3. The section of board described in pt. 5 of the record of pro-

ceedings (No. 300).

4. The section of board described in pt. 6 of the record of proceedings (No. 301).

Precipitating serums reacting to human blood serum and to sheep's blood serums were obtained from N. university.[16]

In addition I used some precipitating serum reacting to human blood which I happened to have on hand from the Saxon serum station (originally Uhlenhuth) and which had a very high titer. By means of preparatory experiments it was established that all of the serums were working very specifically, giving no precipitation or opacity with foreign serums, the Saxon serum giving a much stronger reaction than that from N.[16]

After the preliminary test of the serums, I proceeded to the analysis, by precipitation reaction, of the above-indicated material evidence described in points 2, 3, 5 and 6.

For this purpose parts of the wood on which there were suspected stains resembling blood were removed by means of scraping and cutting with a knife. The scraped particles of wood from each stain were placed in absolutely clean test tubes (those from each stain placed in a separate test tube) and a physiological solution (0.85%) of table salt poured over them, having in mind the desirability of obtaining, after the extraction of the blood, the strongest possible solutions. The particles of wood were allowed to stand in the salt solution at room temperature (in a cool room) for 24 hours. As a control, scraped particles and shavings were also taken from the same section of board, at a point where there were definitely no suspected blood-stains.

From the section of board (No. 298) described in point 2 of the record of proceedings of the court investigator, two samples of wood were removed for analysis:

One (No. 1) from the wall of the blind channel of the bullet which had lodged in the thickness of wood and which had been removed on 24 February, and the other sample (No. 2) from the wall of the other, trans-piercing, bullet channel. In order to remove the sample from the wall of this channel, the channel was opened up by breaking the board apart. . . . . . (by chemist N.) [17] in my presence.

In the same manner the board described in point 3 of the record of proceedings (No. 299) was broken apart in order to open up the bullet channel. The sample of wood (No. 3) was removed from the wall of the channel, which was colored with a brownish color, evidently, by the blood soaking into it. From the section of board described in pt. 5 of the record of proceedings, a scraping of wood (No. 4) was taken from the area of the suspected stain which had the appearance of a bloody running stain (No. 300).

Finally, the last sample (No. 5) was taken from the section of board described in the record of proceedings under pt. 6 (No. 301), that is from the wall of the bullet channel and from that surface of the board which forms the wall of the floor crevice. When, in order to remove the bullet, the board was broken apart on 24 February 1919 (by the court investigator), it was found that the stain of the bullet channel and the running stains on the crevice surface of the board ran directly together, the one into the other, and therefore the scrapings of wood from the wall of the seat of the bullet and from the floor surface of the board were joined and placed in one test tube.

After the particles of wood had stood in the 0.85% solution of table salt the fluids thus obtained were passed through filter paper, and completely transparent filtrates obtained.

All of the filtrates (Nos. 1-5), except the fluids from the unstained wood, gave a distinct albuminous reaction when boiled with acetic acid and when subjected to Heller's test with nitric acid. *In this manner it was established that the liquid which had saturated the floor boards was undoubtedly albuminous.*

In order to determine whether this was not albumin from blood serum and in particular whether these stains were not from human blood, the filtrates were also analysed according to Uhlenhuth's method.

For this purpose three sets of small, absolutely clean test tubes were prepared, with nine in each set.

Into each of tubes Nos. 1-5 in each set 0.9 cc. of the respective filtrate-extracts obtained from the stains was poured. Into No. 6 the same quantity of extract from the wood was poured. Into No. 7 the same quantity of very dilute horse serum was poured.

Into No. 8—dilute sheep serum.

Into No. 9—dilute human serum (a mixture of 10 serums of normal and syphilitic subjects).

To each of the test tubes of the first set there was added 0.1 cc. of precipitating serum reacting to human blood.

To each of the test tubes of the second set there was likewise added 0.1 cc. of the same kind of serum from the Saxon station (originally Uhlenhuth).

To each of the test tubes of the third set there was added 0.1 cc. of precipitating serum reacting to sheep's blood.

152

The test was made at room temperature. In addition to these test tubes three other test tubes were set up, as control test tubes, containing all three precipitating serums diluted 1:10 with physiological solutions of table salt, in order to be assured that, with prolonged standing, spontaneous opacity would not occur in the solutions of precipitating serums.

Observation was continued for three hours.

The results of the test with all precipitating serums have been set forth in the table following (on p. 189 [154]).

In this manner: 1) the precipitating anti-sheep serum gives a positive reaction only to sheep serum, causing no change in the extracts from the material evidence or in the other, control, test tubes; 2) the precipitating serums reacting to human blood, both from N.[18] and from the Saxon station, showed positive reactions to human serum (test tubes Nos. 9 of sets I and II) and to all of the extracts from the material evidence, while showing no opacity with horse or sheep serum or in the other, control, test tubes.

On the basis of the positive reaction obtained by the Uhlenhuth method, the specificity of which has been scientifically proven, it must be concluded that the extracts obtained by us from the suspected stains on the wood by letting them stand in a physiological solution of salt, are solutions of human blood serum, and that the stains on the floor boards described in the record of proceedings of the court investigator in the matter...under points Nos. 2 (in both bullet marks), 3, 5 and 6, undoubtedly came from human blood."

C) Scientific Analysis of a Part of the Floor Made at the Request of the Member of the Court, Sergeyev.

Method of examination: after microscopic examination of the suspected stains on the excised piece of wood, scrapings were taken from the more stained areas.

The first portion of scrapings was used for a Van Deen test for the presence of blood. For this the particles were moistened with distilled water and then, after three hours, dried with Swedish blotting paper. The edge of the dampened sheet of paper was moistened with tincture of guaiac and ozonized oil of turpentine (turpentine); in the event of the presence of blood the edge of the dampened sheet of paper takes on a bluish color.

The second portion of scrapings was used for a Benzidine test. For this the scrapings were soaked in distilled water. To the watery extract a solution of Benzidine in spirits and acetic acid was added. In the event of the presence of blood the extract normally

[Table appearing on page 189]

	0.9 cc. of extract or solution			0.1 of precipitating serum:		
	Test tube Nos.	Points of record of proceedings of court investigator.	Conventional designation.	Of precipitating albumin of human blood		Of precipitating albumin of sheep's blood
				Of N. 19 (Set I.)	Of Saxon station (Set II.)	Of N. 19 (Set III)
Extracts from the suspected stains on the wood.	1.	pt. 2.	298-A.	Opacity in 10 minutes. +	Distinct opacity at once. +	Liquid transparent even after 3 hours.
	2.	pt. 2.	298-B.	Opacity in 5 minutes. +	Opacity at once. +	The same.
	3.	pt. 3.	299.	The same. +	The same. +	The same.
	4.	pt. 5.	300.	The same. +	The same. +	The same.
	5.	pt. 6.	301.	The same. +	The same. +	The same.
Controls.	6.	Extract from wood.		No opacity. Liquid transparent even after 3 hours.		The same.
	7.	Horse serum.		The same.	The same.	The same.
	8.	Sheep serum.		The same.	The same.	Opacity in 3 minutes
	9.	Human serum.		Opacity in 3 minutes +	Distinct opacity at once. +	Liquid transparent even after 3 hours.
	10.	Physiological solution of salt (0.85%)		No opacity even after three hours.		

Note: A positive reaction of precipitation (opacity) is indicated by the mark +.

19 Translator's Note: University not named.

takes on a greenish-bluish color upon the addition of hydrogen peroxide.

The third portion of scrapings was used for a Teichmann test for the presence of blood. For this the scrapings were thoroughly soaked in distilled water. The extracts thus obtained were then dried on glass slides at 60° C. Small particles of table salt were placed on the stains thus produced on the slides and cover-glasses placed on them. Glacial acetic acid was caused to flow beneath the cover glasses. After one minute's activity of the acid at room temperature the preparations were heated over a spirit lamp until the appearance of bubbles, and then, after cooling, were examined under the microscope with magnification 400 times. With this method of examination, in the event of the presence of blood, Teichmann crystals are obtained which dissolve in ammonia and in strong sulfuric acid, and which do not dissolve in water, ethylether or chloroform.

The fourth portion of scrapings was used for spectroscopic examination. For this the scrapings were soaked at 38° C. in a saturated (at room temperature) water solution of borax. The solution thus obtained was examined with a spectroscope. With such an examination of extracts from stains containing blood, two more or less clear absorption bands are normally produced in the yellow and green fields of the spectrum.

The fifth portion of scrapings was soaked in a physiological solution of table salt and Pagin's [Paccini's?] fluid. The liquid obtained after soaking the scrapings was examined under a microscope with magnification 350 times, first without staining, and then stained with hematoxylin and eosin.

The sixth portion of scrapings was used for making a Uhlenhuth biological test for the presence of human blood. For this the scrapings were thoroughly soaked in a 0.8% water solution of table salt, and the extracts thus obtained were filtered. The completely transparent filtrates were poured into narrow test tubes in quantities from 2.0 to 4.0 cc. and to each of the filters [sic] there was added 0.2 cc. of Uhlenhuth reactive serum. In the event of the presence of blood, or of a liquid containing human albumin, the mixture in the test tube quickly becomes opaque and after a while flakes appear in them, settling to the bottom of the test tubes.

Results of the analysis. Upon examination of the stain for the presence of blood, the Van Deen and Teichmann tests gave a positive result.

Upon spectroscopic examination of the extracts from the given stain, two fairly clear absorption bands were produced in the yellow and green fields of the spectrum. Upon microscopic examination of the scrapings from the given stain an insignificant quantity of deformed red blood corpuscles were found, for the most part having become colorless.

The Uhlenhuth biological test (titer 1:1000 and 1:2000) gave a positive result.

Opinion. On the basis of the microscopic and spectroscopic examinations and the chemical test for Uhlenhuth's reaction, it must be concluded that on one side of the excised piece there are unquestionable traces of blood, which must be accepted as human since the Uhlenhuth reaction was positive.

It is demonstrated that between 17 and 22 July 1918, when Ipatiev renewed the interrupted possession of his house, a murder occurred in it.

This did not occur on the upper floor, where the Imperial Family lived: there is not even a hint that violence was employed there, against anyone.

The bloody carnage took place in one of the rooms of the lower, basement, floor.

The selection alone of this room speaks for itself: the murder was strictly premeditated.

From it there is no escape: behind it there is a deep store-room without exit; its only window, with two sashes, is covered on the outside with a thick iron grating. It is deeply sunk in the ground and completely concealed from the outside by a high fence. This room is, in full degree, a torture-chamber.

The murder was perpetrated with revolvers and bayonets.

More than 30 shots were fired, because it cannot be assumed that all of the blows were trans-piercing and that no bullets remained in the bodies of the victims.

Several people were murdered, because it cannot be supposed that one person could change his position in the room to such an extent and submit to so many blows.

Some of the victims were, before death, in positions along the east and south walls, others were nearer to the center of the room. Several were hit while they were already lying on the floor.

If the Imperial Family and those living with them were murdered here, there is no doubt that they were lured here from their living quarters by some false pretext.

Our ancient law calls such murders "foul."

CHAPTER NINETEEN

[pp. 192-194]

Effects of the Imperial Family Discovered in Ekaterinburg and
Its Environs.

Who was murdered in the Ipatiev House?

At the same time that the court investigator, Nametkin, went there, a rumor was started to the effect that the Imperial Family had been taken away, rescued, and that in order to conceal their deliverance other people had been shot instead.

The valet, Chemodurov, testified at the investigation: "From the effects of the Tsar I packed and brought the following to Ekaterinburg: one dozen day shirts, 1½ dozen night shirts, 1½ dozen silk body shirts, 3 dozen socks, about 150-200 handkerchiefs, 1 dozen sheets, 2 dozen pillow slips, 3 terry-cloth sheets, 12 face towels and 12 towels of Yaroslav linen: in the line of clothing, four khaki shirts, 3 tunics, 1 overcoat of officer's cloth, 1 overcoat of common soldier's cloth, 1 short coat of Romanov sheepskin, five sharovary [wide trousers], 1 grey cloak, 6 service caps, 1 [civilian] cap: in the line of footwear, seven pairs of kid and box-calf boots."

What happened to all these things?

It would be natural to suppose that all such things were taken away by people interested in helping the family.

Was this so?

Inexorable facts say no.

Many medicines and various articles for treatment of the Tsarevich were found in the Ipatiev House. The boy was ill the whole time he was there. Why did they not take, why abandon, the things he needed the most?

More than 60 icons belonging to the Imperial Family were found in the Ipatiev House. Among them were:

1. A holy picture of the Mother of God with the Tsarina's inscription on it: "Blessing to our dear Olga from Papa and Mama. Keep safe November 3, 1912."

2. A holy picture of the Mother of God with the Tsarina's inscription: "Blessing to dear Tatiana, January 12, 1918, Tobolsk, Papa and Mama." This was her parents' last gift to Tatiana Nicholayevna, on her angel's day.

3. Two identical holy pictures of the Mother of God with the Tsarina's inscriptions. On one: "Keep and preserve T. Mama. Christmas tree 1917. Tobolsk." On the other: "Keep and preserve A. Mama. Christmas tree 1917. Tobolsk." These were their mother's last Christmas tree gifts to Tatiana Nicholayevna and Anastasia Nicholayevna.

4. Icons of Rasputin with his inscriptions.

"The Stairway," "On the Endurance of Sorrow," "Prayers," "The Bible", "Guide to Prayer for Those Making Preparation for Holy Communion," "Favors of the Mother of God," "Prayerbook," "Letters on the Christian Life," "The Life and Miracles of the Holy Saint Simeon Verkhotursky," "The Life of Our Holy Father Seraphim Sarovsky," "The Acathistus of the Mother of God," "The Twelve Apostles," "My Life in Christ," "Comfort in the Death of Loved Ones," "Collection of Devout Readings," "Conversations on the Sufferings of Philaret," "The Canon of the Great Andrei Kritsky," "A Collection of Divine Services, Prayers and Hymns"—these are the books of the Tsarina and Tatiana Nicholayevna which were left in the Ipatiev House. They contained their whole moral outlook, their whole soul.

Many things were stolen by the guards. Among these were the diary of the Tsarevich and his favorite dog, a spaniel called Joy.

Scorched remnants of clothing and linen, buttons, needles, thread, articles of feminine handwork, the remains of various handbags, purses, cases and all kinds of brushes and similar items—that is what had been stuffed into the stoves of the Ipatiev House.

And in the *rubbish pit* were found:

1. An officers' cockade and ribbon of St. George. Chemodurov testified: "The ribbon of St. George was taken from the Emperor's overcoat. The Emperor never parted with this overcoat and always went about in it."

2. A holy picture of Saint Seraphim Sarovsky and a holy picture

of Saint Simeon Verkhotursky, which belonged to the Tsarina.

3. A small portrait frame and a small pendant frame with the remains of destroyed photographs: portraits of the parents and brother of the Tsarina.

4. A very much disfigured ikon with the Tsarina's inscription: "Keep and preserve. Mama. 1917. Tobolsk." This was his mother's last Christmas tree gift to her beloved son. The ikon had hung at his bed in Ekaterinburg.

Items of value required for household purposes had been stolen.

In April, 1919 there was a secret Bolshevik organization operating in the Admiral's territory. It was exposed.

A participant in the organization, a red officer, Loginov,[20] testified in my presence, in reply to a question, that in November, 1918 he had gone to Moscow on organization business. There was also a woman doctor with him, Golubeva, director of a Bolshevik hospital train, and her civilian husband who was a worker of some kind.

In Moscow they all stayed in one apartment. When he went to bed Loginov, not having a pillow, asked Golubeva for one of hers. "She said that she could not give me a pillow because there were two people in her party, herself and her husband. In addition, she said, one of the pillows was 'historic'. Her words intrigued me and I asked her to explain. Then she told me that the pillow she called historic had been given to her by Goloshchekin from a collection of things that had belonged to the Imperial Family. Golubeva also told me that she had, in addition, some boots, likewise given to her by Goloshchekin, that had been among the Imperial possessions. Golubeva did not tell me in detail where, when and under what circumstances she had obtained these things from Goloshchekin. She only said that it was very difficult to get any of the Imperial belongings from Goloshchekin, that he gave them only 'for patronage'. Golubeva's story inspired and now inspires my full belief. Golubeva is a well-known Bolshevik, an active worker. Her position would certainly make it appropriate for her to receive something from the Imperial belongings from Goloshchekin."

Things of no material value, but which were most treasured by the family, had been destroyed or scorned and tossed aside.

Very nearly the most treasured object of the Empress was her ikon of the Feodorov Mother of God. This was found in the Ipatiev House. Its diamonds had been removed.

Chemodurov states: "The Empress never went anywhere without this ikon. To take this ikon away from the Empress would be the same as taking her life."

At the conclusion of this book there is a list of those effects of the Imperial Family which were left in the Ipatiev House and which were found by various people.

Photograph No. 56 shows the diary of the Tsarevich.

Photograph No. 57 shows a book belonging to Olga Nicholayevna with a poem inserted in it, written in her own hand, and with an inscription of the Tsarina.

Photographs Nos. 58-59 show holy pictures belonging to the Imperial Family.

Photographs Nos. 60-61 show holy pictures given to them by Rasputin, with his inscriptions.

Photographs Nos. 62-63 show various effects of the Imperial Family taken from various people. Among them are an umbrella of the Empress, toys of the Tsarevich.

CHAPTER TWENTY

1. [pp. 194-196]

The Mine in the Tract of the Four Brothers.

I NOW LEAVE THE IPATIEV HOUSE to look elsewhere for an explanation of the bloody tragedy which its basement concealed.

Twenty versts [13.2538 miles] [21] from Ekaterinburg, on the shore of Lake Isetsk, there was a small village, Koptyaki, with several dozen cottages. Engulfed in the primeval remoteness of the Ural backwoods, it was almost concealed from human eyes by an ancient pine forest. And this circumstance, indeed, determined the way of life of this out-of-the-way village. Fishing and hay-mowing—these were its interests in the summer time. Government employees of modest means went there to their dachas in the summer, from Ekaterinburg, but they used peasant cottages and did not spoil the general tenor of life.

The road which leads there from Ekaterinburg passes through Verkh-Isetsk, which is almost a suburb of the city.

Beyond Verkh-Isetsk the road first passes a little way through meadow land, then enters the forest through which it proceeds without interruption to Koptyaki itself.

Near Verkh-Isetsk the road is crossed by the railroad line to Perm. This is grade-crossing No. 803, at which there is a house for the guard.

Further on towards Koptyaki, 9 versts from the village, the road is crossed by the "mining-plant line". This is crossing No. 184, which also has a house for the guard.

Photograph No. 64 shows a view of this crossing.

Approximately 4½ versts from Koptyaki there are two old pine stumps quite close to the road. According to legend there were at one time four pine trees growing from them. The local people call them the "Four Brothers." This name has been applied to the entire tract characterized by this landmark.

These two stumps are shown in Photograph No. 65.

In this remote tract, west of the road, there is an old mine, 4 versts from Koptyaki. At one time iron ore was obtained there by open pit and shaft mining. This was long ago. The mine was abandoned for many years, during which its appearance greatly changed. The open workings had become a lake, the shafts had caved in and were overgrown with trees and grass.

Photographs Nos. 66-68 show views of these places.

Only one shaft remained in good condition and was called "open".

In Photograph No. 69 it is shown as it looked when I found it; in Photograph No. 70 as it looked after my excavations.

The walls of the shaft were faced with firm planks. An interior wall of similar planks divided it in two: one side was used for descent underground and for removal of ore, the other for pumping out water.

In Photograph No. 70 a sentry is standing near the former.

The depth of the shaft is 5 sazhenes, 7 vershoks [36 feet, ¼ inch]. It is always flooded with water; the ice at the bottom almost never melts.

When the shaft was being worked and clay thrown out, a large, clay-surfaced area was created. This area surrounds the shaft on almost every side and is devoid of growth.

An old birch tree grows near this clay-surfaced area.

Five forest trails lead to the mine from the main, Koptyaki, road. They all converge at the open shaft. There are so many because at one time they were used to move ore from various shafts to the Koptyaki road. These trails are obscure and abandoned; in the summer time they are overgrown with high grass.

In the very center of one of these trails, which is the closest of all to the Four Brothers, there is a pit. Ore was sought here. The trail passes around this pit on both sides.

This area is shown in Photograph No. 71.

Between grade crossing No. 184 and the described mine there are other mines along the Koptyaki road.

They are nearer to Ekaterinburg. It is much easier to get to them because the Koptyaki road is bad for driving in places.

But none of them has those other advantages which distinguish
the mine in the tract of the Four Brothers. The latter is completely
hidden from outside view by dense growth of young forest. Nowhere else is there such a convenient, clay-surfaced area, devoid of
growth, with a deep shaft adjacent.

2. [pp. 196-199]

17-18 July at the Mine.

In the early morning of July 17, 1918 the quiet life of Koptyaki,
and the peacefulness of the remote mine, were broken by a series of
the most mysterious occurrences.

On this early morning Nastasya Zykova had to go to Ekaterinburg.
She went with her son, Nicholas, and his wife, Maria. Nastasya
was transporting fish for sale and Nicholas had been called up by
the Red Army.

The sun had not yet risen. It was early morning dawn. Within
the ancient pine forest the darkness of night remained.

When the Zykovs passed the mine and were approaching the
Four Brothers, a cortege of some kind appeared coming towards
them. There were wagons and mounted and foot personnel of the
Red Army. As soon as the Zykovs were seen, two horsemen immediately rode up to them.

Here is the graphic testimony of Nastasya Zykova: [22] "Two horsemen rode to meet us. One was in sailor's uniform and I recognized
him readily. It was the sailor Vaganov, from Verkh-Isetsk. The other was in soldier's uniform: in a soldier's overcoat and military cap.
The horsemen came towards us quickly: Vaganov leading, the
soldier behind him. As soon as they came up to us, Vaganov
shouted: 'Turn back!' He took out his revolver and held it over
my head. We turned our horses quickly, sharply. Our wagon nearly
turned over. They pranced about us and Vaganov shouted: 'Don't
look back g. v...... m...... I'll shoot!" Our horse raced off with
all the spirit that was in him. They escorted us, Vaganov all the
while keeping his revolver over my head and crying: 'Don't look
back, citizens, g...... v...... m......!' In this fashion we raced
to the place beyond which lies Big Meadow. They continued with
us for about a half verst, or three quarters of a verst, and then fell
back. We did not look back, of course, after they told us I
did not understand what it was all about, but it appeared to me that
troops were coming. We returned to Koptyaki and told the people

what we had seen. I don't know what happened after that."

The Zykovs were greatly frightened. They were met on the road by the peasant, Zvorygin [23] who, it happened, was going to town after them: "We had gone about two versts from Koptyaki, and Nicholas Zykov with his mother and his wife came racing to meet us. He shouted: 'Hey, Uncle Feodor, don't go on! They chased me off there. A fellow threatened me with a revolver and shouted: 'Don't look back!' "

In a fright the Zykovs raced to the village and raised a great commotion. Here is the testimony of the peasant, Alferov: [24] "On Wednesday morning early, after St. Peter's Day, I was on the street. I intended to go out to the mowing. I looked and saw Nicholas Zykov going down the street in a wagon with his mother and his wife. He was riding along shouting and waving his hand: 'Run! Get out of Koptyaki! They are bringing weapons out there. Troops are coming.' Here he stopped his horse. At his word people ran out. We began to question Nicholas as to what he was talking about. He began to tell us and explained: 'We had just passed Big Meadow and were coming to the Four Brothers, when three horsemen came towards us. They shouted: 'Turn back! Turn back!' I began to turn the wagon and the women looked back. One of the riders shouted: 'Don't look back!' And there, on the road, they are moving weapons.' They were driving the horse hard, and those fellows even escorted them a way along the road, never permitting them to look back. At this point we did not know what to think."

At this time a Siberian army was moving on Ekaterinburg and threatened the Bolshevik occupation. This was known in Koptyaki and the people were lying low, awaiting the outcome.

At the same time the muzhiks were much concerned because their economic interests were involved.

Here is the testimony of the peasant, Shveikin: "We muzhiks became disturbed. We were all needed at the mowing, and now troops were coming. Troops were coming. That meant there would be a battle."

They [the villagers] decided to find out just what was happening on the Koptyaki road and sent the peasants Shveikin, Papin, Zubritsky and the officer, Sheremetevsky, who was hiding in Koptyaki, to investigate.[25]

They went off and were mystified: all was quiet in the forest and the Koptyaki road was deserted.

Condemning the Zykovs for their "ranting", the investigators were going past the mine when they heard from there the unusual sound of many horses neighing. At this moment they came to the first turn-off trail after the Four Brothers, leading to the mine.[26] They were amazed by the trail's appearance.

Sheremetevsky and Papin testify:

Sheremetevsky: "This trail, until then difficult to discern and overgrown with grass, as is normally the case with abandoned, unused forest trails, was at that moment trampled down. It was quite evident from its appearance that some sort of vehicles had passed by there, taking this turn-off to the mine from the Koptyaki road."

Papin: "The grass was all quite trampled down along it, and in some places the small trees were bent over."

They were about to go down the trail towards the mine when a Red Army soldier came out armed with a rifle, two revolvers, a sabre and grenades. He told the investigators that there was going to be training in bomb-throwing at the mine and ordered them to leave.

From that moment all movement was stopped on the Koptyaki road, and the mine was shut off with barriers.

But human necessities had their effect nevertheless. Many people needed to go from Koptyaki to Ekaterinburg and back. As a result it was possible to precisely determine the time and place at which the road was closed.

Movement along the Koptyaki road was stopped in the early morning of July 17. It was renewed at 6 o'clock in the morning of July 19.

The barrier on the Koptyaki side was approximately one verst from the village.

The barrier on the Ekaterinburg side was near grade-crossing No. 184.

Photograph No. 72 shows a view of this place.

During all of this time the explosion of grenades could be heard at the mine.

The Bolsheviks fled from Ekaterinburg on July 25.

On July 27 the peasants, Papin and Michael Alferov, went to the city on business. They went to Verkh-Isetsk and reported the mysterious shutting off of the mine to the military authorities there.

When they went back, that day, to Koptyaki they were overcome with curiosity to see what had happened at the mine. Coming to the turn-off mentioned above they left their horses and followed this turn-off, on foot, to the mine. But they had scarcely arrived there when they were seized by an unaccountable fear.

Papin testifies: "For some reason we became terrified. We decided to get some people together in the proper manner and come. So at this time we left without touching anything."

On the morning of July 28 seven peasants from Koptyaki: Nicholas Papin, Michael Babinov, Michael Alferov, Paul Alferov, Jacob Alferov, Nicholas Logunov and Alexander Logunov set out for the mine.[27] They went there on foot by the trail nearest to Koptyaki.[28] They examined the mine carefully and made some valuable discoveries.

They showed extreme care and in no way disturbed the condition of the turn-off where the meeting had occurred between the Red Army soldier and the investigators.

The report made by the peasants was not ignored in Verkh-Isetsk. In the evening of July 28 the local forester, Rednikov, came to the mine with the peasants: Nicholas Bozhov, Alexander Zudikhin, Ivan Zubritsky and Nicholas Tetenev.[29]

On July 28 and 29 they thoroughly examined both the trail to the mine which is closest to the Four Brothers, and the mine itself.

On July 30 the court investigator, Nametkin, went there. He was accompanied by Doctor Derevenko, the valet Chemodurov and many officers. Several valuable discoveries were made.

Nametkin's attention was attracted by the open shaft. It was examined under the direction of assistant prosecutor Magnitsky.

I examined the mine and the area surrounding it from May 23 to June 17, 1919.

When I reported the results of the investigation to Admiral Kolchak he ordered excavations to be made. They were begun on June 6 and interrupted on July 10.

Photographs Nos. 73-74 show the nature of this work.

CHAPTER TWENTY-ONE

[pp. 199-206]

A Motor-Truck at the Mine.—Sulphuric Acid, Gasoline.

What happened, then, at the mine during the period July 17-19, 1918?

The watchman at grade-crossing No. 184, Jacob Lobukhin,[30] testified: "One night last summer during hay-mowing time (I don't remember the month or the date), while I and my family were sleeping, I was awakened by the noise of an automobile. This was surprising because such a thing had never happened before—that an automobile should pass my house—and at night at that. I looked out of the window and saw a motor-truck going along the road to Koptyaki. I did not see what was in it. I did not notice that at all. I only noticed that four men with rifles were sitting in it, apparently in military uniform. This was at dawn. . . . Then day came. People going towards Koptyaki came back and said that passage to Koptyaki was not permitted. I cannot say exactly where the barrier was, but the people said that, from my crossing, it was beyond the log road, or on it. Passage was prohibited for from three to four days."

Movement along the Koptyaki road was stopped in the early morning of July 17. There is no doubt that the mysterious motor-truck went from Ekaterinburg towards Koptyaki under cover of night on July 17.

It did not go all the way to Koptyaki and was concealed somewhere in the woods. Where was it?

Its destination was the mine in the tract of the Four Brothers. It went there by the same turn-off trail on which the meeting took place between the Red Army soldier and the investigators,[31] and went right on to the open shaft.

The investigators came upon this trail almost at the same time as the truck arrived. Here is the testimony of Shveikin: "I can say very positively that the tracks were quite pronounced, both along the Koptyaki road and along the turn-off from the Koptyaki road on which the Red Army soldier had approached us. The tracks from the Koptyaki road thus went also along this turn-off. They were very noticeable along the turn-off. It was evident that someone had just recently passed, right before us. I thus affirm that these were the tracks of an automobile; they were very pronounced, both wide and deep, and the grass was trampled down all along the turn-off."

Other peasants who came to the mine on July 28 also saw the automobile tracks. Here is the testimony of Michael Babinov: "There were tracks at the mine. They, these same tracks, were on the trail which leads here from the Four Brothers. I know this trail very well. And now I say to you positively that something very heavy went over this trail, and the grass along it was all completely trampled. There were wheel tracks of some sort of vehicle right in the ruts of the road, but there were automobile tracks in addition. These tracks were near the ruts, but wider. Furthermore, I examined these tracks more thoroughly where the automobile had turned. It came here, to the open shaft, along the trail and turned around right on the grass plot opposite the shaft. It was at this turn that I noticed its tracks."

On the same day the forester, Rednikov, was at the mine with other peasants. They testified:

Rednikov: "I then turned special attention to the condition of the tracks. It was quite clearly evident that automobiles had come here. I cannot say whether one automobile came here, or more than one, but automobile tracks were clearly visible on the trail. The first trail from the Four Brothers had automobile tracks—here, the same one marked on the drawing you have shown me. Its tracks here were quite clear. A heavy automobile passed here, made heavy tracks, broke and twisted many young trees along the road. . . . The automobile tracks led right to the open shaft and there ended."

Zubritsky: "This path (the first turn-off to the mine from the Four Brothers) was heavily trampled, the small trees were broken. It was plain to see that a heavy automobile had passed here and made heavy tracks along this trail. These tracks went right to the open shaft which I am looking at now on the photograph."

I won't exhaust the reader's attention: the testimony of the other peasants is identical.

On July 30 the court investigator for important cases, Nametkin, went to the mine with some officers, students of the Academy of the General Staff.

I do not want to cast reflections upon anyone, but everybody, indeed, is entitled to expect that a court investigator would give, in his report, a clear picture of the condition of the mine and of all tracks that were there; and that I would present all this in the words of the original report.

There is not a word about them.

An extremely distressing blunder was made. The court investigator and the officers did not follow the example of the peasants. Going to the mine from Ekaterinburg, they did not follow in the tracks of reason, but in those of fantasy, their own and others'. Instead of following the tracks of the automobile, going from the city by way of the dirt road, they went by railroad, and precisely from the opposite direction: from Koptyaki.

The Imperial Family was murdered and the corpses hidden in the bottom of the open shaft in the tract of the Four Brothers. The Imperial Family was rescued. Some other people were murdered and their corpses were hidden in this shaft.

The open shaft conceals the whole solution of the riddle. To resolve it is not difficult. It is only necessary to lower oneself to the bottom of the shaft.

So it was decided in Ekaterinburg. Therefore Nametkin and the officers got on the train in Ekaterinburg, went by the mine-plant line to the station of Iset, from there to Koptyaki and from Koptyaki to the mine along the turn-off trail nearest to Koptyaki.[32]

There were no corpses at the bottom of the shaft. Energies quickly flagged. The court investigator went off to the city after remaining at the mine for an hour and a half.

A distorted idea of the appearance of the place was obtained. The trail which the motor-truck took to the mine was lost for Nametkin.

The peasants took a dim view of the educated people and of the work of the investigator. Michael Alferov testified: "The commission went everywhere here, but it was obvious that they had no sense. They did not look at the tracks, and trampled what there were."

Sergeyev shared the mistake of Nametkin and did not once go to the mine.

I went there on foot from the Ipatiev House. An annoying year had passed. But previous experience had taught me to be cautious. They had trampled, but perhaps they had not yet trampled everything.

I stated above that in the center of the fateful road (number 1) by which the motor-truck went to the mine there was a hole in which a search for ore had been made. (Photograph No. 71).

This place riveted my attention.

It would be difficult for an automobile to pass there. The woods interfered. The automobile would have to stay close to the hole and might fall in.

And it did fall in. This is slightly noticeable in the photograph.

A heavy plank was lying on the bottom of the hole. On it there were strange impressions: some parts of a very heavy object had pressed against the plank and left deep marks.

On the side of the road I found three planks in the woods and the cavity made by a fourth. Anyone acquainted with life in the woods knows that a plank lying for many years sinks gradually into the ground, and that the mark of its resting place remains for a long time. It was from here that the plank in the hole had been taken.

When and why did they take it there?

The forester, Rednikov, and the peasants testified:

Rednikov: ". . . the automobile slid near the hole while passing it on the right side going towards the mine. A plank lay on the bottom of the hole, at one end, where the slide occurred."

Bozhov: "There is a hole in this road, in the middle of it, more than half way to the mine. I remember it. A plank lay on the bottom. Some kind of vehicle had slipped along the edge of this hole."

Tetenev: "We went there by the first turn-off leading to the mine from the Four Brothers. It was quite plain to see that automobiles had passed along this turn-off and trampled the road there right up to the open shaft. And at one point the wheel of an automobile had slipped. This was near the hole which is right on this turn-off. The automobile was skirting the hole and since there was little room for it to pass it had fallen in with one wheel. The slide was clearly visible. I see the photograph of this hole which you have shown me. That is the one I am talking about."

Near the point where the slide occurred I found a thick rope, right on the road. It was very dirty and soaked with some kind of petroleum. After a year it still soiled the hands and made them oily.

Photograph No. 75 shows its appearance.

Why was a rope left there? By accident?

The motor-truck left the mine on July 19, during the night.

The grade-crossing guard, Lobukhin, and his son, Vasili, saw it pass over the crossing towards the city. Beyond the crossing it got stuck in a swamp. It was pulled out and a ramp made for it.

Photograph No. 76 shows a view of this place.

Here is the testimony of Vasili Lobukhin: [33] "About 12 o'clock at night a motor truck passed along the road from Koptyaki and went over our grade-crossing; it must have been the same one which had come at night from the city. . . . There were 10-12 wagons with it, and apparently several dray-carts. The motor-truck, wagons and carts passed towards the city directly from our crossing. The automobile got stuck there, in a ravine. One of the men took a board from our fence and put a ramp there."

This automobile could have passed through Verkh-Isetsk only on the morning of July 19. And so it did. It was seen at that time.

How did it look?

The witnesses Nicholas and Alexandra Zubritsky testified:

Zubritsky: "One of the left wheels, I don't remember which, was apparently damaged: it was wound around with ropes."

Zubritskaya: "Its left rear wheel was wound around with a thick rope: apparently the tire had been damaged. The motor-truck stopped after passing a little way. Some people got out and began to retie the wheel which had been tied with rope."

No, the rope at the mine was not an accident.

Did Nastasya Zykova see the motor-truck when it was going to the mine?

I believe that it was more than the darkness of night which prevented her from telling the whole truth to the court investigator.

Nastasya was being sly. I permitted her this because I was seeking the truth by legal means.

She recognized the sailor, Vaganov, but not the other man. I am convinced that she also knew the other man, but named only Vaganov because he was dead at the time she was questioned. The "pride and joy of the revolution" did not escape from Ekaterinburg and hid himself in his cellar. Some Verkh-Isetsk workers found him there and killed him on the spot.

At home in Koptyaki Nastasya was more frank. After she had raced back to Koptyaki the whole village heard her. The peasant Shveikin testifies: "When Nastasya came she alarmed the entire population. Troops were coming. She said that her party encountered troops at the Four Brothers. They had appeared just as her party approached that point. The troops, she said, were coming and bringing something behind them in an automobile. Thus she spoke also of an automobile . . . Nastasya told us all this on the street, in the presence of all those gathered around."

Where did the motor-truck come from on its way to the mine?

All automobiles in Ekaterinburg had been appropriated by the Bolsheviks. It could have come only from the Soviet garage.

The garage had been placed under special direction. The brothers Peter and Alexander Leonov were working there, out of necessity. During the night, on July 17, the former was on duty in the office and the latter was assisting him.

The Leonovs [34] testified that late at night on July 16 a motor-truck was dispatched to the building of the Cheka. They sent the chauffeur, Nikiforov, back and took the automobile to the Ipatiev House. It was returned in the morning of July 19.

Here is how the Leonov brothers describe its appearance:

Peter: "The entire platform of the truck was stained with blood. It was apparent that the platform had been washed and swept with a broom. But the blood, nevertheless, was clearly visible on the floor of the platform."

Alexander: "I remember very well that the platform had a large, washed, bloodstain."

The peasants found many small bonfires at the mine. They had been lighted for smoke and served to protect the horses from mosquitoes and gadflies.

One of these locations appears in Photograph No. 77.

The testimony of Zudikhin: "It was apparent that horses had been tied here; the trees were broken and chewed."

The testimony of Zubritsky: "It also looked as if horses had been tied here, and that they had dug up the earth with their hooves. It seemed to me at the time that a smudge had been lit near a small pine here to protect them from mosquitoes."

Near one of these spots I found some small pine boards. They had been cut off of a very thick pine board and were charred. The locality presented a clear picture: there was damp forest all about; it was necessary to make a smudge as quickly as possible; some small pieces had been cut from a large pine board and used for kindling.

Where did this board come from?

The Leonov brothers, describing the blood-stained truck upon its return from the mine, testify that its platform was damaged: pieces had been hacked from the edges of the planks.

The Ural gadfly is strong! Communism does not teach care of the goods of others!

The small pine boards which I found are shown in Photograph No. 75.

Small boards of another kind were found near the small bonfires where the smudge was made.

Ends of new rope were scattered in various areas of the mine, principally near the open shaft.

The peasants and the forester, Rednikov, state their significance categorically.

Gabriel Alferov: "Not far from the trail opposite the shaft, not at all far from the trail leading to the shaft, I saw several small boards from a broken box. It was easily seen that these boards were from a box. They were white and not planed, as boxes usually are . . . The bit of rope was new, cut. One end of it was passed through a loop, and it was the thickness of a little finger. It was plain to see that this was binding from the box."

Zubritsky: "Small, thin boards were scattered in this smudge, so, approximately, a half inch, and it was plain to see that they were from a box. There was also some cut, new binding from a box, the thickness of a little finger. There were several pieces of this and they had bends in them from the corners of the box.

Rednikov: "I assure you categorically, positively, that cuttings of rope binding from a box were scattered near the shaft. The rope was of the thickness of a little finger, absolutely new, and it was completely clear that this was binding from a box: it retained the characteristic bends from passing around the corners of the box. There was a loop in one end of it, such as there is in binding. It had not been untied, but cut or hacked, as was clearly to be seen from its appearance."

What was brought to the mine in these boxes?

On July 17, 1918 an employee of the commissariat of supply, Zimin, appeared in the chemist shop of the "Russian Company," in Ekaterinburg and in the name of the oblast commissar, Voikov,[35] presented a written requisition to the manager, Metsner:

"I instruct you, without delay or excuses, to deliver to the bearer of this five pouds of sulphuric acid from your supply.

Obl. Commissar of Supply Voikov."

The acid was delivered to Zimin at that time, and he signed a receipt indicating its delivery at Voikov's personal order.

Late in the evening of the same day Zimin came to the shop again and presented a second order from Voikov:

"I instruct you to deliver to the bearer of this three additional containers of Japanese sulphuric acid.

Obl. Commissar of Supply Voikov."

This acid was also delivered to Zimin upon his receipt indicating delivery pursuant to the same order.

In all, 11 pouds and 4 pounds [358.28428 English pounds] of acid were delivered. The money for this was paid to the shop on July 18, in the amount of 196 roubles and 50 kopecks.

Photograph No. 78 shows Voikov's orders.

Late in the evening of July 17, and during the day on July 18, this acid was brought to the mine in wooden boxes by personnel of the Red Army and by one of the employees of the commissariat of supply.

During the period that the mine was blocked off a large quantity of gasoline was also brought there.

It was brought in motor-trucks. These did not go farther than grade crossing No. 184, where they remained. The gasoline was brought from the grade crossing to the mine by horses.

On July 18 the engineer, Kotenev,[36] went from the city towards Koptyaki. He was not allowed to go beyond the grade crossing. He saw a can of gasoline: "A metal gasoline drum stood on the motor-truck. I affirm that this was, indeed, a gasoline drum. Gasoline is always put in such drums. . . . I can tell you exactly the quantity of gasoline which the drum which was on the motor-truck should contain. It was a 10–11 poud drum."

Vasili Lobukhin stated: "On July 18, a motor-truck, which must have started out (from Ekaterinburg) in the early morning, passed at about 7 o'clock and went along the Koptyaki road, but stopped about 150 sazhenes [1,050 feet] from our grade crossing. I did not see very well just what was on it. It looked to me like there were drums or boxes on it. After dinner still another motor-truck passed and stopped at the same place. This time I saw clearly that in this motor-truck they were carrying gasoline in drums. I took a mind to ask for some gasoline, got a bottle and went to the place where these two motor-trucks were standing on the Koptyaki road; and this time I did see clearly what was on the first truck, the one that came first. On the second there were about three drums of gasoline, or maybe two. The drums were all of metal. There were about five people near the two trucks. . . . I asked them to pour me out a little gasoline. They gave me a bottle."

Many people saw these men moving gasoline. Evaluating the testimony of the witnesses, I say that 40 pouds [1,289.72 pounds], at the very least, were brought to the mine.

Rednikov and the peasants, investigating the shaft on July 28, and the court investigator, Nametkin, on July 30, found that the ice had been broken in its large well and completely destroyed in the small one.

Later I established by examination of the shaft that the bottom of the small well had, in addition, been spread with clay from the adjacent area to the depth of 12 vershoks [21 inches].

The peasants found the remnants of a large bonfire in this area, and another a little further off, near an old birch.

The remnants of these bonfires remained until I came. The first is seen in Photograph No. 79, the second in Photograph No. 80.

What did the motor-truck bring to the mine during the night, on July 17?

What was burned in the two large bonfires?

What was hidden in the bottom of the shaft?

Why were sulphuric acid and gasoline brought there?

The best answer to all of these questions is given by the objects found in the mine.

CHAPTER TWENTY-TWO

[pp. 206-218]

Effects of the Imperial Family Found at the Mine.——
Conclusions.

The following were found at the mine in the tract of the Four
Brothers:[37]

1. *A miniature of St. Nicholas the Miracle-Worker.*

2. *A miniature of Bishops Guri, Aviv and Samon.*

3. *A miniature of the Savior.*
These are shown in Photograph No. 81.
The miniatures are of excellent workmanship. Heavy blows have
been inflicted on their faces.
They were padded at the back so they could be worn on the
breast. The padding of the third miniature was preserved in good
condition.
Tegleva and Ersberg stated that these miniatures belonged to the
children; the one representing Nicholas the Miracle-Worker to Olga
Nicholayevna. Ordinarily these miniatures hung at their beds. The
children wore them when travelling.

4. *30 pieces of enamel from these miniatures.*

5. *Three pieces of metal coating from one miniature.*
These are shown in Photograph No. 82.
There is similar coating on the three miniatures described above,
but these pieces were of a different size and belonged to a fourth

176

miniature.

They had been slightly sooted by fire.

6. *A silver frame from a miniature.*

This is shown in Photograph No. 83.

Because of its size this frame could not have belonged to any of the three miniatures described above, and it could not have been the source of the three mentioned pieces of metal coating. It belonged to a fifth miniature.

Tegleva and Ersberg testified that one of the Empress' miniatures had been in this frame.

The frame was slightly damaged by fire.

7. *Two pieces of zinc from a miniature.*

Tutelberg testified: "I see two zinc fragments with traces of paint. I know that Her Majesty possessed such small, simple miniatures of zinc."

8. *Pieces of white wax, pieces of red wax and part of a stearin candle.*

Nametkin found white wax and stearin candles in the Ipatiev House. Candles of red wax were among the effects of the Imperial Family found in the possession of the guard, Ivan Starkov.

The valet, Volkov, testified: "Their household articles at Tobolsk included red wax candles. They had acquired such candles from the monastery and the cathedral."

9. *A portrait frame.*

This is shown in Photograph No. 84.

It is made of real leather, lined with silk. It bears the mark of "Edward Akkerman, Berlin."

Torn pieces of photograph were found with it. It is impossible to make out the subject.

The witnesses Gilliard, Gibbs, Tegleva, Ersberg, and Zanotti testified that the Imperial Family had many such frames. They us ually took these with them when they travelled.

Tutelberg testified that the Tsar had a portrait of the Tsarina in such a frame.

10. *A military badge.*

This is shown in Photograph No. 85.

This badge was made of silver, plated with gold. One side is covered with white and dark orange enamel.

On the reverse side there is an engraving: "1803 $\frac{17}{V}$ 1903."

The witnesses testified as follows:

Tegleva: "This badge belonged to the Tsarina."

Ersberg: The badge is undoubtedly the Tsarina's. She wore it on a bracelet."

Tutelberg: "This badge belongs to Her Majesty. It was presented to Her Majesty by Orlov, commander of the Regiment of Uhlans, Her Majesty was the patron of this regiment."

11. *A buckle from a man's officer's belt.*

This is shown in Photograph No. 86.

The witnesses testified as follows:

Ivanov: "At the end the Tsar wore a simple yellow belt with an officer's buckle. I see the belt buckle which you are showing me. I believe this buckle is from the Tsar's belt. He had such a buckle on his belt."

Gibbs: "The large buckle is, very probably, from the Tsar's officer's belt."

Tegleva: "The brass buckle from a man's belt is similar to the buckle of the Tsar's belt."

The accused, Yakimov: "I believe that this buckle comes from the Tsar's belt. It is very similar to the buckle on his belt."

It seems to me that the fact that it is the Tsar's is clear, if one compares the picture of it in Photograph No. 86 with Photograph No. 87.

This buckle had been exposed to intense heat of fire.

12. *A buckle from a boy's belt.*

This is shown in Photograph No. 88.

The buckle is of brass, of good workmanship. There is a reproduction on it of the Imperial coat of arms.

It was found with a clasp.

The witnesses testified as follows:

Ivanov: "I definitely accept it as a buckle belonging to Alexei Nicholayevich. It is the very one that he wore on his belt."

Tegleva: "The buckle from a boy's belt is undoubtedly the buckle from a belt belonging to Alexei Nicholayevich."

The witnesses Gilliard, Gibbs, Ersberg, Tutelberg, Zanotti, Volkov, Kobylinsky, and Bittner identified it in the same categorical fashion.

The buckle had been subjected to intense heat by fire.

13. *Two matching, ladies' jeweled shoebuckles.*

These are shown in Photograph No. 89.

CHAPTER TWENTY-TWO

The witnesses testified:

Tegleva: "The two shoe buckles are buckles from shoes belonging to one of the Grand Duchesses. They all had such buckles on their shoes. There were similar buckles on those of the Empress, too."

Zanotti: "The two shoe buckles are precisely the same as those on the shoes of the Grand Duchesses and the Tsarina."

The witnesses Gilliard, Gibbs, Ersberg, Tutelberg, Kobylinsky, Bittner, and Volkov gave testimony to the same effect.

A commission of experts affirmed: "These buckles are buckles from ladies' shoes. They undoubtedly came from fine, expensive shoes. The workmanship of the buckles alone attracts attention. The setting of the stones is well made, with great care. It is for this reason that the stones are still in the settings, even though the buckles and stones have both been exposed to intense heat of fire."

14. *A ladies' shoe buckle.*

This is shown in Photograph No. 90.

Zanotti testified: "The single buckle is from a shoe. The shoes of the Grand Duchesses and the Tsarina had precisely the same kind of buckles."

It had been exposed to intense heat of fire.

15. *A white vial of salts.*

This is shown in Photograph No. 91.

16. *A broken green vial.*

Tegleva, Ersberg, Tutelberg, and Zanotti testified that such vials of salts were used by the Grand Duchesses and the Tsarina; they usually took them with them when travelling.

17. *A lens from spectacles.*

This is shown in Photograph No. 92.

A commission of experts identified it as an optical lens which had formerly been in a frame.

The witnesses testified as follows:

Gilliard: "The lens which you have shown me suggests a lens from Her Majesty's glasses."

Tutelberg: "In Tobolsk, the Tsarina wore glasses when she was working. Her Majesty began, undoubtedly, to have trouble with her eyes, from excessive watering, while in Tobolsk. A doctor in Tobolsk prescribed glasses. They were large, in tortoiseshell frames."

Kobylinsky: "In Tobolsk the Tsarina wore large glasses, with horn rims I believe, when she was working. They had lenses of the same size as this. . . . These glasses were prescribed for her by

Doctor Grigorzhevsky in Tobolsk."

18. *The frame and holder from a lorgnette.*

19. *Two lenses from a pince-nez.*
These are shown in Photographs Nos. 93-94.
A commission of experts affirmed: "Both lenses, judging from their size and the grinding of the edges, are from the same pince-nez. Both lenses are convexo-convex, which indicates use by a far-sighted person."
The witnesses testified as follows:
Gilliard: "Botkin sometimes used a pince-nez which was mounted only at the bridge of the nose."
Kobylinsky: "The lenses from a pince-nez that you have shown me, because of their shape, very strongly suggest the lenses of Botkin's pince-nez. Botkin always took off his glasses and his pince-nez when he was reading. He was evidently far-sighted."

20. *False teeth.*
This is shown in Photograph No. 95.
Gilliard, Gibbs, and Ersberg testified that Doctor Botkin wore false teeth.

21. *A small brush, scorched.*
This is shown in Photograph No. 96.
Kobylinsky testified that Doctor Botkin always carried such a small brush for his mustache and beard.

22. *A collar button.*

23. *A tie clasp.*
These objects appear in Photograph No. 97. The guards, Proskuryakov and Yakimov, stated that Doctor Botkin wore starched linen at the Ipatiev House.

24. *Scorched parts of burned corsets.*
a) six pairs of front stays;
b) side bones;
c) clasps;
d) fasteners and hooks;
e) hooks for laces.
These objects are shown in Photographs Nos. 98—103.
A commission of experts asserted that these were parts of six corsets. With respect to the quality of the corsets, it stated: "The corsets were of good workmanship. The material remaining on

some of the clasps is from elastic garters. The scorched material on several of the fasteners is material of the corset itself. This material is knit: it is knit of silk."

The witnesses testified as follows:

Tegleva: "I affirm that the Empress and the Grand Duchesses, and Demidova, always wore corsets. Only the Tsarina sometimes removed her corset when she put on a dressing-gown. In general she insisted upon this with the Grand Duchesses and used to say that to go without a corset was indecent."

Zanotti: "The Grand Duchesses and the Tsarina customarily wore corsets. Demidova also wore a corset."

25. *More than forty similar pieces of an object or objects destroyed by fire.*

A commission of experts testified: "These objects are parts of footwear that has been burned by fire. These are pieces of leather, soles, cork and cobbler's wax fused into a mass by fire. The appearance of these objects indicates that the footwear was machine made, of good workmanship. The material found in several of the pieces is characteristic of such footwear—a material, used in the manufacture of footwear, containing cork. The presence of this material in itself also points to the high quality of the footwear."

26. *An iron boot guard.*

27. *Seven men's buckles.*
These are shown in Photograph No. 104.

A commission of experts affirmed: All of these buckles except the largest come from men's pants, or men's vests. The last buckle is from a vest. Two of them are mates. They are all of good workmanship: all foreign but one. The largest is a buckle of Russian handwork.

28. *Coil springs.*
These are shown in Photograph No. 105.

29. *A buckle.*
This is shown in Photograph No. 106.

These springs and the buckle are parts of men's suspenders, destroyed by fire.

30. *Two metal buckles.*

A commission of experts affirmed that these are both parts of women's attire.

Tutelberg testified that one of them is from a belt belonging either to the Tsarina or the Grand Duchesses. Tegleva testified that the other was from a belt belonging to Demidova.

The first is shown in Photograph No. 107.

Both buckles were badly scorched.

31. *Six military-style buttons.*

These are shown in Photograph No. 108.

Markings on the reverse side indicate they were manufactured in the Vunder plant in "St. Petersburg."

A commission of experts affirmed: "All of these buttons are of a good type. If they are from the Vunder plant they were not in common use because the buttons of this plant were more expensive than others."

They had been damaged by fire.

32. *Buttons and parts of buttons.*

These are shown in Photograph No. 109.

Tegleva, Ersberg, Tutelberg, and Zanotti tesitfied that among these buttons some were of a type used on the sleeves of the blouses of the Grand Duchesses, some of a type used on the Empress' garters, and that the large buttons were from the Tsarina's lilac suit.

The buttons had been severely damaged by fire.

33. *Hooks, eyes, buttons.*

These are shown in Photograph No. 110.

Tegleva, Ersberg, Tutelberg, and Zanotti testified that such objects had been sewn on the garments of the Grand Duchesses and the Tsarina by their dress-maker, Brissac.

They were all severely damaged by fire.

It strikes the eye that many of the hooks and eyes were considerably stretched apart. Sometimes the hooks were not separated from the eyes.

34. *Pieces of fabric.*

Among these, the witnesses Tegleva, Ersberg, Tutelberg, Zanotti, Gilliard, and Kobylinsky recognized material from the apparel of the Grand Duchesses, the Tsarina, Demidova, and Botkin.

It is very noticeable that the cloth has either been roughly torn from the garment or in some cases roughly cut with the aid of a knife.

Many of the pieces are half burned.

35. *Pieces of cloth.*

The witnesses testified as follows:

Ivanov: "I see the pieces of burned cloth which you have shown me. I am of the firm belief that these are remnants of cloth from an overcoat belonging to Alexei Nicholayevich. His coat was made of precisely the same cloth."

Kobylinsky: "I knew Alexei Nicholayevich's overcoat very well. I see the pieces of burned cloth. I believe that these are pieces of his overcoat. The color of the cloth, its quality, and the threadbare condition definitely suggest his overcoat."

36. *A piece of khaki-colored fabric.*

Chemodurov, in whose possession this piece was found, testified that it had been cut from the Tsarevich's knapsack.

37. *Pieces of lead foil.*

38. *Four nails.*

39. *A used revolver bullet.*

40. *Two copper coins of two-kopeck denomination.*

The witnesses testified as follows:

Ivanov: "Alexei Nicholayevich, being a boy, liked to collect lead foil, rifle and revolver bullets. He carried many such things in his pockets."

Gibbs: "He had several whims: in Tobolsk he collected old nails."

Tegleva: "I remember that he collected lead foil."

41. *An American suitcase key.*

42. *Parts of a small hand-bag or coin purse.*

43. *A pen-knife.*

44. *A safety-pin.*

All of these objects had been damaged by fire.

45. *Splinters of glass.*

Several of these undoubtedly came from a watch, small frames, others from smelling-salt vials.

46. *A jeweled cross.*

This is shown in Photograph No. 111.

Its principal metal is platinum. It contains emeralds, brilliants and pearls.

A commission of experts affirmed: "The cross is of fine, artistic work. It has undoubtedly been exposed to fire. This is indicated by the appearance of the platinum and, primarily, by the fact that the bead on one of the sharp projections is a burned pearl."

47. *A brilliant.*

This is shown in Photograph No. 111.

Its principal metal is platinum, at the bottom there is green gold. It is studded with diamonds. Its weight is 10 carats.

A commission of experts affirmed: "The brilliant shows high quality workmanship and is undoubtedly only part of another ornament: a pendant. The appearance of the platinum indicates that the stone was exposed to fire, but it has not lost its quality or value."

The witnesses testified as follows:

Tutelberg: "I can positively identify both the brilliant and the cross. These things belonged to Her Majesty. The brilliant was a gift to Her Majesty from His Majesty on the occasion of the birth of one of the Grand Duchesses. The cross was a gift to Her Majesty from the Empress Maria Feodorovna."

Zanotti: "The cross and the brilliant undoubtedly belonged to the Empress. I do not recall the source of the cross. It was given to her either by the Tsar or by the Empress Maria Feodorovna. The large brilliant was a gift from the Tsar, I believe, on the birth of one of the Grand Duchesses."

48. *An earring.*

This is shown in Photograph No. 112.

Its principal metal is platinum. The principal stone is a pearl, the smaller is a brilliant. The fastening of the earring is gold.

A commission of experts affirmed: "The earring is of very fine, highly artistic workmanship. The pearl is of the best quality. The earring was not exposed to fire."

The witnesses testified as follows:

Gilliard: "I think this earring belonged to the Tsarina. Her Majesty did have such earrings. She loved them very much and I often photographed Her Majesty while she was wearing them."

Gibbs: "The earring is undoubtedly the Tsarina's. These were her favorite earrings and she wore them often."

Tegleva: "The earrings and the fragments from them are undoubtedly earrings of the Tsarina, which she loved very much."

Ersberg: "The earring is undoubtedly an earring of the Tsarina. These were her favorite earrings, with which she never parted, and I believe she was wearing them when she left Tobolsk."

I could only show Tutelberg and Zanotti a photograph of the earring. They testified as follows:

Tutelberg: "I see the photograph of the earring. I affirm positively that this photograph shows one earring of a pair belonging to Her

Majesty. These were Her Majesty's most beloved earrings. She left Tobolsk wearing them."

Zanotti: "Of the things which you have shown me and their pictures I can identify. . . . The earring is also hers. She loved these earrings and wore them more often than others."

49. *Parts of a pearl and a part of a broken gold ornament (see No. 114).*

A commission of experts affirmed: ". . . They are real pearl. It was exposed to fire. It is possible that these parts at one time formed a single pearl. The large splinter indicates that it was a type of pearl of very high quality and value. It is entirely possible that these splinters formed a single pearl, the mate to the earring just referred to."

50. *Parts of a pearl.*

A commission of experts affirmed in respect to these splinters of pearl:

With respect to the 1st: "It is part of a large pearl of very fine quality and was separated from it by a blow or by pressure."

With respect to the 2d and 3rd: "Both splinters are parts of a pearl of very great size and very high quality."

With respect to the 4th and 5th: "The same conclusions as with respect to the 2d and 3rd."

With respect to the 6th :"This splinter is also part of a large pearl, of high quality, but it comes from a different pearl, not the one from which the splinters described in the previous points might have come."

51. *Thirteen round pearls.*

These are shown in Photograph No. 115.

A commission of experts affirmed: "All of them are of high quality and, apparently, all were part of one string."

Tegleva, Ersberg, Tutelberg, and Zanotti testified that the Empress and the Grand Duchesses possessed many strings of such pearls.

52. *Part of a broken ornament with brilliants.*

This is shown in Photograph No. 116.

A commission of experts affirmed in connection with the principal (large) part: "The ornament has real brilliants of high quality, set in pure silver, and in the setting there is brazing of gold. This ornament is a part of something else that was larger. It has marks indicating that its destruction was caused by the blow of some hard object."

With respect to the 1st piece: "This metal is silver. This piece is the result of separation from the previously described ornament, and it was apparently separated from it by the blow of some sharp object."

With respect to the 2d: "The metal of the piece is silver. This piece was also produced as a result of its separation from an ornament, and it is clear that this separation was produced with the aid of a sharp, cutting object. This piece was also exposed to fire, as was the last mentioned piece, but to a greater degree."

With respect to the 3rd and 4th: "The same conclusions as with respect to the 2d."

Tutelberg testified: "I see part of an ornament with brilliants. It definitely suggests a brooch belonging to Her Majesty. It is a part of it, of the brooch."

53. Thirteen splinters of emerald.

A commission of experts testified: "The splinters are part of an emerald. They were separated from some large emerald of very fine quality. This separation was brought about with the aid of a hard, heavy object. The emeralds were not exposed to fire, but were apparently trampled because the polish of one of them is gone."

Tutelberg testified: "Her Majesty had a great many of the sort of things that contained emeralds. These are splinters from a very large emerald. But I hesitate to say from precisely what object the splinters have come. It is possible that it is a broken emerald egg of Her Majesty's."

54. Two splinters of sapphire.

A commission of experts affirmed: "These splinters are apparently from different stones. They both come from stones of high quality. They were separated from the whole stone by a strong blow with some kind of heavy object."

55. Two brilliants, a ruby, two almandines, two adamants.

A commission of experts affirmed with respect to the brilliants (1 and 2): "Both stones are real brilliants of the highest quality. They were obviously part of the design of some large ornament."

With respect to the almandines (3): "This stone is an almandine of high quality. It is a splinter from a larger stone and was separated from it with the aid of a strong blow of some heavy object. It obviously was part of the multi-stone setting of some jeweled ornament of round form". . . . (4) "This stone is an almandine of good quality. It is a splinter from a larger stone, separated from it with the aid of some heavy object."

With respect to the ruby (5): "The stone is a ruby of average quality. It was in a setting of some kind."

With respect to the adamants: "An auxiliary part of an ornament consisting of a string."

Tutelberg testified with respect to the adamants: "These are from the chain of a bracelet belonging to Her Majesty. In the chain of this bracelet there were pearls and, between them, just such beads."

56. *Two gold chains.*

These are shown in Photograph No. 117.

A commission of experts testified: "Both chains are of gold. They are guard chains for the clasps of bracelets and were apparently torn from them."

Tutelberg testified: "I see the parts of bracelets. Her Majesty and the Grand Duchesses had several bracelets of this type, with such chains. They were all wearing such bracelets when they left Tobolsk."

Tegleva and Ersberg gave similar testimony.

57. *Part of a gold object.*

A commission of experts affirmed: "It is part of a gold ring from which it has been separated with the aid of some heavy object."

58. *A gold flake.*

A commission of experts testified: "It was produced as a result of its separation from some other large object with the aid of a sharp, cutting instrument, of which it bears the marks."

59. *Two parts of gold ornaments.*

A commission of experts affirmed: "Both parts are gold. One of them is most probably part of an earring; the other, part of a bracelet."

60. *A gold ornament with three diamonds.*

A commission of experts identified this as an auxiliary part of a large ornament.

The three latter objects are shown in Photograph No. 118.

Tutelberg testified: "This is an eyelet for fastening jeweled ornaments. Her Majesty had many such eyelets."

61. *Topazes.*

These are shown in Photograph No. 119.

Gilliard, Gibbs, Tegleva, Ersberg, Tutelberg, and Kobylinsky testified that the Tsarina and the Grand Duchesses wore necklaces of such topazes.

The accused, Yakimov: "The Grand Duchesses wore—I don't remember who exactly, all, I believe—necklaces of white beads on their necks, very similar to those at which I am now looking."

Zanotti: "The topazes are from a necklace. Both the Grand Duchesses and the Tsarina possessed such necklaces. These necklaces were given to them by Rasputin."

How did the Imperial jewels get in the mine?

We have seen that the Empress, subjected to crude treatment during her first days at Ekaterinburg, wrote to Tobolsk and asked that special attention be given to her jewels. Before her children left Tobolsk the jewels were sewn in their clothing.

Tegleva testified: "We took several brassieres of heavy linen. We put the jewels in wadding, covered the wadding with two brassieres and then sewed the brassieres together. In this fashion the jewels were sewn between two brassieres, which were then covered with wadding on both sides. The jewels of the Empress were sewn in two pairs of brassieres. In one of such double brassieres the weight of the jewels together with the brassieres and wadding was 4½ pounds. The other was of the same weight. Tatiana Nicholayevna wore one of them, and Anastasia Nicholayevna the other. In these (in both double brassieres) were sewn brilliants, emeralds, amethysts.

The jewels of the Grand Duchesses were sewn into a double brassiere in the same fashion, and it (I don't know how much its contents weighed) was worn by Olga Nicholayevna.

In addition they put many pearls on their bodies, under their blouses.

We also sewed jewels into the hats of the Grand Duchesses, between the lining and the velvet. Among the jewels of this type I remember a large pearl necklace and a brooch with a large sapphire and brilliants.

The Grand Duchesses had blue outer garments of cheviot. These garments (summer clothes which they wore when they left) did not have buttons but sashes, on each of which there were two buttons. We ripped off these buttons, and in place of the buttons sewed jewels, brilliants I believe, wrapping them first in wadding and then with black silk.

In addition the Grand Duchesses had grey garments of English tricot with black stripes. These were fall clothing which they wore also during the summer, in bad weather. We also ripped the buttons off of these and sewed on jewels, after wrapping them in wadding and black silk."

62. *24 pieces of lead, 2 bullets from a revolver of the Nagant type and one steel jacket from such a bullet.*

The shape of the pieces of lead was very distinctive. The lead had been melted in fire and then, cooling, had retained the irregular shape of a congealed mass.

The empty bullet jacket was blackened with smoke. The lead had flowed out of it in the heat of the fire.

63. *A human finger and two pieces of human skin.*

This finger is shown in Photograph No. 120.

A commission of experts affirmed:

1. The finger consists of two phalanxes: the nail and the middle. It is most probably an index finger.

2. This finger belongs, in all probability, to the hand of a person accustomed to manicuring, and it has a well-groomed appearance.

3. The committee of experts is more inclined to believe that this finger is that of a woman who had long, thin fingers.

4. It was removed along the line of the middle-phalanx joint. The edges of the joint and skin are even. Therefore the committee of experts postulates that most probably of all the finger was cut off by some sharp, cutting object.

5. The finger belongs to an adult of middle age.

6. Both pieces of skin were removed from a human hand, but from exactly what part of the hand, and exactly which, it is not possible to determine.

64. *The corpse of a female dog.*

Photograph No. 121 shows a view of this.

The dog was found on June 25, 1919 in the bottom of the open shaft. Thanks to the low temperature in the shaft, the corpse was well preserved.

The right front paw is broken. A hole had been broken in the skull, and this, in the opinion of a doctor, was the cause of its death.

Gibbs testified: "Anastasia Nicholayevna had a small dog of some Japanese breed. It was a very small dog with long fur. Its color was red-black. . . . It had these distinguishing marks: it had large, round eyes; its teeth were exposed and always visible, its tongue was long, hanging out of its mouth, I don't remember on which side. Its nickname was "Jemmi". Such dogs are very small and are often carried in the arms. It belonged to Anastasia Nicholayevna. They all loved this dog, particularly the Empress. I saw the dog today at the shaft. I affirm that this dog which I saw at the shaft, is Jemmi. I noted its fur and the shape of the eye sockets and the teeth. It is undoubtedly she."

Tutelberg, Tegleva, and Ersberg also recognized her.

In Photograph No. 122 Jemmi is in the arms of Anastasia Nicholayevna.

65. *Splinters of the bone of a mammal.*

These are all badly burned, cut and chopped.

The overthrow of the Admiral's government prevented me from conducting the scientific examination of these bones that I desired. However, Doctor Belogradsky, to whom I showed them during his questioning, testified: "I do not exclude the possibility that these bones are all human. The appearance of these bones indicates that they were chopped and exposed to the action of some kind of agent."

All of these bones were found by me alone. More of them, however, were actually found.

The forester, Rednikov, testifies: "I affirm categorically that at that time we found several splinters of shattered and burned bones in the bonfire at the shaft. These were splinters of large bones of a large mammal and, as it seemed to me at the time, splinters of tubular bones. They were badly burned."

Rednikov found many other valuable things. In their case Nametkin's mistake had fatal results. No one realized what had happened at the mine, and all of these valuable objects were thrown away.

66. *Pieces of greasy masses, mixed with earth.*

All of these masses were found in the vicinity of the open shaft: in the clay area, in the fires or near them, near the open shaft in the grass.

Articles noticeable to the eye, as for instance, the finger, Jemmi's corpse, many bones, were found in the bottom of the open shaft (in the small well), where they had been covered with earth from the clay area.

The mine gave up the secret of the Ipatiev House.

During the evening of July 16 the Imperial Family, and those living with them, were alive.

Early in the morning of July 17, under cover of the darkness of night, an auto truck carried their corpses to the mine in the tract of the Four Brothers.

On the clay area, at the open shaft, the corpses were stripped. The clothing was crudely removed, torn away and cut with knives. Several of the buttons were destroyed in the process, hooks and eyes stretched.

The concealed jewels were of course exposed. Several of them which fell with many others on the clay area remained unnoticed, and were trampled in the upper layers of this area.

The main purpose was to destroy the bodies. For this it was necessary, first of all, to dissect the corpses, to cut them up. This was done on the clay area.

The blows of the sharp, cutting instruments, cutting the corpses apart, cut some of the jewels that were trampled in the earth.

A commission of experts established that several of the jewels were destroyed by strong blows of some hard objects: not sharp, cutting instruments. These were jewels that had been sewn into the brassieres of the Grand Duchesses and destroyed by the bullets entering their bodies at the time of the murder.

The dissected bodies were burned in the bonfires with the aid of gasoline and destroyed with sulphuric acid. The bullets which remained in the bodies fell into the fires. The lead was melted, ran onto the ground and then, cooling, acquired the shape of hardened drops. The empty bullet casing remained.

The corpses, burned on the bare ground, gave up fat. Running out it impregnated the soil.

The torn and cut pieces of clothing were burned in the same fires. In several there were hooks, eyes and buttons. They were preserved in burnt form. Several hooks and eyes, having been burned, remained fastened together, unseparated.

Noticing some of the objects remaining, the criminals threw them into the shaft, after having first broken the ice in it. Then they covered them with earth.

Here we have the same picture as in the Ipatiev House: the concealment from the world of the evil that had been committed.

Thus it is the very best, the most valuable witnesses, which speak of the crime; mute objects.

Now let us listen to what the cunning human tongue has to say about it.

CHAPTER TWENTY-THREE

[pp. 218-238]

Testimony of Witnesses and Statements of the Accused
Regarding the Murder of the Imperial Family.

The Popov House, in which the exterior guard was billeted, was
located on the opposite side of Voznesensky Alley from the Ipatiev
House (Photograph No. 37).

The guard occupied only the upper floor. Private individuals were
living on the lower floor.

A peasant, Buivid,[38] who lived on the lower floor, testified: "The
night of the 16th to 17th of July is well impressed upon my memory,
because I did not sleep very well that night, and I recall that about
12 o'clock that night I went out in the yard and walked towards
the fence. I felt sick and I stopped there. After a little while I heard
muffled volleys—there were about 15—and then individual shots—
about 3 or 4. These shots were not from rifles. It was after 2 A.M.
The shots came from the Ipatiev House, and they had a muffled
sound, as though they came from the basement. After this I went to
my room quickly, because I was afraid I might be seen from above
by the guards of the house in which the former Emperor was
imprisoned.

"When I came into the room my room-mate asked me: 'Did you
hear?'

"I answered: 'I heard shots.'

" 'Did you understand?'

" 'I understand,' I said, and we fell silent . . . .

"In about 20 minutes I heard the gates of the fence open at the

Ipatiev House and an automobile come out quietly into the street. It made little noise and turned into Voznesensky Prospect, but in which direction I do not know."

The night watchman, Tsetsegov,[39] testified: "I am the night watchman on Voznesensky Prospect. I recall that during the night of the 16th to 17th of July, at 3 A.M.,[40] I heard the sound of an automobile behind the fence of the Ipatiev House in which the former Emperor was imprisoned. Then I heard the sound of the same automobile going in the direction of Glavny Prospect.[41] I did not see the automobile because I was afraid to go near the Ipatiev House. We were forbidden to do so."

The guard, Michael Ivanov[ich] Letemin, was from the Sysertsky plant in Ekaterinburg uezd. He was a tailor by profession, a rather illiterate, ignorant man. In the past he had been tried for attempted corruption of morals. He joined the guard solely for the pay. He was the only one of the entire guard who lived with his family in a private apartment. He did not leave town with the Reds because he did not consider that his participation in the guard was in any way reprehensible. He was found quickly in Ekaterinburg through recognition of the spaniel, Joy, which had belonged to the Tsarevich, and which Letemin appropriated after the murder.

In response to questioning by Sergeyev, Letemin testified:

"On July 16 I was on duty at post No. 3 (at the side gate, inside the yard) from 4 o'clock in the afternoon until 8 o'clock in the evening, and I recall that when I came on duty the former Tsar and his family were coming back from a walk. I did not see anything unusual at that time.

"On July 17 I came on duty at 8 o'clock in the morning. First I went into the guard quarters and there saw the boy (Leonid Sednev) who had been in the service of the Imperial Family. The boy's presence was very surprising to me and I asked: 'Why is he here?' One of the comrades, Andrei Strekotin, to whom I had directed the question, only waved his hand in reply. Taking me aside, he told me that the Tsar had been killed during the preceding night, with the Tsarina and their entire family, along with the doctor, the cook, a man-servant, and a woman who was with the Imperial Family.

"Strekotin stated that on that night he had been at the machine-gun post in the large room on the lower floor and that during his shift (he was supposed to be on duty from 12 o'clock midnight until 4 o'clock in the morning) he had seen the Tsar, the Tsarina, all the Imperial children, the doctor, two servants and a woman all brought down from upstairs and placed in the room which adjoined the store-room.

"Strekotin told me that as he watched, the commandant, Yurovsky, read a paper and said: 'Your life is finished.' The Tsar did not hear clearly and questioned Yurovsky. The Tsarina and one of the Imperial daughters made the sign of the cross.

"At this moment Yurovsky shot the Tsar and killed him on the spot. Then the Letts and the leader of the guard detachment, Paul Medvedyev, began to shoot.

"I understood from Strekotin's story that all were definitely killed.

"I do not know how many shots were fired at the time of the shooting. I did not ask.

"I do recall that, during the conversation, I remarked to Strekotin: 'There must have been a lot of bullets left in the room.' Strekotin replied, 'Why a lot? The woman who waited on the Tsarina tried to protect herself from the shots with a pillow, and they did fire a lot of bullets into the pillow.'

"The same Strekotin, incidentally, told me that after the Tsar they killed the 'black' servant. He was standing in the corner and, after the shot, sat down and died immediately.

"I do not know any other details of the shooting.

"After hearing the story I said: 'So many people were killed, there must have been a very great deal of blood on the floor.' In reply to this, one of the comrades—I don't remember precisely who—said that they had sent to the detachment for more personnel and all the blood was washed away.

"I was unable to talk any longer at this time as I had to go on guard. After doing my stint I returned to the guard quarters where I was told that we would probably have to 'go to the front'. I said that I would not go to the front because I had not 'signed up' for that, having signed up only for service in a guard detachment at a designated building.

"After we had talked a little about this, the conversation came back to the murder of the Tsar and his family. The chauffeur, Lyukhanov, who was in the guard quarters at this time, said that he had taken all of the victims to the forest in a motor-truck. He also said he had difficulty making his way. It was dark and there were stumps along the road. Lyukhanov said nothing about the direction in which the victims were taken, or what had been done with the corpses, and I did not ask him.

"I wanted to know more about how the victims were taken out

of the house, assuming that in this case also a lot of traces of blood must have been left in the course of removal of the bloody bodies. Someone in the detachment—I don't recall who exactly—said the corpses were carried out to the yard through the servants' entrance, and from there to an automobile which was standing at the main entrance. They said the bodies were carried on stretchers, that the bodies had been covered, and that the traces of blood were swept away with sand.

During the period of the 18th, 19th, 20th and 21st of July the possessions of the Imperial Family were brought from the rooms which they had occupied, as well as from the store-rooms and storehouses, to be taken away in an automobile. The removal of these things was arranged by two young men, assistants to Yurovsky. They took the things to the railroad station because, as a result of the approach of the Cheko-Slovaks, the Soviet authorities had already decided to leave Ekaterinburg.

"With respect to the murder of the Imperial Family, an Austrian by the name of Rudolph, who had acted as servant for the commandant, also told me that on that night the commandant advised him in advance not to be afraid if he heard something during the night."

The guard, Philip Polievktov [ich] Proskuryakov, also came from the Sysertsky plant. He joined the guard for the pay. He remained with the guard until the last moment and left for the front with the other guards. Later, however, he took off from there and returned to Ekaterinburg, where he was found by the agent, Alexeyev.

His statement to Alexeyev was transcribed as follows:

"I, Alexeyev, agent of the Criminal Investigating Division, interrogated the detained, Philip Proskuryakov, regarding the circumstances of the case and he, Proskuryakov, professed complete ignorance of all aspects thereof, explaining that he was never in the guard of the Ipatiev House, where the Tsar and his family were held, and knew nothing about the matter. He had been mobilized along with others for the guard of the Ipatiev House, but had fled while on the road and was not in the guard.

"Upon further questioning on the following day, February 22, after confrontation with Paul Spiridonovich Medvedyev, who contradicted him and stated that he had incorrectly testified that he was not in the guard of the Ipatiev House, and that he, Philip Proskuryakov, was in the guard of this house until the termination of the presence there of the Tsar and his family, he, Proskuryakov, changed his original testimony and explained that he was actually in the guard of the Ipatiev House, where the Tsar and his family were, but knew nothing about the matter and did not know where either the Tsar or his family were. He did not know whether they were dead or alive.

"Upon further questioning as to all the details of his presence in the guard of the Ipatiev House, he, Proskuryakov, still refused to give any further essential information about the matter and finally confirmed only the facts that Paul Medvedyev had, on one evening— whose date he did not remember—not long before the departure of the Bolsheviks from the city of Ekaterinburg, come into the guard quarters where the guard of the house was; that he, Proskuryakov, was one of the guards; that Medvedyev had forewarned the guard that there would be shooting that night, and that they should not be alarmed but should at that time be prepared for any eventuality; that Medvedyev had also told them that the family would be shot that night. What happened that night he, Proskuryakov, did not know, because after Medvedyev came he went to sleep on the stove in the guard quarters and slept the whole night through. In the morning he heard from a Red Army man, Andrei Starkov, that the family had been taken away from the house.

"Upon subsequent questioning, Proskuryakov still further changed the last part of his testimony to state that he had heard from Red Army personnel who were in the guard of the house that the Tsar Nicholas II and his family had been shot and taken away somewhere in an automobile. On this occasion Proskuryakov stated that he had not himself then seen the Tsar Nicholas II and his family and did not know whether they had actually been shot and carried off, that he did not carry their corpses out, and that he was not among those other persons who had washed away the blood in the room of the shooting. He did not hear whether Medvedyev had ordered the guard to carry out the corpses and wash away the blood.

"Finally, to a question put by me, agent of the Criminal Investigating Division, on February 28, he, Proskuryakov, confirmed his previous testimony to the effect that he knew nothing about the case, and that he did not know whether the Tsar Nicholas II and his family were shot during the night on July 17, new style, adding that at the time this took place he, Proskuryakov, and a Red Army man, Yegor Stolov, who was in the guard of the Ipatiev House, had been confined by the detachment leader, Paul Medvedyev, to the bathhouse of the guard quarters, where they remained for two days under arrest for getting drunk, and that therefore he, Proskuryakov, did not know what took place on that night in the Ipatiev House, where the Tsar and his family were."

In reply to my questioning, Proskuryakov stated:

"They were murdered during the night of Tuesday to Wednesday. I don't recall the date. I remember that we received our pay on Monday. This means that was on the 15th of July, new style. (We were paid twice a month: on the 1st and 15th of each month.) On the day after we were paid, that is on Tuesday the 16th of July, I stood at my post until 10 o'clock in the morning at the shelter near Voznesensky Prospect and Voznesensky Alley. Yegor Stolov, my roommate, was standing, during these hours in the lower rooms of the house. Having finished our tour of duty, Stolov and I went to have a drink. We, Stolov and I, got drunk on denaturat, and went home at evening since we had to go on duty at 5 o'clock.

"Medvedyev saw that we were drunk and placed us under arrest in the bathhouse, in the courtyard of the Popov House. There we went to sleep. We slept until 3 o'clock A.M. (1 o'clock sun time). Medvedyev came to us at 3 A.M., woke us up and said, 'Get up. Come with me.' We asked him, 'Where?' He answered, 'When you are called, come!'

"I say it was 3 o'clock because Stolov had a watch and he looked at it at that time. It was exactly 3 o'clock. We got up and followed Medvedyev.

"He took us to the lower rooms of the Ipatiev House. All of the worker-guards were there except those then standing at their posts.

"There was a sort of cloud of powder smoke in the rooms, and the smell of powder. In the rear room, with the grating on the window, the one next to the store-room, there were bullet marks on the walls and on the floor. There were a particularly large number of bullets (not bullets themselves, but their holes) in one wall—the same wall appearing in the photograph you have shown me—but there were also bullet marks on other walls. There were no marks of bayonet blows anywhere on the walls of the room. On the walls and the floor, where there were bullet holes, there was blood around them. There were spatters and stains of blood on the walls. On the floor there were small pools. There were also drops and pools of blood in all of the other rooms through which it was necessary to pass in order to get to the yard of the Ipatiev House from the room in which the bullet marks were. There were similar traces of blood in the yard, on the stones, in the direction of the gate.

197

"It was clear that many people had been shot in this very room with the grating not long before our arrival, of Stolov and myself. Seeing all this I asked Medvedyev and Andrei Strekotin what had happened.

"They told me that the entire Imperial Family had just been shot, and all the people with them except the boy.

"We all began to wash the floors to remove the traces of blood. In one of the rooms there were some 4-5 brooms already. Exactly who brought them there I do not know. I believe they had been brought from the yard. . . . .

"At Medvedyev's order Kronidov brought sawdust from under the shed in the yard. We all washed the floors with cold water and sawdust, washing away the blood. We washed the blood from the walls, where the shooting took place, with wet rags.

"All of the workers except those on their posts took part in this clean-up.

"Many people participated in the clean-up of the room in which the Imperial Family was killed. I recall that there were two Letts working there, Medvedyev himself, the Smorodyakovs, father and son, Stolov. And I was cleaning up in that room. There were also others, whom I have forgotten.

"In the same manner, that is, with water, we washed away the blood in the courtyard, and from the stones.

"I personally did not find any bullets during the clean-up. Whether others found any, I do not know. When Stolov and I came into the lower rooms there was no one there except several Letts, Medvedyev, our workers, and the Zlokazovsky workers. Yurovsky was not there. And Nikulin, as Medvedyev then said, was in the upper rooms, to which the doors from the lower rooms had been locked on the side of the upper rooms. I did not see any gold objects or any kind of jewels taken from the corpses anywhere in the lower rooms.

"I remember well that it was precisely Andrei Strekotin who stood at the machine-gun in the lower rooms. I remember this very well. He must have seen everything.

"I questioned Medvedyev, and Stolov also questioned him.

"Both he and Strekotin spoke in agreement, relating the following.

"In the evening Yurovsky told Medvedyev that the Imperial Family was to be shot during the night, and ordered him to forewarn the workers of this and take the revolvers from those who were on posts. . . . Pashka Medvedyev carried out Yurovsky's orders exactly, took the revolvers, gave them to Yurovsky, and at 11 o'clock in the evening warned the detachment that the Imperial Family was going to be shot.

"At midnight Yurovsky awoke the Imperial Family, ordering them all to get dressed and go down to the lower rooms. According to Medvedyev, Yurovsky ostensibly explained to the Imperial Family that the night would be a 'dangerous' one, i.e., as I understand it, he told them that it would be dangerous to remain on the upper floor because of possible shooting in the streets and therefore ordered them to go downstairs.

"These, Yurovsky's, orders were carried out and they all went downstairs.

"There were the Tsar himself, the Tsarina, the Tsarevich, all four daughters, the doctor, the man servant, the maid, the cook.

"Yurovsky had apparently ordered that the boy be taken to the quarters of our detachment for three days. I personally saw him there before the murder.

"All were taken to the same room in which there were [later] many bullet marks on the walls and the floor. They stood in two rows, turning the corner slightly, along not one, but two walls.

"Yurovsky began to read them some kind of paper. The Tsar did not hear it all and asked Yurovsky, 'What?' He, in Pashka's words, raised his hand with the revolver and replied to the Tsar, showing him the revolver, 'Here's what!'

"Pashka himself told me that he shot 2-3 bullets at the Tsar and other persons whom they shot. I am telling the absolute truth. Never at any time did he say to me that he, allegedly, did not himself shoot, but went out to hear the shooting from outside. In this he lies.

"When they had all been shot, Andrei Strekotin, as he said to me himself, took all of their valuables from them. Yurovsky immediately took them and carried them upstairs. After this all of the bodies were loaded on an auto-truck—one, apparently—and carted away somewhere. The driver of this auto-truck was a worker from the Zlokazovsky plant, Lyukhanov. I am telling you this on the word of Medvedyev. . . . .

"I do not know in which direction they were taken.

"Medvedyev himself must not have known this because Yurovsky arranged the matter secretly."

The guard, Anatoli Alexandrov [ich] Yakimov, came from the Yugovsky plant, in Perm uezd. By profession he was a lathe operator, and he had worked in the Motovilikhinsky plant. He went to war as a volunteer. After the revolution of 1917 he became a member of the regimental committee of the 494th, Vereisky, regiment. After the collapse of the front he came home and went to work in the plant of the Zlokazovskys in Ekaterinburg.

He joined the guard because the work was easy and the pay good.

He was an erratic non-conformist by nature. He dreamed of the "better" life and considered the Tsar an enemy of the people.

He condemned the Bolshevik terror, but remained in the guard to the end, occupying the responsible post of corporal of the guard.

Upon the evacuation of Ekaterinburg he left with the Reds. But when they also evacuated Perm he did not go with them, but fought against them in the ranks of the army of the Admiral.

The agent, Alexeyev, traced him to Perm and arrested him.

On questioning, Yakimov told the following:

"On July 15th, Monday, the boy who lived with the Imperial Family, and wheeled the Tsarevich in a chaise, appeared in our quarters in the Popov House. He attracted my attention at that time. Undoubtedly he also attracted the attention of other guards. No one knew what it meant, however—why they had brought him over to us. It was undoubtedly done at Yurovsky's order.

"On July 16 I was the corporal of the guard on duty. I was on duty from 2 o'clock in the afternoon to 10 o'clock in the evening. At 10 o'clock I placed sentries on all posts.

"Post No. 3 (in the yard of the house near the wicket gate) was occupied by Brusyanin. Post No. 4 (at the wicket gate in the board enclosure near the main entrance leading to the upper floor) was occupied by Lesnikov. Post No. 7 (in the old shelter between the wall of the house and the inner board enclosure) was occupied by Deryabin. Post No. 8 (in the garden) was occupied by Kleshchev.

"The sentries which I placed at 10 o'clock in the evening should have been changed at 2 A.M. by the new corporal of the guard to whom I turned over the duty—Constantine Dobrynin.

"Having turned over my duty, I went to my quarters. I remember that I had tea and then went to bed. I must have gone to bed at about 11 o'clock.

"At about 4 o'clock in the morning, it must have been, when it was already light, I was awakened by Kleshchev's voice. Romanov and Osokin, who slept with me, also awoke. He said excitedly, 'Get up men! I have news to tell you. Go into that room!' We got up and went into the next room, where there were more people, which was the reason Kleshchev had called us in there.

"When we were all together, Kleshchev said: 'Today the Tsar was shot.'

"We all began to ask how it happened. Kleshchev, Deryabin, Lesnikov, and Brusyanin told us the following. It was principally Kleshchev and Deryabin who spoke, supplementing each other's words. Lesnikov and Brusyanin also said that they had seen it themselves. The story boiled down to this.

"At 2 o'clock A.M. Medvedyev and Dobrynin came to them at their posts and warned them that they would have to remain at their posts beyond 2 A.M. that night because the Tsar was to be shot. Having received this warning, Kleshchev and Deryabin went to the windows: Kleshchev to the window of the anteroom on the lower floor, which is shown on your drawing as number I. The window in it, looking onto the garden, is exactly opposite the door from the anteroom into the room where the murder took place, i.e., into the room marked on the drawing as number II. Deryabin went to the window which is in the room that looks out onto Voznesensky Alley.

"In a short time—this was all, according to them, during the period from midnight until 1 A.M. old time, or from 2 to 3 A.M. according to the new time which the Bolsheviks had put into effect, moving the clock two hours ahead—people came into the lower rooms and went into the room marked number I on the drawing of the lower floor. Kleshchev observed this procession himself, since it was visible to him from the garden, through the window. They all, unquestionably, went from the yard, through the door of the passageway marked number XII on the drawing, and on through the rooms marked numbers VIII, VI, IV, I, into the room marked number II.

"Yurovsky and Nikulin walked in front. Behind them came the Tsar, the Tsarina and the daughters: Olga, Tatiana, Maria, and Anastasia, as well as Botkin, Demidova, Trupp and the cook, Kharitonov. The Tsar himself carried the Tsarevich in his arms. Behind them came Medvedyev and the Letts, i.e., those ten men who lived in the lower rooms and who had been sent from the Cheka at Yurovsky's request. Two of them had rifles.

"When they had all been brought into the room marked number II, they were placed as follows: in the center of the room stood the Tsar, next to him, at his right, the Tsarevich sat on a chair, and to the right of the Tsarevich stood Doctor Botkin. All three, i.e., the Tsar, the Tsarevich, and Botkin were facing the door which led from the room marked number II into the room marked number I.

"Behind them, against the wall which divides the room numbered II from the room numbered III (the door to this room was locked and sealed; some things were kept there) stood the Tsarina with her daughters. I see the photograph of this room which you have shown me, in which the murder took place. The Tsarina with her daughters stood between the arch and the door to the sealed room, right here, where, as appears in the photo, the wall has been picked at.

"To one side of the Tsarina and her daughters, in the corner, stood the cook and the man servant, and on the other side of them, also in a corner, stood Demidova. But on exactly which side, to the right or left, the cook and the man servant stood, and on which Demidova stood, I do not know.

"Yurovsky was in the room, to the right of the entrance. Nikulin stood to the left of him, just opposite to the door leading from the room in which the murder took place to the anteroom marked number I. Next to Nikulin stood those Letts who were also in the room. There were also Letts in the doorway. Behind them stood Medvedyev.

"I am describing this disposition of the people mentioned from the accounts of Kleshchev and Deryabin. They supplemented each other. Kleshchev could not see Yurovsky. Through the window, Deryabin saw that Yurovsky said something, waving his arm. He probably saw part of the figure, mainly Yurovsky's arm. Exactly what Yurovsky said, Deryabin could not relate. He said the words were not audible to him. But Kleshchev stated positively that he heard Yurovsky's words. He said—I remember this well—that Yurovsky spoke to the Tsar thus: 'Nicholas Alexandrovich, your relatives have tried to save you, but did not succeed. And we ourselves must shoot you.'

"And at that very moment, after Yurovsky's words, several shots rang out.

"Only revolvers were fired. Neither Kleshchev nor Deryabin as I recall, said that Yurovsky fired, i.e., they did not speak about him at all, whether he shot or not. It seems to me that this was not visible to them, judging from Yurovsky's position in the room.

"But they could see Nikulin well. They both said that he fired.

"In addition to Nikulin, several of the Letts fired.

"The firing, as I have already said, was exclusively from revolvers. No one shot from a rifle.

"After the first shots, there was a 'woman's scream', as they said, the cry of several feminine voices. Those who were shot began to fall, one after another. The Tsar, they said, fell first, and after him the Tsarevich. Demidova very likely ran about. They both stated that she was protected by a pillow. Whether or not she was wounded by bullets, she was, according to them, nailed to the wall with bayonets by one or two Russians from the Cheka.

"When all were on the floor they were examined and several finished off with shots and slashes. Of the Imperial Family, as I recall, only Anastasia was mentioned as having been stabbed with bayonets.

"Someone brought several sheets, presumably from the upper rooms. The murder victims were wrapped in these sheets and carried to the courtyard through the same rooms through which they had been led to execution. From the courtyard they were carried to an automobile standing at the gate of the house, in the space between the facade, at the main entrance to the upper floor, and the outer board enclosure. This is where automobiles customarily stood.

"Lesnikov and Brusyanin saw this.

"All of the bodies were brought to the motor truck, and all were put in the one truck.

"A cloth was brought from the store-room and put in the automobile. The corpses were placed on it and covered over with the same cloth. There was no mention of who went for the cloth in the store-room. Of course we did not ask questions the way you are now doing. Had I known beforehand, I might have asked.

"The driver of this automobile was Serge Lyukhanov. He was specifically named by both Brusyanin and Lesnikov.

"Lyukhanov drove the automobile with the corpses to the gate which led into Voznesensky Alley and on down Voznesensky Alley past the Popov House.

"After the corpses had been carried out of the house, two of the Letts—a young man with glasses and another young man, about 22, blond—swept the blood with brooms and washed it away with water, with the aid of sawdust. Kleshchev and Deryabin said the bloody sawdust was thrown out somewhere.

"I definitely do not know who else took part in the clean-up of blood. From what they said, it appeared that those who were on duty at posts were not disturbed for this purpose. They all remained at their posts until replaced.

"The stories of Kleshchev, Deryabin, Brusyanin and Lesnikov sounded so much like the truth, and they themselves were so upset and shaken by all that they had seen, that there was not a shadow of doubt on the part of anyone who heard them that they were telling the truth. Deryabin was especially upset, and also Brusyanin. Deryabin cursed outright and called the murderers 'butchers' for this deed. He spoke of them with revulsion. Brusyanin could not endure the sight when they dragged the bodies out in white sheets and put them in the automobile. He ran from his post to the back yard.

"The story of the murder of the Tsar and his family made a strong impression on me. I sat and shook. I did not go back to bed, and at about 8 o'clock in the morning I went to see my sister, Capitolina. I was on good terms with her. I went to her to share my thoughts with her. They weighed very heavily on my soul, and I went to her in order to speak with someone close to me. . . .

"I was with my sister for about two hours, and at approximately 10 in the morning I went back to the Popov House.

"I do not recall how I passed the time until 2 o'clock in the afternoon, when I went on duty again. At that time I replaced Ivan Starkov. At that time I placed a guard on every post except Post No. 7. Starkov told me that it was no longer necessary to place a guard at this post (beneath the windows of the house). Obviously a guard had not been placed there since Deryabin's departure from this post. At that time I so understood Starkov. We both realized why it was no longer necessary to place a guard there and said nothing further about it.

"Having placed the guards, I went to the commandant's office. There I found Nikulin and two of the Letts, non-Russians. Medvedyev was also there. They were all unhappy, worried, depressed. Not one of them said a word.

"On the table in the commandant's office lay many different kinds of valuables. There were stones, earrings, pins with stones, and beads. Many were ornamented. Some were in cases. The cases were all open.

"The door leading from the anteroom into the rooms which had been occupied by the Imperial Family was closed as before, but there was no one in the rooms. This was obvious. No sound came from there. Before, when the Imperial Family lived there, there were always sounds of life in their rooms: voices, steps. At this time there was no life there. Only their little dog stood in the anteroom, at the door to the rooms where the Imperial Family had lived, waiting to be let in. I well remember thinking at the time: you are waiting in vain.

"Another thing I noticed at that time: before the murder there had been a bed and a divan in the commandant's office. On that day, i.e., at 2 o'clock in the afternoon of July 17, when I came into the commandant's office there were two additional beds. A Lett was lying on one of them. Then Medvedyev told us the Letts were no longer going to live in the room where the murder took place, in which they had lived before. Obviously, two beds had been moved at that time into the commandant's office. Excuse me. As far as I can remember, Medvedyev said that the Letts (all 10 of them) were no longer going to live in the lower part of the house and, as I then understood him, had already returned to the Cheka except for those two, probably, who still remained in the commandant's office. But I only saw these two in the house once, on that same day—July 17. I never saw them or any of the others again, even once.

"From 2 o'clock in the afternoon of July 17 I was on duty until 10 o'clock in the evening. I did not see Yurovsky in the house at all on that day. I do not believe he could have been in the house without my seeing him. I do not believe he was in the house at all on that day, at least from 2 o'clock in the afternoon until 10 o'clock in the evening.

"Nor were any of the things removed from the house on July 17. I do not know whether there was any sorting out or packing of things on that day.

"On July 17 Medvedyev told us that they were going to send all of us guards to the front. Therefore, on the 18th of July, in the morning, I went to the Zlokazovsky plant to get some money that was due us on account of previous time, and to get my things. At 2 o'clock in the afternoon I was back with the guard, and I went on duty at 2 o'clock. Some things were removed from the Ipatiev House on this day, July 18. On one occasion I personally saw trunks and boxes being carried out to a light automobile. The automobile went off somewhere with these things. The driver was Lyukhanov, and Beloborodov was carrying things out to the automobile. . . .

"The valuables that had been in the commandant's office still lay there on that day, July 18, looking just as they had before. I did not see Yurovsky in the house during that day, July 18. This I remember well. I believe I did see him about 6 o'clock in the evening.

"About July 19 Yurovsky was in the house from the morning.

"Some things were also removed from the house on that day, but I have retained absolutely no recollection of it.

"I do not know what happened to the boy who had been in our quarters. With respect to him I can say this. I saw this boy from a distance on one of the days following the murder. He was sitting in the room where the Sysertsky workers ate dinner and was crying bitterly, so that I could hear his sobs from a distance. I did not go to him myself, and I did not speak to him at all. I was told —I don't recall by whom, precisely—that the boy had learned about the murder of the Imperial Family and of the others who were with it, and had begun to cry.

"I do not recall exactly when this was. On July 17, still not calmed down after this evil deed, I could stand it no longer and went to see Medvedyev in his room. This was after 2 o'clock in the afternoon, i.e., after my tour of duty began. . . . .

"I asked him about the murder. Medvedyev told me that some time between midnight and 1 A.M. Yurovsky himself woke the Imperial Family and said to the Tsar: 'They are preparing to attack the house. I must take you to the lower rooms.' Then all went downstairs. When I asked exactly who had fired, Medvedyev told me that the Letts fired. I did not question him any further about this particular point.

"When I asked him where they had taken the bodies he told me that Yurovsky, the Letts and Lyukhanov had taken them beyond the Verkh-Isetsky plant in an automobile and that they were all buried there in one hole, as he said, previously prepared in a wooded place near a swamp. I remember he said the automobile got stuck and reached the prepared grave with difficulty."

The guard, Paul Spiridonov[ich] Medvedyev, was from the Sysertsky plant.

By profession he was a shoemaker. He also worked in the plant.

He had studied in the local village school but did not finish the course. He was not very literate.

In 1914 he was mobilized, but was able to avoid military service by obtaining employment in a plant which was doing defense work at that time.

In April 1917 he joined the Bolshevik party in Sysert, and for three months made the required payments to the party treasury.

From the very first days after the Bolshevik seizure of power he was in a Bolshevik military unit and went off to fight against Ataman Dutov. He returned from the front in April 1918 and joined the guard at the Ipatiev House.

From the very first up until the very last he occupied a special position among the workers of this guard. He was in no sense a corporal of the guard as Michael Letemin describes him, but was "leader" of the entire detachment.

He played a definite role in the removal of Avdeyev from the Ipatiev House, assuming the role of informer against him to the Chekist, Yurovsky, regarding those indulgences which Avdeyev allowed the Imperial Family during the second half of his service.

For this he was made Yurovsky's right hand man, enjoying his exclusive confidence.

Medvedyev, of course, left Ekaterinburg with the Reds. He was in Perm when it was taken by the Admiral's army. There he was given a responsible commission by Commissar Goloshchekin himself: to blow up the bridge across the Kama after the Bolshevik departure from the city. The explosion failed for technical reasons. Medvedyev was tracked down and arrested by Alexeyev.

In reply to questioning by Alexeyev he stated:

"On July 16, 1918, new style, at about 7 o'clock in the evening, Yurovsky ordered him, Medvedyev, to take the revolvers from all of the guards on posts in the guard of the house. Altogether the guards of the house had 12 revolvers, all of them of the Nagant type. Having collected the revolvers, he took them to the commandant, Yurovsky, in the office in the house, and laid them on the table.

"Earlier, during the morning of that day, Yurovsky had arranged for the removal of the boy who was the waiter's nephew from the house to the guards' quarters in the neighboring Popov House.

"Yurovsky did not tell him [Medvedyev] why all this was being done, but shortly after he brought the revolvers in to Yurovsky the latter said to him: 'Today, Medvedyev, we are going to shoot the whole family.' Yurovsky ordered him to warn the guard command not to be alarmed if they heard shots. It was about 10 o'clock in the evening when he told him to warn the command about this.

"At this time he, Medvedyev, warned the detachment and then returned to the house.

"At about 12 o'clock midnight the commandant, Yurovsky, woke the Imperial Family.

"Nicholas II himself and his whole family, as well as the doctor and servants got up, dressed, washed; and in approximately an hour's time all eleven people left their rooms.

"All of them were calm in appearance and did not seem to be conscious of danger.

"From the upper floor of the house they went down the stairway leading to the outside of the house.

"Nicholas II himself carried his son, Alexei, in his arms.

"After they went down, they went into the room which is at the end of the house.

"Several of them had pillows with them. The maid carried two pillows.

"Then the commandant, Yurovsky, ordered chairs to be brought. Three chairs were brought in.

"At this time two members of the Extraordinary Investigating Commission were already in the house by special appointment. One of them, as he [Medvedyev] later learned, was Yermakov (he does not know his other names) from the Verkh-Isetsky plant, and the other was completely unknown to him.

"The commandant, Yurovsky, his assistant, and these two persons went down to the lower floor, where the Imperial Family already were.

"Downstairs, in this room where the Imperial Family were, there were seven Letts from the guard. The other three Letts were also downstairs, but in a special room.

"The revolvers had already been distributed by Yurovsky to the seven Letts who were in the room, to the two members of the investigating commission, to Yurovsky himself, and to his assistant. Eleven revolvers were distributed in all. Yurovsky permitted him, Medvedyev, to take one revolver back. In addition, Yurovsky had a Mauser revolver.

"Thus there were 22 people assembled altogether in the room downstairs, 11 who were to be shot and 11 men with weapons, all of whom he had summoned.

"Seated in the chairs in the room were the wife of Nicholas II, Nicholas II himself, and his son, Alexei. The rest stood on their feet near the walls, still calm.

"After several minutes Yurovsky came to him, Medvedyev, in the adjoining room, and said to him: 'Go outside, Medvedyev, and look in the street to see if there are any unauthorized people around. And listen for the shots to see if they can be heard.'

"He, Medvedyev, went outside and as soon as he did, heard shots from the firearms. He went back into the house to tell Yurovsky that the shots could be heard.

"When he entered the room where the Imperial Family were, they had already all been shot and were lying on the floor in various positions. Near them was a mass of blood. The blood was thick, 'like liver'. With the exception of the Tsar's son, Alexei, all were, apparently, already dead. Alexei was still groaning.

"In his, Medvedyev's, presence, Yurovsky shot Alexei two or three more times with a Nagant, and then he stopped groaning.

"The appearance of the victims so affected him, Medvedyev, that he became sick and went out of the room.

"Yurovsky then ordered him to run over to the detachment and tell them not to be alarmed if they had heard shots. As he went over to the detachment two more shots followed in the house. He met the corporals of the guard, Ivan Starkov and Constantine Dobrynin, who were running over from the detachment.

"The latter, meeting him in the street near the house, questioned him. 'You will have to be able to say that they really shot Nicholas II and not someone else in his place—that you recognized him.' He told them that he had personally seen that they were shot, i.e., Nicholas II and his family, and he told them to go to the detachment and quiet the guards so they would not be aroused.

"In this manner he, Medvedyev, saw that the following had been shot: the former Emperor Nicholas II, his wife, Alexandra Feodorovna, his son, Alexei, his daughters: Tatiana, Anastasia, Olga, and Xenia,[42] Doctor Botkin, and the servants: the cook, the waiter, and the maid.

"Each had several gunshot wounds in various parts of their bodies. The faces of all were covered with blood, and the clothing of all was also bloody.

"The deceased evidently knew nothing of the danger which threatened them up until the last moment of the shooting.

"He himself, Medvedyev, did not take part in the shooting.

"When he, Medvedyev, returned to Yurovsky in the room, Yurovsky ordered him to bring several men from the guard to carry the bodies of the victims to an automobile. He summoned more than 10 men from the guard, but does not remember precisely whom. Stretchers were made from the shafts of two sleighs standing in the yard, under the shed. Sheets were tied to them with rope, and in this manner all of the bodies were carried to the automobile.

"While still in the room, from all of the members of the Imperial Family, whichever had them, rings, bracelets and 2 gold watches were taken. These things were immediately given to the commandant, Yurovsky. How many rings and bracelets were taken from the deceased he does not know.

"Then all eleven corpses were taken from the courtyard to the automobile. The automobile in which the corpses were placed was a special truck, brought to the courtyard in the evening.

"The two members of the investigating commission went off in this automobile with the corpses, one of them being Yermakov, and the other of the above description, whom he did not know. The driver of this automobile, apparently, was Lyukhanov, by family name, a man of average height, stocky, in appearance more than thirty years old, with a bumpy (pimply) face.

"The corpses of the murder victims were placed in the automobile on a grey military cloth and covered over with the same cloth. The cloth was taken from that place in the house where it had been kept in one piece.

"He, Medvedyev, does not know for certain where the corpses were taken and at that time asked no one about this.

"After the corpses were taken from the house, the commandant, Yurovsky, ordered the detachment summoned to wash the floor in the room where the shooting took place, and also to wash the blood on the wall of the house, at the main entrance in the courtyard, and where the automobile had stood. This order was then carried out by those who constituted the guard.

"When all this was done, Yurovsky left the courtyard and went to the office in the house. He, Medvedyev, went off to the Popov House, where the guard quarters were, and did not leave the quarters until morning.

"*The guard of the house remained on duty and was not removed until July 20, in spite of the fact that there was no one left in the house. This was done in order to keep the people from becoming excited and to give the appearance that the Imperial Family was still alive.*[43]

"On July 17, he, Medvedyev, went into the house and, coming to the upper floor, found great disorder in the house. The Imperial effects were all rummaged through and thrown about in various places. Several gold and silver objects—rings, bracelets and others, were lying in the office on the tables. There were a great many gold and silver things, covering all the tables.

"In the office at that time were the assistant to the commandant, and Letts. They were examining the things.

"The commandant himself, Yurovsky, was not there.

"Walking about the room, he, Medvedyev, went to one table on which a book, "The Law of God," was lying. He picked up the book and noticed money under it, 60 roubles in ten rouble notes. He took this money for himself, saying nothing to anyone.

"Then he took three silver rings which had fallen on the floor, and on which some prayers were inscribed, and several handkerchiefs. In addition to this, the former assistant to the commandant, Moshkin, gave him some men's socks, one pair, and a lady's blouse.

"He did not take any other things.

"On the following day his wife, Maria Danilov[n]a, came to him, Medvedyev. He gave her the aforesaid things and went home with her.

"At that time the commandant, Yurovsky, gave him 8,000 roubles for distribution to the families of men in the guard.

"He returned to Ekaterinburg on July 21. At that time the guard of the house had been removed."

In response to questioning by Sergeyev, Medvedyev stated:

"I went on duty in the evening of July 16. At about eight o'clock in the evening the commandant, Yurovsky, ordered me to take all the Nagant type revolvers from the detachment and bring them to him. From those who were at their posts and from several others I took, in all, 12 revolvers and brought them to the office of the commandant.

"Then Yurovsky said to me: 'Today all must be shot. Warn the commmand not to be alarmed if they hear shooting.'

"I guessed that Yurovsky was talking about shooting the whole Imperial Family, and the doctor and servants who lived with them. But I did not ask when and by whom the decision to shoot them had been made.

"I should tell you that during the morning the kitchen-boy in the house had, at Yurovsky's order, been taken to the quarters of the guard detachment (the Popov House).

In the lower floor of the Ipatiev House there were Letts from the 'Lettish commune', billeted there after Yurovsky assumed the duties of commandant. There were ten of them. I do not know the names or surnames of any of them.

"At about 10 o'clock in the evening I warned the detachment, in accordance with Yurovsky's order, that they should not be disturbed if they heard shooting. I told Ivan Starkov that the Imperial Family was going to be shot.

"I definitely do not remember exactly which men of the detachment were on post at that time, and I cannot name them. I also cannot remember from which I took revolvers.

"At about 12 midnight Yurovsky woke the Imperial Family. Whether he told them why he was disturbing them, or where they were supposed to go—I do not know. I confirm that it was precisely Yurovsky who went into the rooms where the Imperial Family were. Yurovsky did not give either me or Constantine Dobrynin the duty of awakening the sleepers.

"In approximately an hour the whole Imperial Family, the doctor, the maid servant and the two men servants had gotten up, washed and dressed.

"Even before Yurovsky went to awaken the Imperial Family, two members of the extraordinary commission had come into the Ipatiev House. One, as it turned out later, was Peter Yermakov, and the other a person whose name and surname are unknown to me.

"At about two o'clock the Tsar, the Tsarina, the four Imperial daughters, the woman servant, the doctor, the cook, and the man servant came from their rooms. The Tsar carried the Tsarevich in his arms.

"The Tsar and the Tsarevich were dressed in field shirts. They had service caps on their heads. The Tsarina and her daughters wore dresses, without outer clothing. Their heads were uncovered. The Tsar walked in front with the Tsarevich. Behind them were the Tsarina, their daughters and the others.

"They were accompanied by Yurovsky, his assistant and the two members of the extraordinary commission whom I mentioned. I was also there.

"While I was present no member of the Imperial Family asked any questions of anyone. Also there were no tears, no sobbing.

"Having gone down the stairs leading from the second floor anteroom to the lower floor, they went into the courtyard and from there through the second door (counting from the gate) to the inner rooms of the lower floor.

"Yurovsky indicated the way.

"They went into the corner room of the lower floor, adjacent to the sealed storeroom.

"Yurovsky ordered chairs to be brought. His assistant brought three chairs. One chair was given to the Tsarina, another to the Tsar, the third to the Tsarevich.

"The Tsarina sat at the wall in which there is a window, nearer to the rear post of the arch. Behind her stood three of the daughters (I know all of them very well by sight because I saw them taking walks almost every day, but I do not know the names of each very well.) The Tsarevich and the Tsar sat next to each other, almost in the center of the room. Doctor Botkin stood behind the chair of the Tsarevich. The maid servant—I do not know her name, she was a tall woman—stood at the left door post of the door leading into the sealed storeroom. With her stood one of the Imperial daughters (the fourth). The two men servants stood in the left corner (from the entrance), against the wall adjacent to the storeroom.

"The maid servant had a pillow in her arms. The Imperial daughters had also brought small pillows with them. They put one of the pillows on the seat of the Tsarina's chair, another on the seat of the chair of the Tsarevich.

"At the same time eleven men came into the same room: Yurovsky, his assistant, two members of the extraordinary commission and seven Letts.

"Yurovsky sent me out, saying: 'Go out into the street and see if there is anyone out there and if the shots can be heard.'

"I went out into the courtyard, which is enclosed with a high wall and, not reaching the street, heard the sound of shots. I went back into the house at once (about 2-3 minutes had passed) and, going into the room where the shooting took place, saw that all members of the Imperial Family: the Tsar, the Tsarina, the four daughters, and the Tsarevich, were already lying on the floor with many wounds in their bodies. The blood ran in streams.

"The doctor, the maid servant and the two men servants had also been killed. When I came in the Tsarevich was still alive—he was groaning. Yurovsky went over to him and shot him point blank two or three times. The Tsarevich became quiet.

"The scene of the murder, the odor and sight of blood, made me feel sick.

"Before the murder Yurovsky handed out all the Nagants. He also gave me a revolver, but I, I repeat, did not take part in the shooting.

"In addition to a Nagant, Yurovsky had a Mauser.

"When the murder was completed Yurovsky sent me to the detachment for men to wash the blood from the room.

"On the way to the Popov House I met the guard corporals, Ivan Starkov and Constantine Dobrynin, running from the detachment. The latter asked me: 'Have they shot Nicholas II? Look and see that they have not shot someone else in his place. You will have to answer questions.'

"I replied that Nicholas II and all his family had been killed.

"I brought about 12-15 men from the detachment, but I do not remember whom, precisely, and cannot name one of them for you. The men whom I brought were first occupied in carrying the corpses of the murder victims to an auto truck that had been brought up to the main entrance.

"They carried the corpses out on stretchers made from sheets stretched on shafts taken from sleighs that were standing in the courtyard.

"Placed in an automobile, the corpses were wrapped in a piece of military cloth taken from the small storeroom in the entrance passageway of the lower floor.

"The driver of the automobile was the Zlokazovsky worker, Lyukhanov.

"Peter Yermakov and the other member of the extraordinary commission sat in the truck and took away the corpses. In what direction they went, and where they put the corpses, I do not know.

"The blood in the room and in the courtyard was washed away, and everything put in order.

"At 3 o'clock A.M. everything was finished. Yurovsky went into his office, and I returned to my place with the detachment. At about 9 o'clock in the morning I awoke and went to the commandant's room.

"The chairman of the Oblast Soviet, Beloborodov, was already there, as were also the Commissar Goloshchekin and Ivan Andreyevich Starkov, the corporal of the guard who was going on duty.

"There was complete disorder in every room. All the things were thrown about, the suitcases and trunks opened. Piles of gold and silver objects were spread out on all the tables in the commandant's room. There were jewels lying there, taken from the Imperial Family prior to the shooting, and gold objects they had worn—bracelets, rings, watches.

"The jewels were packed in two trunks brought from the carriage barn.

"The commandant's assistant was also there. You have asked if the last name 'Nikulin' were known to me, and now I recall that this was the last name of that assistant.

214

"From what Nikulin said I know that he had formerly been with the Extraordinary Investigating Commission.

"You say that according to information in your possession, Andrei Strekotin was at the machine-gun post in the large room on the lower floor, and I now recall that A. Strekotin was actually standing at the machine-gun at that time. The door leading from the room in which the machine-gun stood at the window into the formal anteroom was open. The door leading into the room where the shooting took place was also open.

"Walking about the rooms I found six ten rouble notes in one of them, under a book, "The Law of God", and I took this money for myself. I also took several silver rings and some other trinkets.

"On the morning of the 18th my wife came to me. I went off with her to the Sysertsky plant, having been assigned to distribute money to the families of men serving in the detachment.[44]

"I returned to Ekaterinburg on July 21. All the possessions of the Imperial Family had already been taken away, and the guard removed.

"I left Ekaterinburg on July 24.

"In Perm Commissar Goloschchekin appointed me to a unit that was to make preparations for blowing up a bridge over the Kama in the event of the appearance of White Guards. I did not succeed in blowing up the bridge in accordance with the instructions given to me, nor did I wish to, having decided to give myself up voluntarily. I received the order to blow up the bridge when it had already come under fire from Siberian troops and I went off and gave myself up voluntarily.

"*I did not concern myself with the question of who was determining the fate of the Imperial Family and whether he had authority to do so, but simply fulfilled the orders of those whom I was serving.*"[45]

Did Medvedyev commit murder himself, or was he only a witness of the murder?

His wife, Maria, testified:

"The last time I came to my husband in the city, in the early part of July of this year (reckoning by old style) . . . .

"Left alone with me, my husband told me that the Tsar, the Tsarina, the Tsarevich, all of the Grand Duchesses and all the servants of the Imperial Family had been killed several days before. My husband did not give me the details of the murder at that time. In the evening my husband sent the detachment to the railroad station. On the following day we went home because the commandant had given him two days' leave so that he could distribute money to the families of the Red Army personnel.

"Once home Paul Medvedyev told me several details of how the murder of the Tsar and his family was accomplished.

"According to Paul, during the night, at about 2 o'clock, he was ordered to awaken the Tsar, the Tsarina, all the Imperial children, those with them and their servants. Paul sent Constantine Stepanovich Dobrynin to do this.

"All those who were awakened got up, washed, dressed and were taken to the lower floor, where they were placed in one room. Here they were read a paper which said: 'The revolution is dying, and you must die also.'

"After that they began to shoot at them and they were all killed to the last man. My husband also fired. He said that he was the only one of the Sysertsky workers who took part in the shooting. The others were 'not ours', i.e., not from our plant, but whether they were Russians or non-Russians—this was not explained to me.

"There were 12 men shooting. They did not shoot with rifles, but with revolvers. Al least that is what my husband told me.

"They took the murder victims a long way into the woods and threw them into some holes, but my husband did not tell me anything about the locality, and I did not ask.

"My husband told me all this quite calmly. Toward the last he became unresponsive, did not recognize anyone and acted as though he had ceased to have any concern for his family."

Did Yakimov witness the murder with his own eyes, or did he know about it only through the words of others?

On the morning after the murder he went to his sister, Capitolina Agafonova "to share his thoughts with her".

Agafonova testified in response to my questioning: [46]

"I was in the kitchen when my brother came. He greeted me and then went silently to our room. He appeared to be extremely upset. I noticed this at once and followed him.

"I asked my brother: 'What's the matter?'

"He asked me to close the door to the kitchen, sat down and was silent. His face showed the greatest dejection, fright. He was trembling all over.

"Again I asked my brother: 'What's the matter?'

"I thought he must have had some kind of an accident. He still remained silent and said nothing. It was apparent that he was suffering.

"The thought first struck me: have they really killed Nicholas?

"I don't recall in what words, but I first asked him precisely about this. My brother answered my question with something like 'Of course.'

"I recall that I asked him about the fate of the other members of the family. He replied that they had all been killed, i.e., the Tsar himself, as well as all his family and all those with them except the kitchen-boy.

"I do not recall whether I asked him if he had taken part in the murder himself. It is possible that I asked him this question, seeing his disturbed condition. I do not remember this. I only recall that he said that he had witnessed the scene of the murder himself, with his own eyes. He said that this scene of their murder had so shaken him he could not bear it, and that from time to time he had gone out of the room into the open air. He said that his comrades in the guard rebuked him for this, suspecting him of feeling remorse, or pity, or in general, sympathy for the sufferings of the deceased. At the time I understood from him that he was himself in the room where the murder took place, or else near it, and had witnessed the entire murder with his own eyes."

In the evening of July 17 Yakimov came to see Agafonov to say goodbye.

Agafonov testified: [47] "At about six o'clock in the evening of that same day Yakimov came to us to say goodbye. His appearance greatly shocked me. His face was pinched, his pupils dilated, and his lower lip trembled when he talked. Looking at my brother-in-law I was convinced, without being told, of the truth of everything that my wife had passed on to me of what he had said. It was plain that during the preceding night Anatoli had lived through and experienced something terrible, staggering."

CHAPTER TWENTY-FOUR

1. [pp. 239-244]

The Role of Yermakov in the Murder.

We know how the Imperial Family was killed.

They were killed by Chekists under the leadership of Yurovsky.

In all probability, Medvedyev also took part in the murder.

All of these people are known to us already. But Medvedyev names Yermakov and some other person as being among the murderers.

Peter Zakharov[ich] Yermakov was a native of Verkh-Isetsk.

When the Bolshevik leaders abroad were in need of funds, they obtained them from Russia, through robbery and murder.

They had their own local people for this purpose.

Yermakov was one of such people, having for a long time been associated with Goloshchekin.

He had been exiled for one of such crimes, returning home in 1917.

After the uprising of October 25, he became military commissar of Verkh-Isetsk and was responsible to Goloshchekin, the oblast commissar.

He was also connected with Goloshchekin, and with Yurovsky, through the Cheka, in which he sometimes filled the role of executioner.

His close assistant was the sailor, Stepan Vaganov, whom we already know.

As military commissar of Verkh-Isetsk, Yermakov had a special Red Army unit which included:

1. Yegor Skoryanin
2. Michael Shadrin
3. Peter Yaroslavtsev
4. Vasili Kurilov
5. Michael Kurilov
6. Peter or Serge Puzanov
7. Nicholas Kazantsev
8. Michael Sorokin
9. Ilya Perin
10. Gregory Desyatov
11. Ivan Prosvirnin
12. Victor Vaganov
13. Yegor Shalin
14. Polikarp Tretyakov
15. Alexander Medvedyev
16. Ivan Zaushitsin
17. Alexander Rybnikov
18. Guskin
19. Oreshkin

All of these men were Russians, for the most part inhabitants of Verkh-Isetsk, where Bolshevik propaganda was very strong.

Yermakov took the bodies of the Imperial Family to the mine in a motor truck.

Vaganov, who had so frightened the Zykovs, was one of those mounted Red Army soldiers who accompanied the automobile.

Yermakov and Vaganov were in charge of the armed guard on the Koptyaki road, which was manned by designated Red Army personnel from Yermakov's unit.

On the morning of July 17, the peasant, Karlukov,[48] was on the way to his mowing, not far from the mine. He was coming from Verkh-Isetsk and somehow, bypassing grade crossing No. 184, managed to come out on the Koptyaki road.

He testified: "Yermakov and Vaganov came out of the woods on to the road, and Vaganov ordered me not to go any farther, threatening to shoot if I did not obey. Other Red Army personnel were visible further off in the woods."

The Soviet press has several times attempted to give Yermakov the role of leader in the murder.

This is not correct.

Yermakov was not involved in the murder for the purpose of the murder itself. Yurovsky had sufficient executioners at his disposal in the Ipatiev House to slaughter defenseless people in the torture chamber.

Yermakov was brought into the murder for another purpose. A convenient mine was selected for the destruction of the bodies. This could have been done only by a man well acquainted with the depths of the forest in Ekaterinburg's vicinity. Yurovsky did not know them, but Yermakov did.

Yermakov's role was purely to carry out orders. On the night of

July 17 he rode to the mine in a motor truck, in streams of blood.

He returned to Verkh-Isetsk in the same automobile with empty gasoline drums.

The witnesses testify:

Zudikhin: "I knew Yermakov at Verkh-Isetsk. For a long time he was engaged in robbery on the main roads, obtaining money in this fashion. He was sent to a labor camp and was in exile. After the revolution he returned to Verkh-Isetsk, and when the Bolsheviks seized power he became our military commissar. His assistant was the sailor, Stepan Vaganov, a hooligan and very much of a tramp. Commissar Goloshchekin was in close relationship with them both."

Bozhov: "Who showed them this mine? It was Yermakov, from Verkh-Isetsk. He knows this mine. Yermakov and Vaganov were both close to Goloshchekin."

The peasants took the correct view of the case and correctly defined Yermakov's position in it.

He appears in Photograph No. 124, Vaganov in Photograph No. 125.

2.

The Role of Yurovsky.

The man directly in charge of the murder was Jacob Yurovsky.

And he also worked out the plan of the murder, in detail.

The boy, Leonid Sednev, was taken to the Popov House at Yurovsky's order. When did this happen?

The guard, Letemin, first saw him in the Popov House on July 17.

The guards, Proskuryakov and Yakimov, said that they saw him there on July 15, but the guard, Medvedyev, said that Sednev was brought there on the morning of July 16.

I believe that Medvedyev is correct because Starodumova and Dryagina, who washed the floors of the Ipatiev House in the morning on that day [the 16th], saw Sednev still there.

The removal of Sednev from the Ipatiev House is the earliest fact known to us which reveals Yurovsky's intention.

It occurred on July 16.

The novices, Antonina and Maria, always used to bring food for the Imperial Family, early in the morning.

Antonina testified: "On July 15 Yurovsky told us to bring fifty eggs on the following day, and a chetvert [2.099 hectoliters] of milk, and he *had us pack the eggs in a basket*. He also gave us a note from one of the Grand Duchesses to get thread. We brought all this on Tuesday. On Wednesday we brought another chetvert of milk. We came, and we waited and waited. No one took it from us. We asked the guards where the commandant was. They told us the commandant was eating dinner. We asked: 'What kind of dinner at 7 o'clock?' Well, we went from one to another, and they told us: 'Go away! Don't bring things any more!' And they didn't take our milk."

Maria gave exactly the same testimony.

Why did Yurovsky arrange for these eggs on July 15, asking that they be packed in a basket?

There is a small clearing in the woods near the open shaft where the bodies were destroyed. In it there is a solitary pine stump, very convenient to sit upon.

From there one can very conveniently observe what is going on at the shaft.

I found an egg shell near this stump on May 24, 1919, beneath the previous year's leaves and dead grass.

Early in the morning of July 15 Yurovsky was already getting ready to go to the mine, and he was taking care of his provisions.

The clearing described above is shown in Photograph No. 126. The figure of a soldier shows the location of the pine stump.

On the same day, May 24, in this same clearing, at a distance from the bushes and trees, I found several sheets of paper under the previous year's grass. They had been torn from a booklet and were soiled with human feces.

This booklet was a medical textbook of small format, pocket-size. One of the sheets still showed the name of that part of the book, "Alphabetical Index", from which the sheets had been torn.

Someone had satisfied his needs in this clearing. Nothing appropriate had been at hand. He took his booklet from his pocket and used the least important pages.

A doctor with practical knowledge of medicine would not carry a textbook in his pocket. This indicates a partly-trained person. Yurovsky was such a person—a medical attendant, half-trained.

Recall the road over which the motortruck came to the mine with the corpses. Its passage was hindered by the woods and by the hole into which it fell.

At exactly the place where the forest meets the road at this hole (Photograph No. 71), I found two pine saplings which had been cut down with an axe.

My report states: "Two young pine saplings attract attention: they are just opposite the cave-in and contiguous to the rut of the road. Both saplings, it is plain to see, were cut above the roots with an axe, and fell to the side, away from the rut of the road, in the direction of the woods, obviously with the purpose of allowing a vehicle to proceed without striking against them."

Several paces away, in the collapsed shaft, I found an axe with a broken haft.

It is shown in Photograph No. 127.

Is this only a coincidence?

Not long before the murder of the Imperial Family the peasant, Volokitin,[49] was walking along the Koptyaki road. He was going from Koptyaki to Ekaterinburg.

This is his testimony: "I well remember that during the first days of the month of July I was going to Ekaterinburg along the road which leads from Koptyaki. On this road I encountered three horsemen, riding mounted, in saddles.

Two of them were Magyars. They wore Austrian military clothing. The third was Yurovsky, whom I knew quite well. In Yurovsky's hands I saw a simple carpenter's axe.

This meeting took place at 4 o'clock in the afternoon.

They were riding directly towards grade crossing No. 184 (towards Koptyaki).

Yurovsky flung a few more words at me, asking if there were many berries.

I cannot recall the exact date on which this meeting with Yurovsky occurred, but I am certain it was before I heard of the murder of the *Emperor*, and not long before the day the Bolsheviks made an official announcement about it in the newspapers.

About a day or two afterwards I was again going home along the same road and again met a light automobile.

Several men were sitting in the automobile. Among them, I saw this well, was Yurovsky again. I absolutely did not have time to see who the others were, and did not even notice their clothing.

Their automobile was going in the same direction, toward Koptyaki.

This second meeting took place at about 5-6 o'clock in the afternoon. It is difficult to say exactly, but I believe, nevertheless, that this second meeting with Yurovsky also took place before the Bolshevik's announcement of the murder of the *Emperor*."

There is no doubt that Volokitin met Yurovsky in the woods in peaceful circumstances, i.e., while there was no barricade on the Koptyaki road.

The mine was cordoned off beginning on the morning of July 17.

If we adopt the position most favorable to Yurovsky, i.e., that his second meeting with Volokitin took place on July 16 and that it was separated from the first meeting only by one day, only one conclusion is possible: Yuorvsky was riding along to clear the road for the motor truck with the corpses of the Imperial Family on July 15.

Recall the old birch tree which grew at the open shaft.

On July 30 the court investigator, Nametkin, noticed a notch in the birch tree, in which there was an inscription made with an indelible pencil: "Mine technician I.A. Fesenko, July 11, 1918."

This Fesenko was found by Alexeyev, and questioned by him at my direction.

Fesenko testified [50] that in the summer of 1918 he had been commissioned to search for ore in the wooded area. He did this work in June and July. He was in the tract of the Four Brothers and made the indicated mark on the birch tree there not thinking of why he was doing it.

He further told Alexeyev: "Once during his work in the area near the Four Brothers he had seen horsemen riding, Yurovsky and two unknown persons. One of the latter was called Yermakov by the workers, and the other was an Austrian prisoner, a Magyar or someone else, he doesn't know.

He knew Yurovsky because the latter occupied some sort of important position with the Bolsheviks and was known to many. It was the first time in his life he had seen Yermakov and the prisoner, and he had not known them at all prior to that.

When they met him they first asked him what he was doing there. He told them he was prospecting for ore.

Then they asked him if it was possible to go to Koptyaki by that road and beyond in a motor truck, explaining that they had to transport 500 pouds of grain. . . .

Yurovsky did most of the talking with him.

They met him in the evening, around 5 o'clock. This was about July 11 or after that date, he does not remember exactly, but only knows that it was during those days.

After Yurovsky and Yermakov passed he worked some time longer—a day or two—in the same place. Then the work was stopped because Red Army personnel began to send people away from there because of military activities."

Fesenko and Volokitin are speaking of different events, of two different meetings with Yurovsky.

On July 15, when he met Volokitin, Yurovsky was riding to clear a road which he already knew, along which he was preparing to bring the corpses.

Meeting with Fesenko he was also inspecting this road.

I adopt another hypothesis, also the most favorable to Yurovsky: that his meeting with Fesenko was separated from his first meeting with Volokitin by one day.

On July 14 Yurovsky was looking for the road to the mine.

His work was more responsible than Yermakov's. But it had the same character; it was "black" work.

Was he the person who determined the fate of the Imperial Family?

Yurovsky took up his abode in the Ipatiev House on July 4 and after several days brought the executioners there.

Obviously Yurovsky's criminal activity was instigated in this interval of time, between the 4th and 14th of July, by some other people who had decided the fate of the Imperial Family.

CHAPTER TWENTY-FIVE

[pp. 244-255]

The Roles of Sverdlov and Goloshchekin.

The fate of the Imperial Family was not decided in Ekaterinburg, but in Moscow.

On May 24, 1919, in the same field with the pine stump, I discovered two scraps of newspaper under the previous year's leaves and grass.

These are shown in Photograph No. 128.

They had been used for the same purpose as the sheets from the medical text.

The newspaper is in the German language. From the preserved text it is possible to make out a discussion of the Siberian movement, described as serving the interests of the "Entente".

Only two words are printed in Russian: "Third in. . . ." (Internationale).

The newspaper bears the date of "June 26, 1918" and was published in Moscow.

How did this Moscow newspaper turn up in the forest thicket in the Urals?

The Chekist, Shaya Goloshchekin, played a much bigger role in the Urals than Jacob Yurovsky.

One of the old members of the communist party, he had a personal relationship with the chairman of the TsIK [Central Executive Committee], Jacob Movshev[ich] Sverdlov.

When Jacob Yurovsky established himself in the Ipatiev House, Shaya Goloshchekin was away from Ekaterinburg. At that time he was in Moscow and was living in Sverdlov's apartment.

But Beloborodov advised him by telegraph [51] of the change which had taken place in the Ipatiev House, on the same day that the change occurred.

Beloborodov's telegram contained the following: [52]

MOSCOW
   Chairman of the TsIK Sverdlov
   for Goloshchekin.
Avdeyev replaced his assistant Moshkin arrested in place of Avdeyev Yurovsky internal guard entirely changed replaced by others period.——4558.
4/VII   Beloborodov.
Telegram accepted by Commissar (signature illegible).

This telegram is shown in Photograph No. 129.

A complete series of other documents makes it perfectly clear that on July 8 Shaya Goloshchekin was still in Moscow and was to remain there for still some time.

He was able to return to Ekaterinburg, and did return from Moscow, about July 14.

His return to Ekaterinburg and the series of measures by which Yurovsky prepared for the murder of the Imperial Family coincide in time precisely.

Shaya Goloshchekin was at the mine when the corpses were destroyed there.

He went there for the last time on July 18, in the evening, and returned to Ekaterinburg on the morning of July 19, after being at the mine all night.

The guardswoman at grade-crossing No. 803, Catherine Privalova,[53] testified as follows: "On that day (July 18) a light automobile passed towards Koptyaki. Three or four men were sitting in it. Of them I recognized only Goloshchekin. I had seen him before and knew him by his face. On the next day (July 19) in the early morning, at dawn, while I was driving out the cow, this automobile came back. Goloshchekin was sitting in it again, with several people, but I don't know if they were the same people or others. He was sitting in the automobile and sleeping."

This automobile was also seen in Verkh-Isetsk while returning to the city.

Zubritskaya and the priest, Father Iuda Prikhodko, testified:

Zubritskaya: "There were some people in the automobile. I did

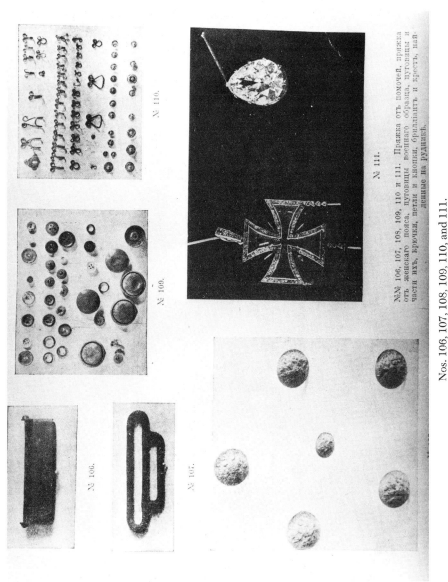

№ 110.

№ 109.

№ 111.

№ 106.

№ 107.

№№ 106, 107, 108, 109, 110 и 111. Пряжка отъ помочей, пряжка отъ женскаго пояса, пуговицы военнаго образца, пуговицы и части ихъ, крючки, петли и кнопки, бриллiантъ и крестъ, найденные на рудникѣ.

Nos. 106, 107, 108, 109, 110, and 111.

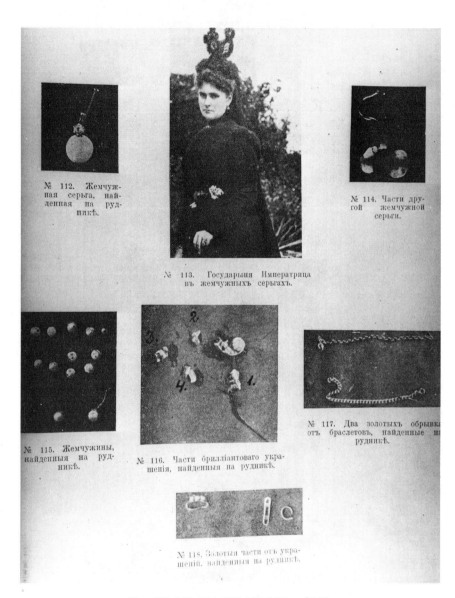

№ 112. Жемчужная серьга, найденная на рудникѣ.

№ 114. Части другой жемчужной серьги.

№ 113. Государыня Императрица въ жемчужныхъ серьгахъ.

№ 115. Жемчужины, найденныя на рудникѣ.

№ 116. Части бриллiантоваго украшенiя, найденныя на рудникѣ.

№ 117. Два золотыхъ обрывка отъ браслетовъ, найденные на рудникѣ.

№ 118. Золотыя части отъ украшенiй, найденныя на рудникѣ.

Nos. 112, 113, 114, 115, 116, 117, and 118.

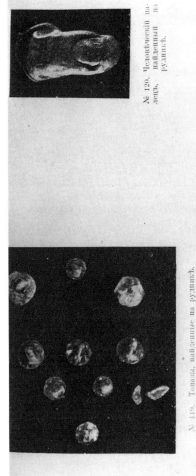

№ 119. Топазы, найденные на рудникъ.

№ 120. Человѣческій па-
лецъ, найденный на
рудникъ.

№ 121. Трупъ собаки „Джемми", принадлежавшей Великой Княжнѣ
Анастасіи Николаевнѣ, найденный на рудникъ.

№ 122. „Джемми" на рукахъ Великой Княжны Анастасіи Николаевны.

Nos. 119, 120, 121, and 122.

№ 125. Расписка Медвѣдева въ полученіи отъ Юровскаго денегъ для раздачи съ сѣверными охранниками послѣ убійства царской семьи.

№ 124. П. Ермаковъ.

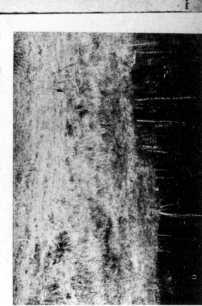

№ 126. Полянка съ сосновымъ пнемъ, вблизи открытой шахты, гдѣ уничтожались трупы царской семьи.

Nos. 123, 124, 125, 126, and 127.

№ 129. Телеграмма Бѣлобородова Голощекину о замѣнѣ внутрен-
няго караула чекистами.

128. Обрывки газеты на нѣм. яз.

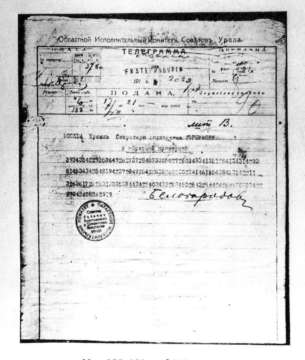

Nos. 128, 129, and 130.

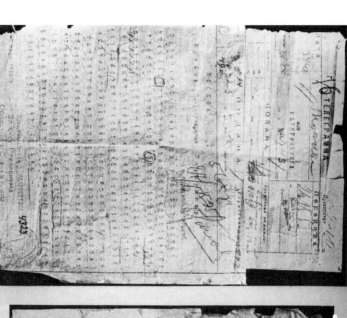

№ 131. (Текстъ телеграммы см. стр. 250).

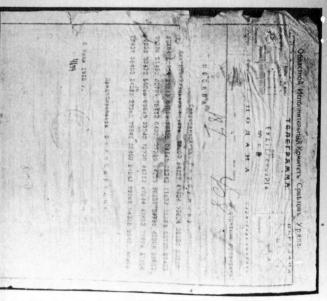

№ 132. (Текстъ телеграммы см. стр. 251).

Nos. 131 and 132.

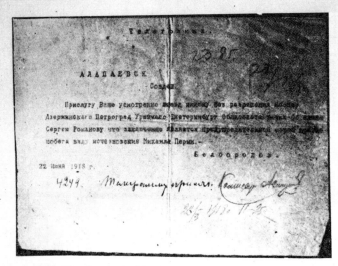

№ 133. Телеграмма Юровскаго.

№ 134. Телеграмма Белобородова екатеринбургскому совѣту.

Nos. 133 and 134.

Областной Исполнительный Комитетъ Совѣтовъ Урала.

ТЕЛЕГРАММА

изъ ЕКАТЕРИНБУРГА

191 г. №

ПОДАНА.

ПЛАТА. ПЕРЕДАНА.

СРОЧНАЯ

МОСКВА два адреса Совнаркомъ Предсѣдателю ЦИК Свердлову

ПЕТРОГРАД два адреса Зиновьеву Урицкому

Алапаевскій Исполкомъ сообщаетъ нападеніи утромъ восемнадцата-
го неизвѣстной бандѣ помѣщеніе гдѣ содержались подъ стражей
бывшіе великіе князья Игорь Константиновичъ Константинъ Константиновичъ Иванъ Константиновичъ Сергѣй Михайловичъ и Палей точка
Несмотря сопротивленіе стражи князья были похищены точка
Есть жертвы обѣихъ сторонъ поиски ведутся точка. 4853.

Предоблсовѣта БѢЛОБОРОДОВЪ

№ 135.   Телеграмма Бѣлобородова о мнимомъ похищеніи алапаев-
скихъ узниковъ.

No. 135.

№ 136. Трупъ Великаго Князя Сергѣя Ми-
хайловича.

№ 137. Трупъ Великой Княгини Елизаветы Федоровны.

№ 138. Трупъ Князя Іоанна Констан-
новича.

№ 139. Трупъ Князя Константина Кон-
стантиновича.

Nos. 136, 137, 138, and 139.

№ 140. Трупъ Князя Игоря Константино-
вича.

№ 141. Алапаевскіе убійцы.

Nos. 140 and 141.

№ 143. Трупъ гр. А. Гейдроехъ, найденный въ Перми.

№ 142. Графиня А. В. Гендрикова.

Nos. 142, 143, and 144.

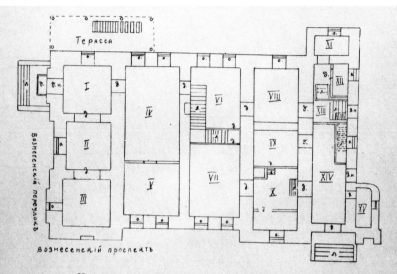

План нижняго этажа дома Н. Н. Ипатьева.

Масштабъ:

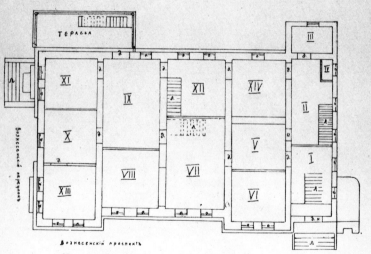

Планъ верхняго этажа дома Н. Н. Ипатьева.

No. 145.

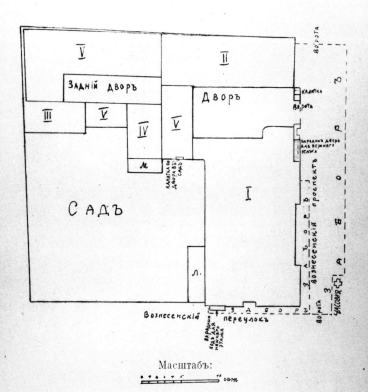

Масштабъ:

План

усадебнаго мѣста Н. Н. Ипатьева въ г. Екатеринбургѣ съ указаніемъ построекъ.

Обозначенія:

  I. Каменный двухъэтажный домъ.
  Л. Терраса.
  II. Каменныя двухъэтажныя службы.
  III. Каменная одноэтажная баня и прачешная.
  IV. Деревянныя службы съ каменнымъ погребомъ.
  М. Досчатая бесѣдка.
  V. Навѣсъ на деревянныхъ столбахъ.

No. 146.

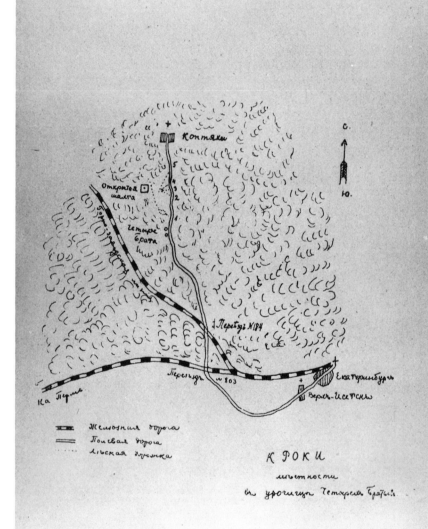

С.

Ю.

Коптяки

Открытая шахта

Четыре брата

ж. Переёздъ № 184

Переёздъ № 803

Ка Пермь

Екатеринбургъ

Верхъ-Исетскiй

Железная дорога
Полевая дорога
лесная дорожка

КРОКИ

местности

въ урочище Четырехъ Братьевъ

No. 147.

No. 148.

No. 149.

not notice their clothing or external appearance. They were all sitting in drooping attitudes, their heads hanging, as though drunk or sleepy, not having had enough sleep."

Father Prikhodko: [54] "A blond man was sitting in the front seat with the driver, and in the back there were four men of Jewish type. All were sprawling, asleep."

The mine connected Shaya Goloshchekin with Jacob Yurovsky.

But there are other facts which connect Goloshchekin with Jacob Sverdlov.

On July 21 the official Bolshevik "Press Bureau" sent a telegram, No. 6153, from Moscow to the oblast soviet in Ekaterinburg. It is dated July 19.[55]

Its contents are as follows:

"July 19. At first session of presidium of TsIK of soviets July 18 Chairman Sverdlov announced receipt by direct wire of advice from the Ural Oblast soviet of shooting of former Tsar Nicholas Romanov period During last days danger of approach of Cheko-Slovak bands posed serious threat to capital of red Ural Ekaterinburg period At same time new conspiracy of counter-revolutionaries exposed with purpose of tearing away crowned executioner from the hands of Soviet Government period In view of all these circumstances presidium of Ural Oblast Soviet resolved to shoot Nicholas Romanov, which was carried out July 16 period *Wife son* [56] of Nicholas sent to safe place period Documents concerning exposed conspiracy sent to Moscow by special courier period Having made this announcement Sverdlov reviewed history of transfer of Romanovs from Tobolsk to Ekaterinburg when a similar organization of white guards was discovered with the purpose of arranging flight of Romanovs period Recently proposed to put former Tsar on trial for all his crimes against people only events now developing prevented calling of this court period Presidium having considered all circumstances compelling Ural Oblast Soviet to take decision to shoot Romanov Central Executive Committee in person of its presidium resolved to accept decision of Ural Oblast Soviet as correct period Then chairman announced that there is now *at disposal of TsIK important material documents of Nicholas Romanov his handwritten diaries which he kept in recent times diaries of his wife and children correspondence of Romanov period* There are also letters of Gregory Rasputin to Romanov his family period All this material will be sorted and published in near future period Continuation follows."

Sverdlov lied when he spoke thus.

On July 17, after 9 o'clock in the evening, he had in his possession a telegram whose contents were as follows: [57]

MOSCOW

Kremlin to Secretary of Sovnarkom Gorbunov
with return confirmation.

39343542293536492627372840333050272623493413512841343142
33514534342548394237234725422938260230234146155438433142
21132636172128313335384434274034332834502843294426284938
333422373426628262919

Beloborodov

This telegram is shown in Photograph No. 130.

It is decoded in the following manner.

The entire encoded text is divided into twelve two-digit groups placed one beneath the other. Then the code takes the following form:

1	2	3	4	5	6	7	8	9	10	11	12
39	34	35	42	29	35	36	49	26	27	37	28
40	33	30	50	27	26	23	49	34	13	51	28
41	34	31	42	33	51	45	34	34	25	48	39
42	37	23	47	25	42	28	38	26	02	30	23
41	46	15	54	38	43	31	42	21	13	26	36
17	21	28	31	33	35	38	44	34	27	40	34
33	28	34	50	28	43	29	44	26	28	49	38
33	34	22	37	34	26	28	26	29	19		

Each letter is encoded with twelve keys, i.e., for each letter there are twelve two-digit figures, depending on the row in which the letter is found.

These keys are as follows:

(Publisher's note: See chart on page 229.)

Decoding the contents of the telegram in this manner we obtain the following:

(Publisher's note: See chart and text on page 230.)

	1	2	3	4	5	6	7	8	9	10	11	12
У —	16	20	11	28	16	26	19	23	12	02	26	14
Ф —	17	21	12	29	17	27	20	24	13	03	27	15
Х —	18	22	13	30	18	28	21	25	14	04	28	16
Ц —	19	23	14	31	19	29	22	26	15	05	29	17
Ч —	20	24	15	32	20	30	23	27	16	06	30	18
Ш —	21	25	16	33	21	31	24	28	17	07	31	19
Щ —	22	26	17	34	22	32	25	29	18	08	32	20
Ю —	23	27	18	35	23	33	26	30	19	09	33	21
Я —	24	28	19	36	24	34	27	31	20	10	34	22
А —	25	29	20	37	25	35	28	32	21	11	35	23
Б —	26	30	21	38	26	36	29	33	22	12	36	24
В —	27	31	22	39	27	37	30	34	23	13	37	25
Г —	28	32	23	40	28	38	31	35	24	14	38	26

	1	2	3	4	5	6	7	8	9	10	11	12
Д —	29	33	24	41	29	39	32	36	25	15	39	27
Е —	30	34	25	42	30	40	33	37	26	16	40	28
Ж —	31	35	26	43	31	41	34	38	27	17	41	29
З —	32	36	27	44	32	42	35	39	28	18	42	30
И —	33	37	28	45	33	43	36	40	29	19	43	31
К —	34	38	29	46	34	44	37	41	30	20	44	32
Л —	35	39	30	47	35	45	38	42	31	21	45	33
М —	36	40	31	48	36	46	39	43	32	22	46	34
Н —	37	41	32	49	37	47	40	44	33	23	47	35
О —	38	42	33	50	38	48	41	45	34	24	48	36
П —	39	43	34	51	39	49	42	46	35	25	49	37
Р —	40	44	35	52	40	50	43	47	36	26	50	38
С —	41	45	36	53	41	51	44	48	37	27	51	39
Т —	42	46	37	54	42	52	45	49	38	28	52	40

1	2	3	4	5	6	7	8	9	10	11	12
П	е	р	е	д	а	и	т	е	С	в	е
39	34	35	42	29	35	36	49	26	27	37	28
р	д	л	о	в	у	ч	т	о	в	с	е
40	33	30	50	27	26	23	49	34	13	51	28
с	е	м	е	и	с	т	в	о	п	о	с
41	34	31	42	33	51	45	34	34	25	48	39
т	и	г	л	а	т	а	ж	е	у	ч	а
42	37	23	47	25	42	28	38	26	02	30	23
с	т	ч	т	о	и	г	л	а	в	у	о
41	46	15	54	38	43	31	42	21	13	26	36
ф	ф	и	ц	и	а	л	н	о	с	е	м
17	21	28	31	33	35	38	44	34	27	40	34
и	я	п	о	г	и	б	н	е	т	п	р
33	28	34	50	28	43	29	44	26	28	49	38
и	е	в	а	к	у	а	ц	и	и		
33	34	22	37	34	26	28	26	29	19		

Here, maintaining the spelling, is the contents of the telegram:
"Передаите Свердлову что все семеиство постигла та же участ что и главу оффициално семия погибнет при евакуации".
["Tell Sverdlov entire family suffered same fate as head officially family will perish in evacuation."]

CHAPTER TWENTY-FIVE

I will speak about this in greater detail.

This telegram immediately drew my attention and led to my expenditure of much time and effort. It held up my departure from Omsk to Ekaterinburg, depriving me of the possibility of questioning Medvedyev personally. I found him ill with typhus.

On February 24 I submitted the contents of this telegram to an experienced person on the Staff of the Supreme Commander in Chief; on February 28 to the Ministry of Foreign Affairs; later to the Commander in Chief of the allied troops, General Janin. The results were pitiful.

In Europe I succeeded in finding the one Russian individual who has always been known as a man of absolutely unique ability and experience in this field. He received the contents of the telegram on August 25, 1920. On September 15 of the same year I had the decoded message from him.

The judgments of those who are not concerned with politics and government, and who are not acquainted with investigatory procedures, usually follow a single pattern; the most simple crimes seem to them extraordinarily mysterious until they are solved, and even the most mysterious crimes seem extraordinarily simple to them after they are solved. One usually encounters judgments such as this: how could the criminals leave such a valuable object undestroyed? Can it be genuine?

The Bolsheviks are people, and like all people they are subject to every human weakness and mistake.

I give them their due. They accomplished the crime, especially the second part. They destroyed the bodies as carefully as they were able.

They lied, I give them their due, intelligently.

But sometimes they overrated themselves, and their caution.

Commissar Voikov, who supplied the sulphuric acid for the mine, was always noted for his inclination to theatrical gestures, for his stupidity and excessive garrulousness, especially in the company of ladies. In such company he was asked once about the fate of the Imperial Family, and pompously replied: "The world will never know what we did with them."

There are no miracles in our investigatory trade. We move towards the truth with patience and effort.

On August 25, 1920 the essence of the Bolshevik lie became entirely clear to me. "We shot the Tsar, but not the *family*."

Putting on a revolutionary face they subordinated moral principle to crime. With this principle they justified the murder of the Tsar.

But what morals could justify the murder of children?

There was only one means left to them: to lie. And they lied.

But they lied for the world. For themselves, and between themselves, they had to speak the truth. This truth could not avoid, it had to accept, the word "family".

This word was given to me with the others on August 25, 1920. A specialist-technician with collossal experience and outstanding abilities far above the ordinary had brought to light the message of the mysterious telegram.

Its key, obviously, was the word "Ekaterinburg," which had 12 letters.

Among the 65 telegrams there are others, also encoded with the same key.

Set forth below are the contents of two which were sent from Ekaterinburg to Moscow on June 26 and July 8, 1918:

MOSCOW

> Secretary of the Council of Peoples' Commissars Gorbunov
> with return confirmation

(Publisher's note: See chart and text on page 233.)

MOSCOW

> Secretary of the Council of Peoples' Commissars Gorbunov
> For immediate reply

(Publisher's note: See chart and text on page 234.)

Both of these telegrams are shown in Photographs Nos. 131-132.

Thus Jacob Sverdlov first spoke about the fate of the Imperial Family on July 18, 1918, in Moscow, in the presence of the presidium of the TsIK.

A press statement about it appeared in Moscow on July 19.

We have the same picture in Ekaterinburg.

There Shaya Goloshchekin first made a statement about the fate of the Imperial Family on July 20.

Printed announcements about it were posted in various parts of the city on July 21.

Statements of witnesses establish that it was Shaya Goloshchekin himself who spoke.

1	2	3	4	5	6	7	8	9	10	11	12
М	и	у	ж	е	с	о	о	б	щ	а	л
36	37	11	43	30	51	41	45	22	08	35	33
и	ч	т	о	в	е	с	з	а	н	а	с
33	24	37	50	27	40	44	39	21	25	35	39
з	о	л	о	т	а	и	п	л	а	т	и
32	42	30	50	42	35	36	46	31	11	52	31
н	и	в	и	в	е	з	е	н	о	т	с
37	37	22	45	27	40	35	37	33	24	52	39
ю	д	а	д	в	а	в	а	г	о	н	а
23	33	20	41	27	35	30	32	24	24	47	23
с	т	о	я	т	к	о	л	е	с	а	х
41	46	33	36	42	44	41	42	26	27	35	16
П	е	р	м	и	п	р	о	с	и	м	у
39	34	35	48	33	49	43	45	37	19	46	14
к	а	з	а	т	с	п	о	с	о	б	х
34	29	27	37	42	51	42	45	37	24	36	16
р	а	н	е	н	и	я	н	а	с	л	у
40	29	32	42	37	43	27	44	21	27	45	14
ч	а	и	п	о	р	а	ж	е	н	и	я
20	29	28	51	38	50	28	38	26	23	43	22
с	о	в	е	т	в	л	а	с	т	и	м
41	42	22	42	42	37	38	32	37	28	43	34
н	е	н	и	е	о	б	л	а	к	о	м
37	34	32	45	30	48	29	42	21	20	48	34
а	н	а	р	т	и	и	и	о	б	л	а
25	43	20	52	42	43	36	40	34	12	45	23
с	о	в	е	т	а	с	л	у	ч	а	е
41	42	22	42	42	35	44	42	12	06	35	28
н	е	у	д	а	ч	и	в	е	с	г	р
37	34	11	41	25	30	36	34	26	27	38	38
у	з	п	о	х	о	р	о	н	и	т	д
16	36	34	50	18	48	43	45	33	19	52	27
а	б	и	н	е	о	с	т	а	в	и	т
25	30	28	49	30	48	44	49	21	13	43	40
в	р	а	г	а	м						
27	44	20	40	25	46						

Chairman of oblast soviet *Beloborodov*. 4323.
June 26, 1918, №.

Similarly, the verbatim text of this telegram is as follows:

"Ми уже сообщали что вес запас золота и платини вивезен отсюда два вагона стоят колесах Перми просим указат способ хранения на случаи поражения советвласти мнение облакома партии и обласовета случае неудачи вес груз похоронит даби не оставит врагам."

["We have already stated that entire supply of gold and platinum removed from here two cars are standing in Perm request advise method of preserving in event of overthrow of Soviet power opinion party oblakom and oblast soviet event failure bury entire load in order not to leave to enemies."]

1	2	3	4	5	6	7	8	9	10	11	12
Г	у	с	е	в	П	е	т	р	о	г	р
28	20	36	42	27	49	33	49	36	24	38	38
а	д	а	с	о	о	б	щ	н	л	ч	т
25	33	20	53	38	48	29	29	29	21	30	40
о	Я	р	о	с	л	а	в	л	е	в	о
38	28	35	50	41	45	28	34	31	16	37	36
з	с	г	а	н	и	е	б	е	л	о	г
32	45	37	37	37	43	33	33	26	21	48	26
в	а	р	д	е	и	ц	е	в	п	о	е
27	29	35	41	30	43	22	37	33	25	48	28
з	д	н	а	м	и	в	о	з	в	р	а
32	33	32	37	36	43	30	45	28	13	50	23
щ	е	н	о	б	р	а	т	н	о	ф	П
22	34	32	50	26	50	28	49	33	24	27	37
е	р	м	к	а	к	п	о	с	т	у	п
30	44	31	36	25	44	42	45	37	28	26	37
а	т	д	а	л	е	е	о	б	с	у	д
25	46	24	37	35	40	33	45	22	27	26	27
и	т	е	Г	о	л	о	щ	е	к	и	н
33	46	25	40	38	45	41	29	26	20	43	35
и	м										
33	40										

Chairman of oblast soviet *Beloborodov*.
July 8, 1918. №. 4369.

In the same fashion the text of this telegram, verbatim, is as follows:

"Для немедленного ответа Гусев Петрограда сообщил что Ярославле возстание белогвардеицев поезд нами возвращен обратно ф Перм как поступат далее обсудите Голощекиным."

["Gusev of Petrograd advised white guard uprising in Yaroslavl we returned train to Perm consult with Goloshchekin how proceed further."]

As a result of my instructions the text of one of the posted announcements was found in Ekaterinburg on July 6, 1919, by employees of the Criminal Investigating Division.

The basic message was the same in both Moscow and Ekaterinburg: the Tsar "had been executed by the will of the people", the family had been spared.[58]

Both Sverdlov and Goloshchekin lied to the same effect. With this common lie they tied themselves together as partners in crime.

But the role of each in this crime was not identical.

Why did Moscow make the first announcement of the Tsar's death, while Ekaterinburg, where he was murdered, announced it only after two days?

The Bolsheviks were fleeing from Ekaterinburg in panic, like cowards. They were so frightened that they left their original telegrams and their original telegraph tapes in the telegraph office.

One of these contains conversations on July 20, 1918 between Jacob Sverdlov in Moscow and a person in Ekaterinburg whose name is not indicated on the tape.

To Jacob Sverdlov's question, "What do you hear?" the unknown person replies as follows:

"The situation at the front is a little better than it seemed yesterday. It appears the enemy has stripped the entire front and thrown all his forces at Ekaterinburg. It is difficult to say if we can hold Ekaterinburg for long. We are taking all measures to hold on. All non-essential people have been evacuated from Ekaterinburg.

Yesterday a courier left, bringing you some documents which will be of interest to you. *Advise* decision of TsIK and *whether we may release to the public the text which you know?"*

Sverdlov replied:

"At the session of the presidium of the TsIK of the 18th it was resolved to accept the decision of the Ural Oblast Soviet as correct. *You may publish your text.* We published a corresponding statement in all the papers yesterday. I have just sent for the exact text and will pass it on *to you.*

"In the meantime I want to tell you the following: 1) hold on no matter what happens we are sending reinforcements in all areas we are sending significant units we hope by their means to smash the Czechs. 2) We are sending several hundred trustworthy party people from the workers of Petersburg and Moscow to all fronts with the special purpose of providing for broad propaganda work among the army and the population. 3) Once again I remind you of the necessity of securing the rear. 4) With respect to the Ger-

THE SOKOLOV INVESTIGATION

mans, after the murder of Mirbach the Germans demanded that they be permitted to send a battalion to Moscow. We categorically refused and were within a hair's breadth of war. The Germans have now withdrawn this demand. Evidently there will not be war in the meantime there is nothing more to say. I will now give you the precise text of our publication.

Headline

The Execution of Nicholas Romanov. . . . . . ." [59]

I will stop here. The transcription continues with the text of the telegram of the Bolshevik "Press Bureau," No. 6153, which is set forth above.

The transcription reveals the reason why Moscow spoke of the Tsar's death before Ekaterinburg. Ekaterinburg did not dare to speak about it on its own, without permission from Moscow.

How could they carry out the murder on their own responsibility when they did not even dare to speak about it without Moscow's permission?

Who spoke with Sverdlov?

This man [the speaker] knew the condition of the front. Goloshchekin knew the front because he was oblast "military" commissar.

Sverdlov was on close terms with him, using the familiar form of address, "ty".

V. L. Burtsev is well acquainted with both Sverdlov and Goloshchekin. He testifies: "I know both Sverdlov and Goloshchekin personally. They are on familiar terms, using the address form 'ty' ".

On July 18 Yakov Sverdlov said that a special courier had been sent from Ekaterinburg to Moscow with documents concerning the discovery of a counter-revolutionary conspiracy to rescue the Emperor, and that the Central Executive Committee already had the diaries and letters of the Imperial Family at its disposal.

The documents on the conspiracy were never sent to Sverdlov from Ekaterinburg for the reason that such a conspiracy never existed.

The diaries and letters of the Imperial Family were actually delivered to Sverdlov, but he did not have them on July 18 and could not have had them.

He was lying again. This is the verdict of logic and the facts.

On the morning of July 15, when he told the novices to bring him eggs, Yurovsky knew he was going to rip open the bodies of the children in the forest thicket.

236

Only a few hours after the departure of the novices, the women came to wash the floors of the Ipatiev House. Recall what Starodumova said about Yurovsky: ". . . he was sitting in the dining room talking with the Tsarevich and *enquiring about his health.*"

As a technician with some experience in uncovering the foul deeds of humanity, I give due recognition to the truth: Yakov Mikhailovich Yurovsky was unquestionably a man of "strong will".

He thought the crime out carefully, and persevered to the end.

He lured the Imperial Family from its rooms with deception, on the pretense of departure from the house. And he took his revolver from his pocket only after they were in the torture chamber.

He moved towards his planned objective with greatest caution because he did not want it prematurely revealed.

The Imperial Family had their diaries and letters with them in the Ipatiev House. There is no doubt that the Empress' letters to the Tsar were his most prized possessions. How could they be gotten away from him before the murder? Such a measure would reveal the intention of murder.

These letters were taken from the Tsar by trampling over his dead body.

The murder took place on the night of July 17.

On July 18 Sverdlov could not have had either the diaries or the letters of the Imperial Family. To understand this one needs only to glance at the geographical map of Russia. It shows how many versts there are between Ekaterinburg and Moscow.

These very valuable articles were sent to Sverdlov by special courier. The courier was Yakov Yurovsky, who left Ekaterinburg with them on July 19.

The coachman, Yelkin,[60] took him to the station from the Ipatiev House. He describes Yurovsky's departure as follows: "The last time I brought a horse to the Ipatiev House for Yurovsky was on July 19. Some young people came out of the house and with the help of an old Red Army man brought out seven pieces of luggage and put them in my carriage. There was a wax seal on one of them, a black leather suitcase of medium size."

Yurovsky was hurrying to bring these documents to Moscow, and was in such haste that he forgot his wallet, with money, in the Ipatiev House.

On July 20, en route, he sent a telegram to Beloborodov from Bisert station: "I left a wallet with about two thousand in money in the house of special assignment. Request you send it to Trifonov by first traveller for me Yurovskys."

Why was the intervention of Trifonov necessary for delivery of the money, and why did the telegram end with the word "Yurovskys" instead of "Yurovsky"?

Yurovsky was too much of a well-known figure among the Bolsheviks. If he had been evacuated to Perm, where he lived at that time, Beloborodov would have known his address at all times.

He left Ekaterinburg on July 19 with his wife and children. He left them at Perm and went on to Moscow alone. Trifonov was a well-known Chekist of Perm. His name was given because he had been appointed to watch over the family in Yurovsky's absence.

"Yurovskys" is not a signature. In the text of the telegram the word "for", already used, has been dropped.

Yurovsky was asking Beloborodov to send his wallet to the Chekist Trifonov so that he could pass it on to his wife. This is the sense of the telegram.

It is shown in Photograph No. 133.[61]

What is the significance of Sverdlov's lie?

The fate of the Imperial Family was decided between the 4th and the 14th of July, when Shaya Goloshchekin was in Moscow and was living in Sverdlov's apartment.

At that time Sverdlov ordered Goloshchekin to send him, after the murder of the family, all intimate documents. It was undoubtedly decided that a special, trusted courier should bring them.

On July 18 Sverdlov received a coded telegram. The Imperial Family had been murdered. Sverdlov celebrated the bloody victory over defenseless people and in the joy of his heart rashly boasted of what he did not yet possess.

With his own vulgarity he determined his own place; chief among the other participants in the murder.

Yakov Movshevich Sverdlov was a petty bourgeois from the city of Polotsk, in Vitebsk guberniya—a Jew. He was born in 1885 in the city of Nizhny Novgorod.

He studied in the Nizhny Novgorod gymnasium but did not finish the course. Then he became an apothecary's apprentice.

In 1907 he was a member of the Perm committee of the Bolshevik party. In the same year he was sentenced by the Kazan Court of Justice to two years' imprisonment.

In 1911 he was exiled to Siberia, fled, and was exiled again.

At Lenin's conference of the RS-DLP in April, 1917, he was a member of the Presidium, as representative of the Urals. Then he was elected a member of the TsIK.

Among a number of other persons he was a member of the military-revolutionary committee which led the uprising of October 25.

Was the fate of the Imperial Family decided only by these two, Sverdlov and Goloshchekin?

On July 20 his conversational partner told him from Ekaterinburg: "Yesterday a courier left bringing you some documents which will be of interest to you. Advise decision of TsIK . . ."

There is no doubt that the form of address, "vy", [you] used in this passage, is collective. It is not addressed to Sverdlov alone.

There were other people in Moscow who participated in the decision with Sverdlov and Goloshchekin regarding the fate of the Imperial Family.

I do not know them.

CONCLUSION

[pp. 267-272]

The violence committed against the Tsar did not only determine the fate of his children. A particular effort is being made to establish the story that the Grand Duke Michael Alexandrovich was saved by flight. One should consider whether he could have made such a decision without regard for what would have happened, in such an event, to his autocratic brother and his family.

To deprive the Tsar of freedom, and thus make his departure from the country impossible, was, in fact, the surest way to guarantee his death and the death of his family.

True, the Tsar himself did not wish to leave Russia. When Yakovlev took him from Tobolsk, the teacher, Bittner, came to say goodbye to him at the last minute. She states: "He was depressed and distraught. I tried to comfort him and said that perhaps it might be better this way. He looked upon the future at that time without hope. When I said that they were, perhaps, taking him out of the country, he replied: 'Oh, God forbid! Anything except to be sent abroad!' "

Languishing in captivity, the Tsar was cut off from the world. He could not know the condition of the nation, and could not understand the extent of the danger which threatened him.

But those who held his fate in their hands knew all this.

What did they do to give him an opportunity to leave Russia and save his children?

I thought I would get a complete answer to this question from the head of the Provisional Government, Prince Lvov. Prince Lvov gave his testimony foggily, attempting in every way to relieve himself of personal responsibility and hide behind the garish, impetuous figure of Kerensky.

In reply to my question, he said: "I affirm that there were discussions at that time between the members of the Provisional Government concerning the departure of the Imperial Family from the country. Evaluating the situation in the country in the summer of 1917, we found that it would be better for them to leave Russia. England and Denmark were mentioned at that time. There was no report on this question. But I believe the Minister of Foreign Affairs, Milyukov, mentioned this possibility, and, as I recall, the initiative in the matter came from several of the Grand Dukes, in particular from Nicholas Mikhailovich and Michael Alexandrovich. Why nothing came of it I do not know."

Milyukov testified: "In the first days of the revolution, when a ruling authority had already been organized in the person of the Provisional Government, in which I was Minister of Foreign Affairs, a number of documents were received, including a telegram from King George of England, addressed to the abdicated Tsar Nicholas II. In this telegram the King expressed his personal feelings for the Tsar as head of state. It contained no concrete proposal with respect to the Tsar's fate. This telegram simply bore, so to speak, a 'complimentary' character. It was delivered to me as Minister of Foreign Affairs. Since there no longer was such a person as that to whom the telegram was addressed (I repeat that it was addressed to the Emperor at a time when he had already abdicated from the throne) I returned it to the English Ambassador, Buchanan. I remember quite well that the question of the fate of the Tsar and his family was raised as soon as a revolutionary authority was set up in the person of the Provisional Government, acknowledging the necessity of Tsar Nicholas II's abdication from the throne. It was recognized as desirable and necessary that Nicholas II and his family should leave the territorial limits of the country and go abroad. I definitely confirm that such was the desire of the Provisional Government, and that the country to which our attention turned was England. As Minister of Foreign Affairs I considered myself obliged, by virtue of the decision of the Provisional Government, which had recognized the necessity of the Tsar's departure from the country, to talk about this question with the Ambassador of Great Britain, Buchanan. After our conversation Buchanan made inquiry of his government. That government stated its readiness to receive the Imperial Family in England and Buchanan, advising of this, said that a cruiser would come to remove the Imperial Family.

This was, I assume, in all probability, brought to the knowledge of the Tsar. The cruiser, however, did not come and there was no departure. There was some hitch, so to speak. I spoke a second time with Buchanan about this question and he told me that the government of England was no longer 'insisting' on the Imperial Family's departure for England. I used the word 'insist' intentionally, but not with the purpose of indicating that the initiative in this matter came from the English government. The initiative came from us, i.e., from the Provisional Government. The term 'insist' was used in 'diplomatic language'. I do not know whether my successor, Tereshchenko, had any conversations with Buchanan on this question, since by that time I no longer had authority."

Kerensky testified: "The Provisional Government decided to make an effort to explore with the English Government the possibility of the Imperial Family's departure for England. The Minister of Foreign Affairs (in the beginning possibly Milyukov) began to have conversations concerning this with the English Ambassador, Buchanan. As a result the following reply of the government of England was transmitted by Buchanan to Tereshchenko, who was at that time Minister of Foreign Affairs and who passed it on to me and Prince Lvov: 'The government of England does not consider it possible to extend its hospitality to the former Tsar while the war continues.' This reply was considered by the Provisional Government in a completely secret session, without a journal of the session." [62]

For about a year, beginning July 25, 1917, our former envoy in Portugal, P.S. Botkin, made continuous requests to responsible, active political figures in France to save the life of the Imperial Family. He spoke of the danger to which they were exposed, and his words, unfortunately, proved to be prophetic. In his last letter, July 2, 1918, he wrote to M. Pichon, Minister of Foreign Affairs: "With great regret I must say that all my efforts were in vain, every step which I took remained fruitless, and as replies to my letters I have only the receipts of the couriers confirming that my letters reached their destinations."

What could the Allies reply?

To those aware of the facts of social and political life, the significance for their governments of the force of "public opinion" is well known. How could they save the Tsar when the Russian government, which they had so warmly welcomed, was itself putting the Tsar on trial, telling the whole world that he was a traitor, or that he had been preparing a separate peace with the enemy to save his own personal and dynastic interests, i.e., a catastrophe for the Allies?

In his memoirs, the business-manager of the Provisional Government, the late Nabokov, acknowledges that the decree which deprived the Tsar of freedom "tied a knot" that was cut in Ekaterinburg.[63]

It was probably not tied by all the members of the Provisional Government. Several, apparently, did not even know anything about it.

From Nabokov's memoirs we know that this question was decided in Prince Lvov's office. Nabokov supplies characteristic detail. When he entered the decree had not yet been signed, but the machinery for putting it into effect had already been prepared. This machinery consisted of members of the State Duma: Bublikov, Kalinin, Gribunin and Vershinin, who arrested the Tsar at the headquarters of the general staff.

How did Prince Lvov carry out this decree?

Sending members of the Duma to arrest the Tsar, he first sent a telegram to staff headquarters, to General Alexeyev.

The aide-de-camp, Mordvinov, now reveals its contents: "The Provisional Government has resolved to grant the Emperor unhindered passage to Tsarskoye Selo and further movement to Murmansk." [64]

General Lukomsky read the telegram. He testified: "On March 20 a telegram addressed to Alexeyev was received from the Provisional Government. It stated that the Provisional Government had assigned special people to 'accompany' the Tsar to Tsarskoye. I assert that I saw this telegram myself. I recall that it was from the head of the government, Prince Lvov, and I assert in the most categorical fashion that not only was there no statement in the telegram with respect to the disposition already made by the Provisional Government concerning the arrest of the Tsar and the Tsarina, but that there was not even a word about it. Its sense was this, that the people assigned by the Government would accompany His Majesty, as the abdicated head of state; that this was a mark of consideration for the Ruler. I know that the persons who came at the instance of the government did not speak to Alexeyev of the Tsar's arrest until the Tsar was already on the train for Tsarskoye. They told Alexeyev about it, and at their request, he told the Tsar about it."

Having abdicated from the throne, the Tsar addressed a letter to Prince Lvov entrusting his fate and the fate of his family to him as head of the new regime.

He got on the train which was leaving Mogilev with no guard whatsoever, relying upon the honor of the new regime.

What did he find on that train?

One question still remains. What was the mutual relationship of the two forces, Bolshevik and German, in regard to the Ekaterinburg tragedy? Did the blood of the Tsar and his family disunite them, or unite them?

I recognize all the seriousness of this question. Within the limits of the possibilities available to me, I will attempt to ascertain the truth. I do not doubt that a complete solution will be found in the future. My duty is to indicate the results I have achieved.

In the Moscow Mission of Count Mirbach there was a Doctor Riezler. He played a large part in it and after the murder of Mirbach was his replacement.

On June 14, 1921 I was received by Riezler in Berlin. He acquainted me with the contents of German official documents. I received copies of them in September of that year.

Here are the contents of the four documents:

1. *Mission in Moscow to the Ministry of Foreign Affairs, July 19, 1918.*

"Whether the firm representation regarding a cautious attitude towards the Tsaritsa should be repeated . . . as a German princess. To extend the representations to the Tsarevich as well would be dangerous because the Bolsheviks are no doubt aware of the monarchists' inclination to put the Tsarevich in the forefront. Bolshevik distrust with regard to German counter-revolution has been still further aggravated as a result of the outspoken statements of General Krasnov."

2. *Mission in Moscow to the Ministry of Foreign Affairs, July 20, 1918.*

"Yesterday I told Radek and Vorovsky that the whole world condemns the execution of the Tsar in the most severe manner, and that the Imperial envoy must firmly warn them against further pursuance of this course. Vorovsky replied that the Tsar was executed only because he would otherwise fall into the hands of the Czechoslovaks. Radek asserted the personal opinion that if we show special interest in the ladies of the Imperial Family of German blood, it might be possible to grant them free exit. It might perhaps be possible to free the Tsaritsa and the Tsarevich (the latter as inseparable from his mother) as indemnification in the matter on a humanitarian basis. Riezler.[65]

244

3. Ministry of Foreign Affairs to the Chargé d' Affaires in Moscow, July 20, 1918.

"I concur in representations on behalf of Imperial Family. Bussche."

4. Mission in Moscow to the Ministry of Foreign Affairs, July 23, 1918.

"I made a corresponding representation on behalf of the Tsaritsa and the princesses of German blood with an indication of the effect of regicide on public opinion. Chicherin listened to my representations in silence. Riezler."

In the general course of world events the death of the Tsar was the inevitable, direct result of his being deprived of freedom. And in July, 1918 there was no longer any force which could prevent it.

FOOTNOTES
FOR
A TRANSLATION OF SECTIONS
OF

NICHOLAS A. SOKOLOV'S

THE MURDER OF THE IMPERIAL FAMILY

1 – 65

[1] From the address of Academy Professor V. O. Klyuchevsky made at a formal meeting of the Moscow Ecclesiastical Academy, September 26, 1892.

[2] Dates throughout are given according to new style. Where old style dates are used, this is indicated.

[3] There were three types of court investigators in Russia: 1) "divisional", 2) "for major cases" and 3) "for especially important cases", divided according to the degrees of importance of the cases themselves. This "importance" was determined by the prosecutor's examination. Investigations by investigators of major cases were initiated by resolution of the prosecutor of the regional court and those made by investigators for especially important cases by resolution of the prosecutor of the regional court, the prosecutor of the court of appeals, or by the Minister of Justice as Procurator General.

[4] M. C. Dieterichs, *The Murder of the Imperial Family and Members of the House of Romanov in the Urals*, part I, page 14.

[5] The witness, Father Storozhev, was questioned by member of the court, Sergeyev, 8–10 October, 1918 in Ekaterinburg.

[6] Photograph No. 29.

[7] The witnesses M. G. Starodumova and V. O. Dryagina were questioned by member of the court Sergeyev on November 11, 1918, in Ekaterinburg.

8 In the interests of technical convenience I have permitted a departure from the original report: the measurements are not given in the Russian system, but in the metric system.

9 On that very night Belshazzar was murdered by his slaves.

10 I made them with the aid of an expert artilleryman 26–27 February 1919 in Omsk.

11 Translator's Note: Should read 1919.

12 Sergeyev designated the area of excision of the wood with pencil outlines.

12a All of the bullets are not shown in this picture. Part of them were distributed by Sergeyev to various people.

13 It must be borne in mind that the piece of floor from room number I is described in the investigation in point 1 of the record of proceedings 17–18 February 1919; the remaining pieces in points 2, 3, 5 and 6 of the same record. In the reports of the scientific analysis the first is conventionally designated number 297, and the rest as numbers 298, 299, 300 and 301, with the use, where necessary, of letters of the Russian alphabet.

14 The bullet was removed in my presence.

15 Translator's Note: Chemist not named.

16 Translator's Note: University not named.

17 Translator's Note: Chemist not named.

18 Translator's Note: University not named.

19 Translator's Note: University not named.

20 Witness S. G. Loginov was questioned by me on April 4, 1919 in the city of Ekaterinburg.

21 Translator's Note: 1 verst equals 0.66296 miles.

22 The witnesses N. P. Zykova and N. S. Zykov were questioned by me on June 27 and 29, 1919 in Ekaterinburg.

23 Witness F. P. Zvorygin was questioned by me at the site (at the mine) on June 28, 1919.

24 Witness G. Ye. Alferov was questioned by me at the site on June 28, 1919.

25 The witnesses N. M. Shveikin, N. V. Papin, P. A. Zubitsky [sic] and A. A. Sheremetevsky were questioned by me at the site on the 9th, 10th and 27th of June, 1919.

26 It is marked number 1 on the drawing.

27 The witnesses M. I. Babinov, M. D. Alferov, P. F. Alferov were questioned by me at the site on June 27, 1919.

28 It is marked number 5 on the drawing.

29 The witnesses V. G. Rednikov, N. Ye. Bozhov, A. R. Zudikhin, I. S. Zubritsky, N. A. Tetenev were questioned by me: the first on August 4, 1919, the second and third on August 5 of that year, and the last on August 7 of that year, in the city of Ishim.

30 Witness J. I. Lobukhin was questioned by me on the site on July 10, 1919.

31 It is marked number 1 on the drawing.

32 It is marked number 5 on the drawing.

33 The witness V. J. Lobukhin was questioned by me at the site on July 10, 1919.

[34] The witnesses P. A. Leonov and A. A. Leonov were questioned by me in the village of Vozdvizhenk, Ekaterinburg uezd, on April 29 and 30, 1919.

[35] Peter Lazarevich Voikov was on Lenin's staff and came with him to Russia. I do not know his nationality.

[36] The witness V. S. Kotenev was questioned by me on July 22, 1919 in the city of Ishim.

[37] Many of these objects were examined, from 10 February to 18 December, 1919, by doctors, opticians, jewelers, shoemakers, tailors, dealers.

[38] The witness, V. I. Buivid, was questioned by the chief of the Ekaterinburg Criminal Investigating Division on August 10, 1918.

[39] The witness, P. F. Tsetsegov, was questioned by the same authority on August 22, 1918.

[40] The Bolsheviks had advanced the time two hours.

[41] The way to Koptyaki.

[42] Alexeyev transcribed Medvedev's statement with literal accuracy.

[43] Translator's Note: Italics are Sokolov's.

[44] At that time Yurovsky gave Medvedev 10,800 roubles. A receipt for this money was found by Sergeyev in one of the stoves on the lower floor of the Ipatiev House. It is shown in Photograph No. 123.

[45] Translator's Note: Italics are Sokolov's.

[46] The witness, C. A. Agafonova, was questioned by Sergeyev on December 6, 1918 and by me on May 19, 1919 in Ekaterinburg.

[47] The witness, G. T. Agafonov, was questioned by Sergeyev on December 6, 1918 in Ekaterinburg.

[48] The witness, S. F. Karlukov, was questioned by agent of the Investigating Division, Sretensky, on May 17, 1919 in Ekaterinburg.

[49] The witness, M. A. Volokitin, was questioned by me at the site on June 21, 1919.

[50] The witness, I. A. Fesenko, was questioned by Alexeyev on August 30, 1919.

[51] The dispatch of this telegram by Beloborodov, the written copy of which serves also as a receipt showing its acceptance for transmission, was discovered on August 25, 1918 by employees of the public prosecutor's office in the building occupied by the Ural oblast soviet. It was sent by the prosecutor of the Ekaterinburg Regional Court to member of the court Sergeyev an August 31 of that year.

[52] The first part of the text of the telegram has no significance in the case. It was definitely determined that it deals with the shipment of money from Ekaterinburg to Perm, whither the Commissar of Finance, Syromolotov, was going for this purpose.

[53] The witness, Ye. P. Privalova, was questioned by me at the site on July 10, 1919.

[54] The witness, Father Iuda Prikhodko, set down his written testimony with respect to the case on June 25, 1920.

[55] This telegram, found by the military authorities in the building occupied by the Ural oblast soviet, was turned over to the court prosecutor by the Ekaterinburg Military-Investigating Commission on July 8, 1919, under No. 8025, and by the prosecutor to me on July 9 of that year as No. 6196.

[56] I will attempt later to explain why Sverdlov said nothing on July 18 about the fate of the Grand Duchesses.

[57] On January 4, 1919 the prosecutor of the Ekaterinburg Regional Court proposed to Sergeyev to remove from the Ekaterinburg Telegraph Office all genuine telegrams of the Bolsheviks. Numbering 65 in all, they were sent to Sergeyev by the Chief of this Office on the 20th and 26th of January, 1919, under Nos. 369 and 374.

[58] Goloshchekin's announcement in Ekaterinburg differs from Sverdlov's announcement in Moscow in that Goloshchekin did not, like Sverdlov, single out information about the fate of the Tsarina and Tsarevich, but spoke generally about the "evacuation" of the family other than the "executed" Tsar. I will attempt to explain this difference later on.

[59] The Ekaterinburg Military-Investigating Commission sent a transcription of this tape to the prosecutor of the Ekaterinburg Regional Court. It was sent to me by the prosecutor on July 9, 1919 under No. 6196.

[60] The witness, A. K. Yelkin, was questioned by Sergeyev on November 27, 1918 in Ekaterinburg.

[61] This telegram was found in the building occupied by the Ural oblast soviet on September 8, 1918 by assistant prosecutor N. I. Ostroumov.

[62] On February 7, 1920, after the death of Admiral Kolchak, I was in Harbin. The situation was difficult. There was no money. In February I addressed a letter to the Ambassador of Great Britain in Peking, Mr. Lampson, and requested that he furnish me with the means to bring the reports of the investigation and the material evidence to Europe. I stated that among the material evidence there were relics of the Imperial Family. On February 23 the Ambassador's secretary, Mr. Keith, came to me and stated that the Ambassador had submitted the request to his government in London. Lampson, apparently, had no doubt of an affirmative reply. My car was attached to Keith's train and put under guard. On March 19 the English consul in Harbin, Mr. Sligh, gave me the English government's reply. It was laconic. "We are unable." With General Dieterichs I turned to the French General, Janin. He told us that he would ask no one, because help in this matter was considered a duty of honor. Thanks to General Janin it was possible to save the reports of the investigation and the material evidence. I cannot pass over in silence the names of two Russians. A merchant in Harbin, I. T. Shchelokov, obtained an ingot of gold from the peasant, F. M. Vlasov, from which the sum of 3,000 yen was realized. With this money I was able to get to Europe and save the investigation.

[63] "Archives of the Russian Revolution," vol. I.

[64] "Russian Chronicle", book 5.

[65] After the murder of Mirbach the Germans demanded that they be allowed to bring a battalion of their troops to Moscow. The Bolsheviks, of course, refused. The Germans made a compromise and were ready to settle their demand with an agreement on the part of the Bolsheviks to preserve the life of the German Princesses, and of the Tsarevich as inseparable from his mother.

Sverdlov, no doubt, knew the intentions of the Germans. On July 18, speaking of the "execution" of the Tsar, he especially singled out the names of the Empress and the Tsarevich, emphasizing that they were still alive. With this he cut the root of the German demand to bring in a battalion, eliminating the question at its root.

For the same reason the Bolsheviks were silent about the fate of the Grand Duchess Elizabeth Feodorovna, knowing full well that the Germans would not believe their assertion regarding her abduction by "White Guards".

Goloshchekin, in Ekaterinburg, had no need to single out the names of the Tsaritsa and the Tsarevich. He spoke, therefore, about the "evacuation" of the whole family together, except the "executed" Tsar.

BIBLIOGRAPHY

FOR

TRANSLATOR'S COMMENTARY

Bulygin, Captain Paul Petrovich, and Alexander Feodorovich Kerensky, *The Murder of the Romanovs*. London, Hutchinson and Company, New York, McBride, 1935.

Bykov, Paul Mikhailovich, *Les derniers jours des Romanov*. Paris, Payot, 1931.

The Last Days of Tsar Nicholas. New York, International Publishers, 1934.

The Last Days of Tsardom. London, Martin Lawrence, Ltd., 1934.

Posledniye dni Romanovykh. Moscow, State Publ., 1930, Sverdlovsk, Uralkniga, 1926.

Article in *Arkhiv Russkoy Revolyutsii, XVII*. Berlin.

Article in *Rabochaya revolyutsiya na Urale*. Ekaterinburg, 1921.

Degras, Jane, ed., *Soviet Documents on Foreign Policy, Vol. I*. London, 1951.

Dieterichs, General Michael Constantinovich, *Ubiistvo tsarskoi sem'i i chlenov Doma Romanovykh na Urale*. 2 vols. Vladivostok, Military Academy, 1922.

Gilliard, Pierre, *Thirteen Years at the Russian Court*. London, Hutchinson and Company, New York, Doran, 1921.

Tragicheskaya sud'ba Russkoi imperatorskoi familii. Revel, EPK, 1921.

Tragiona subda Nikole II i njegov porodice. Zagreb, Kr. Zemaljska Tiskara, 1921.

Le tragique destin de Nicolas II et de sa famille. Paris, Payot, 1921.

Jagow, Gottlieb von, *Documents from the Prussian Archives of the Ministry of Foreign Affairs*. Berlin, Monatshefte, May, 1935.

Janin, General Maurice, *Ma Mission en Sibérie*. Paris, Payot, 1933.

Kennan, George F., *The Decision to Intervene*. Princeton, 1958.

Kerensky, Alexander Feodorovich, and Captain Paul Petrovich Bulygin, *The Murder of the Romanovs*. London, Hutchinson and Company, New York, McBride, 1935.

Leuchtenberg, Duke of, statement in *Papers Relating to the Foreign Relations of the United States, 1918, Russia. Vol. II*. Washington, D.C., 1931.

Markov, Serge Vladimirovich, *How We Tried to Save the Tsaritsa*. London and New York, Putnam's, 1929.

Mel'gunov, Serge Petrovich, *Sud'ba Imperatora Nikolaya II poslye otrecheniya*. Paris, La Renaissance, 1951.

Nicholas II Alexandrovich, Emperor and Tsar, *Dnevnik Nikolaya Romanova, Krasny Arkhiv, XXVII*, 1928.

Sokolov, Nicholas Alexeyevich, *Enquête judiciaire sur l'assassinat de la famille impériale russe*. Paris, Payot, 1924.

So begann der Bolschewismus, Leidensweg und Ermordung der Zarenfamilie. Berlin, Deutsche Verlagsgesellschafft, 1936.

Der Todesweg des Zaren; Dargestellt von dem Untersuchungsrichter. Berlin, Stollberg, 1925.

Ubiistvo tsarskoi sem'i. Berlin, Slovo, 1925.

Tisdall, Evelyn Ernest P., *The Dowager Empress*. London, Stanley Paul and Company, 1957.

Marie Fedorovna, Empress of Russia. New York, John Day Company, 1957.

Wilton, Robert, *Les derniers jours des Romanof*. Paris, Grès et Compagnie, 1920.

The Last Days of the Romanovs. London, Thornton Butterworth, New York, George H. Doran Company, 1920.

Posledniye dni Romanovykh. Berlin, 1923.

INDEX

FOR

TRANSLATOR'S COMMENTARY

AND FOR

A TRANSLATION OF SECTIONS

OF

NICHOLAS A. SOKOLOV'S

THE MURDER OF THE IMPERIAL FAMILY

Translator's Biography

John F. O'Conor is the author of *Cold War and Liberation,* and translated *The Kronstadt Thesis* from the Russian of E. Petrov-Skitaletz.

Mr. O'Conor is a graduate (A.B. 1939 summa cum laude) of Holy Cross College, and of Harvard Law School (LL.B. 1942). During World War II he served as an infantry platoon leader in the Aleutians and in France. From 1946-1956 he practiced law in New York City. Since then he has been engaged in writing and research.

MARYLAND
TERPS #1